Artificial Vi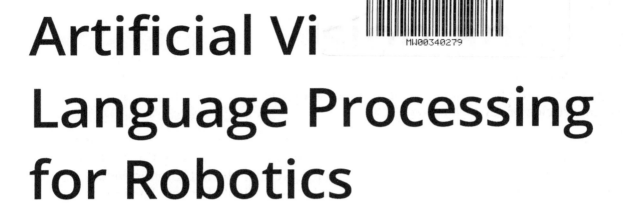 Language Processing for Robotics

Create end-to-end systems that can power robots
with artificial vision and deep learning techniques

Álvaro Morena Alberola

Gonzalo Molina Gallego

Unai Garay Maestre

Artificial Vision and Language Processing for Robotics

Copyright © 2019 Packt Publishing

All rights reserved. No part of this book may be reproduced, stored in a retrieval system, or transmitted in any form or by any means, without the prior written permission of the publisher, except in the case of brief quotations embedded in critical articles or reviews.

Every effort has been made in the preparation of this book to ensure the accuracy of the information presented. However, the information contained in this book is sold without warranty, either express or implied. Neither the author, nor Packt Publishing, and its dealers and distributors will be held liable for any damages caused or alleged to be caused directly or indirectly by this book.

Packt Publishing has endeavored to provide trademark information about all of the companies and products mentioned in this book by the appropriate use of capitals. However, Packt Publishing cannot guarantee the accuracy of this information.

Authors: Álvaro Morena Alberola, Gonzalo Molina Gallego, and Unai Garay Maestre

Technical Reviewer: Rutuja Yerunkar

Managing Editor: Adrian Cardoza

Acquisitions Editor: Kunal Sawant

Production Editor: Samita Warang

Editorial Board: David Barnes, Ewan Buckingham, Jonathan Wray, Simon Cox, Manasa Kumar, Alex Mazonowicz, Douglas Paterson, Dominic Pereira, Shiny Poojary, Erol Staveley, Ankita Thakur, and Mohita Vyas

First Published: April 2019

Production Reference: 1270419

ISBN: 978-1-83855-226-8

Published by Packt Publishing Ltd.

Livery Place, 35 Livery Street

Birmingham B3 2PB, UK

Table of Contents

Neural Networks with NLP   121

Build a Text-Based Dialogue System (Chatbot)   223

Preface

About

This section briefly introduces the author, the coverage of this book, the technical skills you'll need to get started, and the hardware and software requirements required to complete all of the included activities and exercises.

About the Book

Artificial Vision and Language Processing for Robotics begins by discussing the theory behind robots. You'll compare different methods used to work with robots and explore computer vision, its algorithms, and limits. You'll then learn how to control the robot with natural language processing commands. As you make your way through this book, you'll study Word2Vec and GloVe embedding techniques, non-numeric data, as well as recurrent neural networks (RNNs) and their advanced models. You'll create a simple Word2Vec model with Keras, build a convolutional neural network (CNN), and improve it with data augmentation and transfer learning. You'll walk through ROS and build a conversational agent to manage your robot. You'll also integrate your agent with ROS and convert an image to text and text to speech. You'll learn how to build an object recognition system with the help of a video clip.

By the end of this book, you'll have the skills you need to build a functional application that can integrate with ROS to extract useful information from your environment.

About the Authors

Álvaro Morena Alberola is a computer engineer and loves robotics and artificial intelligence. Currently, he is working as a software developer. He is extremely interested in the core part of AI, which is based on artificial vision. Álvaro likes working with new technologies and learning how to use advanced tools. He perceives robotics as a way of easing human lives; a way of helping people perform tasks that they cannot do on their own.

Gonzalo Molina Gallego is a computer science graduate and specializes in artificial intelligence and natural language processing. He has experience of working on text-based dialog systems, creating conversational agents, and advising good methodologies. Currently, he is researching new techniques on hybrid-domain conversational systems. Gonzalo thinks that conversational user interfaces are the future.

Unai Garay Maestre is a computer science graduate and specializes in the field of artificial intelligence and computer vision. He successfully contributed to the CIARP conference of 2018 with a paper that takes a new approach to data augmentation using variational autoencoders. He also works as a machine learning developer using deep neural networks applied to images.

Objectives

- Explore ROS and build a basic robotic system
- Identify conversation intents with NLP techniques

- Learn and use word embedding with Word2Vec and GloVe
- Use deep learning to implement artificial intelligence (AI) and object recognition
- Develop a simple object recognition system using CNNs
- Integrate AI with ROS to enable your robot to recognize objects

Audience

Artificial Vision and Language Processing for Robotics is for robotics engineers who want to learn how to integrate computer vision and deep learning techniques to create complete robotic systems. It will be beneficial if you have a working knowledge of Python and a background in deep learning. Knowledge of ROS is a plus.

Approach

Artificial Vision and Language Processing for Robotics takes a practical approach to equip you with tools for creating systems that integrate computer vision and NLP to control a robot. The book is divided into three parts: NLP, computer vision, and robotics. It introduces advanced topics after a detailed introduction to the basics. It also contains multiple activities for you to practice and apply your new skills in a highly relevant context.

Minimum Hardware Requirements

For the optimal student experience, we recommend the following hardware configuration:

- Processor: 2GHz dual core processor or better
- Memory: 8 GB RAM
- Storage: 5 GB available hard disk space
- A good internet connection

To train neural networks, we recommend using **Google Colab**. But if you want to train these networks with your computer, you will need:

- NVIDIA GPU

Software Requirements

We don't recommend using Ubuntu 16.04 for this book because of compatibility issues with ROS Kinetic. But if you want to use Ubuntu 18.04, there is a version that is ROS supported, named Melodic. During the project, you will need to install several libraries to complete all of the exercises, such as **NLTK** (<= 3.4), **spaCy** (<=2.0.18), **gensim** (<=3.7.0), **NumPy** (<=1.15.4), **sklearn** (<=0.20.1), **Matplotlib** (<=3.0.2), **OpenCV** (<=4.0.0.21), **Keras** (<=2.2.4), and **Tensorflow** (<=1.5, >=2.0). The installation process for each library is explained in the exercises.

To use YOLO in your Ubuntu system, you will need to install the **NVIDIA** drivers of your GPU and the NVIDIA **CUDA** toolkit.

Conventions

Code words in text, database table names, folder names, filenames, file extensions, pathnames, dummy URLs, user input, and Twitter handles are shown as follows: "With the `TfidfVectorizer` method, we can convert the collection of documents in our corpus to a matrix of TF-IDF features"

A block of code is set as follows:

```
vectorizer = TfidfVectorizer()
X = vectorizer.fit_transform(corpus)
```

New terms and important words are shown in bold. Words that you see on the screen, for example, in menus or dialog boxes, appear in the text like this: "**Morphological analysis**: Focused on the words of a sentence and analyzing its morphemes"

Installation and Setup

Before you start this book, you need to install the following software. You will find the steps to install these here:

Installing Git LFS

In order to download all the resources from the GitHub of this book and be able to use images to train your neural network model, you will need to install **Git LFS** (Git Large File Storage). It replaces large files such as audio samples, videos, datasets, and graphics with text pointers inside Git.

If you have not cloned the repository:

1. Install Git LFS

2. Clone the Git repository

3. From the repository folder, execute `gitlfs pull`

4. Done

If the repository is already cloned:

1. Install Git LFS

2. From the repository folder, execute: `gitlfs pull`

3. Done

Installing Git LFS: https://github.com/git-lfs/git-lfs/wiki/Installation

[Recommended] Google Colaboratory

If you have the option, use Google Colaboratory. It is a free Jupyter notebook environment that requires no setup and runs entirely in the cloud. You can also take advantage of running it on a GPU.

The steps for using it are as follows:

1. Upload the entire GitHub to your Google Drive account, so you can use the files that are stored in the repository. Make sure you have made use of Git LFS first to load all the files.

2. Go to the folder where you want to open a new Google Colab Notebook, click New > More > Colaboratory. Now, you have a Google Colab Notebook opened and saved in the corresponding folder, and you are ready to use Python, Keras, or any other library that is already installed.

3. If you want to install a specific library, you can do so using the "pip" package installation or any other command-line installation and adding "!" at the beginning. For instance, "!pip install sklearn", which would install scikit-learn.

4. If you want to be able to load files from your Google Drive, you need to execute these two lines of code in a Google Colab cell:

```
from google.colab import drive
drive.mount('drive')
```

5. Then, open the link that appears in the output and log in with the Google account that you used to create the Google Colab Notebook.

6. You can now navigate to where the files were uploaded using **ls** to list the files in the current directory and **cd** to navigate to a specific folder:

```
[4]  from google.colab import drive

[5]  drive.mount('drive')

[→]  Go to this URL in a browser: https://accounts.google.com/o/oauth2/auth?client_id=9473189898(

     Enter your authorization code:
     ..........
     Mounted at drive

[6]  ls

[→]  drive/  sample_data/

[7]  cd drive/My\ Drive

[→]  /content/drive/My Drive

[8]  ls

[→]  Alemán/                                                    PERSONAL/
     Artificial-Vision-and-Language-Processing-for-Robotics/    RETOS/
     'Colab Notebooks'/                                         TRABAJO/
     INGLES/                                                    UNIVERSIDAD/
     'Neural Networks'/                                         VIU/
     PCCOMPONTENTES_AITA_MAMA.pdf

[9]  cd Artificial-Vision-and-Language-Processing-for-Robotics/Chapter\ 2

[→]  /content/drive/My Drive/Artificial-Vision-and-Language-Processing-for-Robotics/Chapter 2
```

7. Now, the Google Colab Notebook is capable of loading any file and performing any task, just like a Jupyter notebook opened in that folder would do.

Installing ROS Kinetic

These are the steps you must follow to install the framework in your Ubuntu system:

1. Prepare Ubuntu for accepting the ROS software:

   ```
   sudosh -c 'echo "deb http://packages.ros.org/ros/ubuntu $(lsb_release -sc)
   main" > /etc/apt/sources.list.d/ros-latest.list'
   ```

2. Configure the download keys:

   ```
   sudo apt-key adv --keyserver hkp://ha.pool.sks-keyservers.net:80 --recv-
   key 421C365BD9FF1F717815A3895523BAEEB01FA116
   ```

3. Ensure that the system is updated:

   ```
   sudo apt-get update
   ```

4. Install the full framework to not miss functionalities:

   ```
   sudo apt-get install ros-kinetic-desktop-full
   ```

5. Initialize and update **rosdep**:

   ```
   sudo rosdep init
   rosdep update
   ```

6. Add environment variables to the **bashrc** file if you want to avoid declaring them each time you work with ROS:

   ```
   echo "source /opt/ros/kinetic/setup.bash" >> ~/.bashrcsource ~/.bashrc
   ```

   > **Note**
   >
   > It might be appropriate to reboot your computer after this process for the system to implement the new configuration.

7. Check that the framework is correctly working by starting it:

   ```
   roscore
   ```

Configuring TurtleBot

> **Note**
>
> It may happen that TurtleBot is not compatible with your ROS distribution (we are using Kinetic Kame), but don't worry, there are lots of robots that you can simulate in Gazebo. You can look up different robots and try to use them with your ROS distribution.

This is the configuration process for TurtleBot:

1. Install its dependencies:

   ```
   sudo apt-get install ros-kinetic-turtlebotros-kinetic-turtlebot-apps
   ros-kinetic-turtlebot-interactions ros-kinetic-turtlebot-simulator
   ros-kinetic-kobuki-ftdiros-kinetic-ar-track-alvar-msgs
   ```

2. Download the TurtleBot simulator package in your **catkin** workspace:

```
cd ~/catkin_ws/src
git clone https://github.com/turtlebot/turtlebot_simulator
```

3. After that, you should be able to use TurtleBot with Gazebo.

If you get an error trying to visualize TurtleBot in Gazebo, download the **turtlebot_simulator** folder from our GitHub and replace it.

Start ROS services:

```
roscore
```

Launch TurtleBot World:

```
cd ~/catkin_ws
catkin_make
sourcedevel/setup.bash
roslaunchturtlebot_gazeboturtlebot_world.launch
```

Basic Installation of Darknet

Follow these steps for installing Darknet:

1. Download the framework:

```
git clone https://github.com/pjreddie/darknet
```

2. Switch to the downloaded folder and run the compilation command:

```
cd darknet
make
```

You should see an output like the following if the compilation process was correctly completed:

```
gcc -Iinclude/ -Isrc/ -Wall -Wno-unused-result -Wno-unknown-pragmas -Wfatal-erro
rs -fPIC -Ofast -c ./examples/darknet.c -o obj/darknet.o
gcc -Iinclude/ -Isrc/ -Wall -Wno-unused-result -Wno-unknown-pragmas -Wfatal-erro
rs -fPIC -Ofast obj/captcha.o obj/lsd.o obj/super.o obj/art.o obj/tag.o obj/cifa
r.o obj/go.o obj/rnn.o obj/segmenter.o obj/regressor.o obj/classifier.o obj/coco
.o obj/yolo.o obj/detector.o obj/nightmare.o obj/instance-segmenter.o obj/darkne
t.o libdarknet.a -o darknet -lm -pthread  libdarknet.a
```

The Darknet compilation output

Advanced Installation of Darknet

This is the installation process that you must complete in order to achieve the chapter objectives. It will allow you to use GPU computation to detect and recognize objects in real time. Before performing this installation, you must have some dependencies installed on your Ubuntu system, such as:

- **NVIDIA drivers**: Drivers that will allow your system to correctly work with your GPU. As you may know, it must be an NVIDIA model.

- **CUDA**: This is an NVIDIA toolkit that provides a development environment for building applications that need GPU usage.

- **OpenCV**: This is a free artificial vision library, which is very useful for working with images.

> **Note**
>
> It is important to consider that all these dependencies are available in several versions. You must find the version of each tool that is compatible with your specific GPU and system.

Once your system is ready, you can perform the advanced installation:

1. Download the framework if you didn't do the basic installation:

   ```
   git clone https://github.com/pjreddie/darknet
   ```

2. Modify the Makefile first lines to enable OpenCV and CUDA. It should be as follows:

   ```
   GPU=1
   CUDNN=0
   OPENCV=1
   OPENMP=0
   DEBUG=0
   ```

3. Save Makefile changes, switch to **darknet** directory and run the compilation command:

   ```
   cd darknet
   make
   ```

Now, you should see an output similar to this one:

```
gcc -Iinclude/ -Isrc/ -DOPENCV `pkg-config --cflags opencv` -DGPU -I/usr/local/
cuda/include/ -Wall -Wno-unused-result -Wno-unknown-pragmas -Wfatal-errors -fPIC
-Ofast -DOPENCV -DGPU -c ./examples/darknet.c -o obj/darknet.o
gcc -Iinclude/ -Isrc/ -DOPENCV `pkg-config --cflags opencv` -DGPU -I/usr/local/
cuda/include/ -Wall -Wno-unused-result -Wno-unknown-pragmas -Wfatal-errors -fPIC
-Ofast -DOPENCV -DGPU obj/captcha.o obj/lsd.o obj/super.o obj/art.o obj/tag.o o
bj/cifar.o obj/go.o obj/rnn.o obj/segmenter.o obj/regressor.o obj/classifier.o o
bj/coco.o obj/yolo.o obj/detector.o obj/nightmare.o obj/instance-segmenter.o obj
/darknet.o libdarknet.a -o darknet -lm -pthread `pkg-config --libs opencv` -L/
usr/local/cuda/lib64 -lcuda -lcudart -lcublas -lcurand -lstdc++ libdarknet.a
```

The Darknet compilation with CUDA and OpenCV

Installing YOLO

Before performing this installation, you must have some dependencies installed on your Ubuntu system, as mentioned in the *advanced installation of Darknet*.

> **Note**
>
> It is important to take into account that all these dependencies are available in several versions. You must find the version of each tool that is compatible with your specific GPU and system.

Once your system is ready, you can perform the advanced installation:

1. Download the framework:

   ```
   git clone https://github.com/pjreddie/darknet
   ```

2. Modify the Makefile first lines to enable OpenCV and CUDA. It should be as follows:

   ```
   GPU=1
   CUDNN=0
   OPENCV=1
   OPENMP=0
   DEBUG=0
   ```

3. Save Makefile changes, switch to the darknet directory, and run the compilation command:

```
cd darknet
Make
```

Additional Resources

The code bundle for this book is also hosted on GitHub at: https://github.com/PacktPublishing/Artificial-Vision-and-Language-Processing-for-Robotics.

We also have other code bundles from our rich catalog of books and videos available at https://github.com/PacktPublishing/. Check them out!

Links to documentation:

ROS Kinetic - http://wiki.ros.org/kinetic/Installation

Git Large File Storage - https://git-lfs.github.com/

Fundamentals of Robotics

Learning Objectives

By the end of this chapter, you will be able to:

- Describe important events in the history of robotics
- Explain the importance of using artificial intelligence, artificial vision and natural language processing
- Classify a robot depending on its goal or function
- Identify the parts of a robot
- Estimate a robot's position using odometry

This chapter covers the brief history of robotics, classifies different types of robots and its hardware, and explains a way to find a robot's position using odometry.

Introduction

The robotics sector represents the present and the future of humanity. Currently, there are robots in the industrial sector, in research laboratories, in universities, and even in our homes. The discipline of robotics is continually evolving, which is one of the reasons it is worth studying. Every robot needs someone to program it. Even those based on AI and self-learning need to be given initial goals. Malfunctioning robots need technicians and constant maintenance, and AI-based systems need constant data inputs and monitoring to be effective.

In this book, you will learn and practice lots of interesting techniques, focusing on artificial computer vision, natural language processing, and working with robots and simulators. This will give you a solid basis in some cutting-edge areas of robotics.

History of Robotics

Robotics stemmed from the need to create intelligent machines to perform tasks that were difficult for humans. But it wasn't called "robotics" at first. The term "robot" was coined by a Czech writer, Karel Čapek, in his work **R.U.R. (Rossum's Universal Robots)**. It is derived from the Czech word **robota**, which means servitude and is related to forced labor.

Čapek's work became known worldwide, and the term "robot" did too, so much so that this term was later used by the famous teacher and writer Isaac Asimov in his work; he termed robotics as the science that studies robots and their features.

Here you can see a timeline of the important events that have shaped the history of robotics:

Events	Year	Description
Da Vinci's robot	1495	In 1950 a robot design was found in Da Vinci's notes. We don't know if Leonardo ever tried to build this robot, but according to the design the robot seemed to perform human moves in an anatomically perfect way.
R.U.R	1921	Rossum's Universal Robots is a stage play written by Karel Čapek. The play is about an enterprise that builds robots to help humans with their tasks
Robotics laws	1942	These are the three laws mentioned by Isaac Asimov in many of his books and stories: 1. A robot may not injure a human being or allow a human being to come to harm 2. A robot must obey the orders given by a human unless the orders conflict with the other laws. 3. A robot must protect its own existence, except when it conflicts with the previous laws.
Walter's turtle	1953	Walter's turtle was an analog device comprising two sensors, two actuators, and two "neurons". This robot had the following behaviors: • It searched for a light source. • It approached to a faint light source. • It moved away from any bright lights. • It pushed obstacles in its path and turn around
Unimate	1956	It was the first industrial robot. Its task was to transport die castings from an assembly line and to weld these parts onto auto bodies.
Shakey	1969	Shakey was the first general-purpose mobile robot to be able to reason about its own actions. It was also the first robot combining Computer Vision and Natural Language Processing.
Soviet robot on Mars	1971	This was a Soviet robot that was sent to explore Mars.
American robot on Mars	1977	This was an American robot that was sent to explore Mars.

Figure 1.1: History of robotics

Asimov's *The Complete Robot*	1982	*The Complete Robot* was one of Asimov's most important publications. It was a set of some of his stories written between 1940 and 1976.
Robots with human features	Present	Nowadays, a lot of humanoid robots are being developed. Robots perform more and more complex tasks, which also has the potential to improve human results.

Figure 1.2: History of robotics continued

Figures 1.1 and 1.2 give a useful timeline of the beginnings and evolution of robotics.

Artificial Intelligence

AI refers to a set of algorithms developed with the objective of giving a machine the same capabilities as that of a human. It allows a robot to take its own decisions, interact with people, and recognize objects. This kind of intelligence is present not just in robots, but also in plenty of other applications and systems (even though people may be unaware of it).

There are many real-world products already using this kind of technology. Here's a list of some of them to show you the kind of interesting applications you can build:

- **Siri**: This is a voice assistant created by Apple, and is included in their phones and tablets. Siri is very useful as it is connected to the internet, allowing it to look up data instantly, send messages, check the weather, and do much more.

- **Netflix**: Netflix is an online film and TV service. It runs on a very accurate recommendation system that is developed using AI that recommends films to users based on their viewing history. For example, if a user usually watches romantic movies, the system will recommend romantic series and movies.

- **Spotify**: Spotify is an online music service similar to Netflix. It uses a recommendation system to make accurate song suggestions to users. To do so, it considers songs that the user has previously heard and the kind of music added to the user's library.

- **Tesla's self-driving cars**: These cars are built using AI that can detect obstacles, people, and even traffic signals to ensure the passengers have a secure ride.

- **Pacman**: Like almost any other video game, Pacman's enemies are programmed using AI. They use a specific technique that constantly computes the collision distance, taking into account wall boundaries, and they try to trap Pacman. As it is a very simple game, the algorithm is not very complex, but it is a good example that highlights the importance of AI in entertainment.

Natural Language Processing

Natural Language Processing (**NLP**) is a specialized field in AI that involves studying the different ways of enabling communication between humans and machines. It is the only technique that can make robots understand and reproduce human language.

If a user uses an application that is supposed to be capable of communicating, the user then expects the application to have a human-like conversation. If the humanoid robot uses badly formed phrases or does not give answers related to the questions, the user's experience wouldn't be good and the robot wouldn't be an attractive buy. This is why it is very important to understand and make good use of NLP in robotics.

Let's have a look at some real-world applications that use NLP:

- **Siri**: Apple's voice assistant, Siri, uses NLP to understand what the user says and gives back a meaningful response.

- **Cortana**: This is another voice assistant that was created by Microsoft and is included in the Windows 10 operating system. It works in a similar way to Siri.

- **Bixby**: Bixby is a part of Samsung that is integrated in the newest Samsung phones, and its user experience is similar to using Siri or Cortana.

> **Note**
>
> You may be asking which one of these three is the best; however, it depends on each user's likes and dislikes.

- **Phone operators**: Nowadays, calls to customer services are commonly answered by answering machines. Most of these machines are phone operators that work by receiving a keyword input. Most modern operators are developed using NLP in order to have more realistic conversations with clients over the phone.

- **Google Home**: Google's virtual home assistant uses NLP to respond to users' questions and to perform given tasks.

Computer Vision

Computer vision is a commonly used technique in robotics that can use different cameras to simulate the biomechanical three-dimensional movement of the human eye. It can be defined as a set of methods used to acquire, analyze, and process images and transform them into information that can be valuable for a computer. This means that the information gathered is transformed into numerical data, so that the computer can work with it. This will be covered in the chapters ahead.

Here's a list of some real-world examples that use computer vision:

- **Autonomous cars**: Autonomous cars use computer vision to obtain traffic and environment information and to decide what to do on the basis of this information. For example, the car would stop if it captures a crossing pedestrian in its camera.

- **Phone camera applications**: Many phone-based camera applications include effects that modify a picture taken using the camera. For example, **Instagram** allows the user to use filters in real time that modify the image by mapping the user's face to the filter.

- **Tennis Hawk-Eye**: This is a computer-based vision system used in tennis to track the trajectory of the ball and display its most likely path on the court. It is used to check whether the ball has bounced within the court's boundaries.

Types of Robots

When talking about AI and NLP, it is important to take a look at real-world robots, because these robots can give you a fair idea of the development and improvement of existing models. But first, let's talk about the different kinds of robots that we can find. Generally, they can be classified as industrial-based robots and service-based robots, which we will discuss in the following sections.

Industrial Robots

Industrial robots are used in manufacturing processes and don't usually have a human form. In general, they pretty much look like other machines. This is because they are built with the aim of executing a specific industrial task.

Service Robots

Service robots work, either partially or entirely, in an autonomous manner, and perform useful tasks for humans. These robots can also be further divided into two groups:

- **Personal robots**: These are commonly used in menial house-cleaning tasks, or in the entertainment industry. This is the kind of machine that people always imagine when discussing robots, and they are often imagined to have human-like features.

- **Field robots**: These are robots in charge of military and exploratory tasks. They are built with resistant materials because they must withstand harsh sunlight and other external weather agents.

Here you can see some examples of real-world personal robots:

- **Sophia**: This is a humanoid robot created by Hanson Robotics. It was designed to live with humans and to learn from them.

- **Roomba**: This is a cleaning robot made by iRobot. It consists of a wheelie circular base that moves around the house while computing the most efficient way to cover the entire area.

- **Pepper**: Pepper is a social robot designed by SoftBank Robotics. Although it has human form, it doesn't move in a bipedal way. It also has a wheelie base that provides good mobility.

Hardware and Software of Robots

Just like any other computer system, a robot is composed of hardware and software. The kind of software and hardware the robot has will depend on its purpose and the developers designing it. However, there are a few types of hardware components that are more commonly used in several robots. We will be covering these in this chapter.

First of all, let's look at the three kinds of components that every robot has:

- **Control system**: The control system is the central component of the robot, which is connected to all other components that are to be controlled. It is usually a microcontroller or a microprocessor, the power of which depends on the robot.

- **Actuators**: Actuators are a part of the robot that allows it to make changes in the external environment, such as a motor for moving the whole robot or a part of the robot, or a speaker that allows the robot to emit sounds.

- **Sensors**: These components are in charge of obtaining information so that the robot can use it to have the desired output. This information can be related to the robot's internal status or to its external circumstances. Based on this, the sensors are divided into the following types:

- **Internal sensors**: Most of these are used for the measuring position of the robot, so you will usually find them inside the body of these robots. Here are a few internal sensors that can be used by a robot:

  Optointerrupters: These are sensors that can detect any object that crosses the inner groove of the sensor.

Encoders: An encoder is a sensor that can transform slight movements into an electric signal. This signal is later used by a control system to perform several actions. An example is encoders that are used in elevators to notify the control system when the elevator has reached the correct floor. It is possible to know the amount of power given by an encoder by counting the times it turns on its own axis. It is a translating movement that is converted into a certain amount of energy.

Beacons and GPS systems: Beacons and GPS systems are sensors that are used to estimate the positions of objects. GPS systems can successfully perform this task thanks to the information they get from satellites.

- **External sensors**: These are used to obtain data from the robot's surroundings. They include nearness, contact, light, color, reflection, and infrared sensors.

The following diagram gives a graphical representation of the internal structure of a robot:

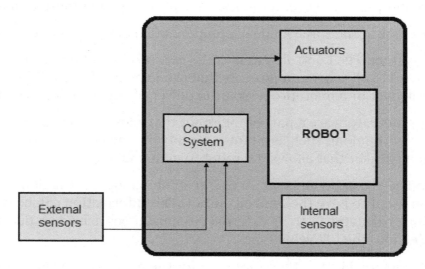

Figure 1.3: Schema of robot parts

To get a better understanding of the preceding schema, we are going to see how each component would work in a simulated situation. Imagine a robot that has been ordered to go from point A to point B:

Figure 1.4: Robot starting to move from point A

The robot is using a GPS, which is an **internal sensor**, to constantly check its own position and to check whether it has arrived at the target point. The GPS computes the coordinates and sends them to the **control system**, which will process them. If the robot hasn't got to point B, the **control system** tells the **actuators** to keep going. This situation is represented in the following diagram:

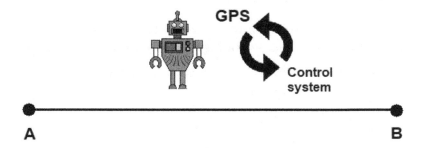

Figure 1.5: Robot in the process of completing the path from A to B

On the other hand, if the coordinates sent to the **control system** by the GPS match the point B, the **control system** will order the **actuators** to finish the process, and then the robot won't move:

Figure 1.6: End of the path! The robot arrives at point B

Robot Positioning

By using one of the internal sensors mentioned in the preceding section, we can calculate the position of a robot after a certain amount of displacement. This kind of calculation is called **odometry** and can be performed with the help of the encoders and the information they provide. When discussing this technique, it's important to keep in mind the main advantage and disadvantage:

- Advantage: It can be used to compute the robot's position without external sensors, which would result in a robot's design being much cheaper.

- Disadvantage: The final position calculation is not completely accurate because it depends on the state of the ground and wheels.

Now, let's see how to perform this kind of calculation step by step. Supposing we have a robot that moves on two wheels, we would proceed as follows:

1. First, we should compute the distance completed by the wheels, which is done by using the information extracted from the engine's encoders. In a two-wheeled robot, a simple schema could be like this:

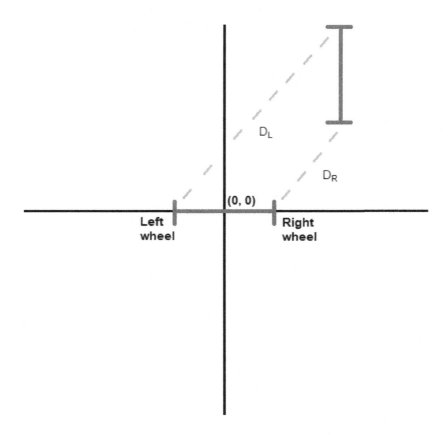

Figure 1.7: Schema of a two-wheeled robot's movement

The distance traveled by the left wheel is the dotted line in Figure 1.6 tagged with D_L, and D_R represents the right wheel.

2. To calculate the linear displacement of the center point of the wheel's axis, we will need the information calculated in the first step. Using the same simple schema, Dc would be the distance:

> **Note**
>
> If you were working with multi-axial wheels, you should study how the axes are distributed first and then compute the distance traveled by each axis.

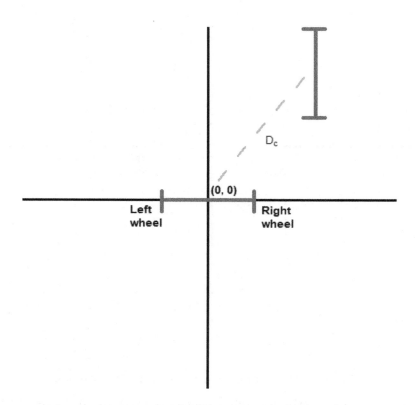

Figure 1.8: Schema of a two-wheeled robot's movement (2)

3. To calculate the robot's rotation angle, we will need the final calculation obtained in the first step. The angle named α is the one we are referring to:

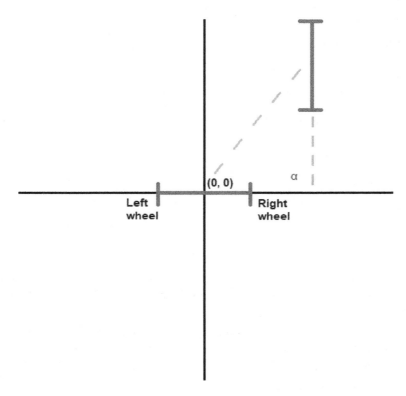

Figure 1.9: Schema of a two-wheeled robot's movement (3)

As shown in the diagram, α would be 90° in this case, which means that the robot has rotated a specific number of degrees.

4. Once you've obtained all the information, it is possible to perform a set of calculations (which will be covered in the next section) to obtain the coordinates of the final position.

Exercise 1: Computing a Robot's Position

In this exercise, we are using the previous process to compute the position of a two-wheeled robot after it has moved for a certain amount of time. First, let's consider the following data:

- Wheel diameter = 10 cm
- Robot base length = 80 cm
- Encoder counts per lap = 76
- Left encoder counts per 5 seconds = 600
- Right encoder counts per 5 seconds = 900
- Initial position = (0, 0, 0)
- Moving time = 5 seconds

> **Note**
>
> Encoder counts per lap is the measurement unit that we use to compute the amount of energy generated by an encoder after one lap on its axis. For example, in the information provided above we have the left encoder, which completes 600 counts in 5 seconds. We also know that an encoder needs 76 counts to complete a lap. So, we can deduce that, in 5 seconds, the encoder will complete 7 laps (600/76). This way, if we would know the energy generated by 1 lap, we know the energy generated in 5 seconds.

For the initial position, the first and second numbers refer to the X and Y coordinates, and the last number refers to the rotation angle of the robot. This data is a bit relative, as you have to imagine where the axes begin.

Now, let's follow these steps:

1. Let's compute the completed distance of each wheel. We first compute the number of counts that each encoder performs during the time it moves. This can be easily computed by dividing the total movement by the given encoder time and multiplying it by the number of counts of each encoder:

   (Moving time / Encoder time) * Left encoder counts:

   (5 / 5) * 600 = 600 counts

(Moving time / Encoder time) * Right encoder counts:

(5 / 5) * 900 = 900 counts

Once this has been calculated, we can use this data to obtain the total distance. As wheels are circular, we can compute each wheel's completed distance as follows:

[2πr / Encoder counts per lap] * Total left encoder counts:

(10π/76) * 600 = 248.02 cm

[2πr / Encoder counts per lap] * Total right encoder counts:

(10π/76) * 900 = 372.03 cm

2. Now compute the linear displacement of the center point of the wheels' axis. This can be done with a simple calculation:

    (Left wheel distance + Right wheel distance) / 2:

    (248.02 + 372.03) / 2 = 310.03 cm

3. Compute the robot's rotation angle. To do this, you can calculate the difference between the distance completed by each wheel and divide it by the base length:

    (Right wheel distance – Left wheel distance) / Base length:

    (372.03 - 248.02) / 80 = 1.55 radians

4. Finally, we can compute the final position by calculating each component separately. These are the equations to use to obtain each component:

    Final x position = initial x position + (wheels' axis displacement * rotation angle cosine):

    0 + (310.03 * cos (1.55)) = 6.45

    Final y position = initial y position + (wheels' axis displacement * rotation angle cosine):

    0 + (310.03 * sin (1.55)) = 309.96

    Final robot rotation = initial robot rotation + robot rotation angle:

    0 + 1.55= 1.55

So, after this process, we can conclude that the robot has moved from (0, 0, 0) to (6.45, 309.96, 1.55).

How to Work with Robots

Like any other software development, the process of implementing applications and programs for robots can be done many different ways.

In the upcoming chapters, we will use frameworks and technologies that make it possible to abstract a specific problem and develop a solution that is easily adaptable to all kinds of robots and devices. In this book, we will be using **Robot Operating System (ROS)** for this purpose.

Another issue to consider before we start working with robots is the programming language to use. You surely know and have used some languages, but which one is the most appropriate? The real answer to this question is that there is no specific language; it always depends on the problem at hand. But during our book, and due to the kinds of activities that we will work on, we are going to use Python, which, as you may know, is an interpreted, high-level, general-purpose programming language that is used in AI and robotics.

By using Python, as with other languages, you can develop any functionality you want your robot to have. For example, you could give your robot the simple behavior of greeting when it detects a person. You could also program a more complex functionality, for example, to dance when it "hears" music.

Now we are going to go through some exercises and activities that will introduce you to Python for robotics, if you haven't used it before.

Exercise 2: Computing the Distance Traveled by a Wheel with Python

In this exercise, we are going to implement a simple Python function for computing the distance covered by a wheel using the same process that we performed in *Exercise 1, Computing a Robot's Position*. These are the steps to be followed:

1. Import the required resources. In this case, we are going to use the number π:

    ```
    from math import pi
    ```

2. Create the function with the parameters. To compute this distance, we will need the following:

    Wheel diameter in centimeters

    Encoder counts per lap

    Number of seconds used to measure encoders' counts

    Wheel encoder counts during the given number of seconds

Total time of movement

This is the function definition:

```
def wheel_distance(diameter, encoder, encoder_time, wheel, movement_time):
```

3. Begin with the implementation of the function. First, compute the distance measured by the encoder:

```
time = movement_time / encoder_time
wheel_encoder = wheel * time
```

4. Transform the obtained distance from above to the one we expect, which would be the distance traveled by the wheel:

```
wheel_distance = (wheel_encoder * diameter * pi) / encoder
```

5. Return the final value:

```
return wheel_distance
```

6. You can finally check whether the function is correctly implemented by passing values to it and make the corresponding calculation manual:

```
wheel_distance(10, 76, 5, 400, 5)
```

This function call should return **165.34698176788385**.

The output in your notebook should look like this:

```
In [1]: from math import pi

        def wheel_distance(diameter, encoder, encoder_time, wheel, movement_time):

            time = movement_time / encoder_time
            wheel_encoder = wheel * time
            wheel_distance = (wheel_encoder * diameter * pi) / encoder

            return wheel_distance


        wheel_distance(10, 76, 5, 400, 5)

Out[1]: 165.34698176788385
```

Figure 1.10: Final distance covered by the wheel

Exercise 3: Computing Final Position with Python

In this exercise, we use Python to compute the final position of a robot, given its initial position, its distance completed by the axis, and its rotation angle. You can do it by following this process:

1. Import the sine and cosine functions:

    ```
    from math import cos, sin
    ```

2. Define the function with the required parameters:

    The robot's initial position (coordinates)

    The completed distance by the robot's central axis

    The angle variation from its initial point:

    ```
    def final_position(initial_pos, wheel_axis, angle):
    ```

    Set a function by coding the formulas used in *Exercise 1: Computing a Robot's Position*.

    They can be coded like this:

    ```
    final_x = initial_pos[0] + (wheel_axis * cos(angle))
    final_y = initial_pos[1] + (wheel_axis * sin(angle))
    final_angle = initial_pos[2] + angle
    ```

    > **Note**
    >
    > As you may guess by observing this implementation, the initial position has been implemented using a tuple, where the first element matches the "X", the second with the "Y", and the last with the initial angle.

    Return the final value by creating a new tuple with the results:

    ```
    return(final_x, final_y, final_angle)
    ```

3. Again, you can test the function by calling it with all the arguments and computing the result by hand:

    ```
    final_position((0,0,0), 125, 1)
    ```

    The preceding code returns the following result:

    ```
    (67.53778823351747, 105.18387310098706, 1)
    ```

Here, you can see the whole implementation and an example of a function call:

```
In [1]:  from math import cos, sin

         def final_position(initial_pos, wheel_axis, angle):
             final_x = initial_pos[0] + (wheel_axis * cos(angle))
             final_y = initial_pos[1] + (wheel_axis * sin(angle))
             final_angle = initial_pos[2] + angle

             return(final_x, final_y, final_angle)

         final_position((0,0,0), 125, 1)

Out[1]:  (67.53778823351747, 105.18387310098706, 1)
```

Figure 1.11: Final position of the robot computed

Activity 1: Robot Positioning Using Odometry with Python

You are creating a system that detects the position of a robot after moving for a certain amount of time. Develop a Python function that gives you the final position of a robot after receiving the following data:

- Wheels diameter in centimeters = 10 cm
- Robot base length = 80 cm
- Encoders counts per lap = 76
- Number of seconds used to measure encoders' counts = 600
- Left and right encoder counts during the given number of seconds = 900
- Initial position = (0, 0, 0)
- Movement duration in seconds = 5 seconds

> **Note**
>
> The functions implemented in the previous exercises can help you to complete the activity. There are a few steps that you can use to proceed ahead with this activity.

Following these steps will help you to complete the exercises:

1. First, you need to compute the distance completed by each wheel.

2. To move on, you need to calculate the distance completed by the axis.

3. Now compute the robot's rotation angle.

4. Then calculate the final position of the robot.

The output would look like this:

```
Out[7]:  (6.4072682633830995, 309.9593745532724, 1.5501279540739117)
```

Fig 1.11: Final position of a robot computed with the activity's Python function

> **NOTE:**
>
> The solution for this activity can be found on page 300.

Summary

In this chapter, you have been introduced to the world of robotics. You have learned about advanced techniques, such as NLP and computer vision, combined with robotics. In this chapter, you have also worked with Python, which you will use in the chapters ahead.

In addition, you have made use of odometry to compute a robot's position without external sensors. As you can see, it is not hard to compute a robot's position if the data required is available. Notice that although odometry is a good technique, in future chapters we will use other methods, which will allow us to work with sensors, and that may be more accurate in terms of results.

In the following chapter, we will look at computer vision and work on more practical topics. For example, you will be introduced to machine learning, decision trees, and artificial neural networks, with the goal of applying them to computer vision. You will use them all during the rest of the book, and you will surely get the chance to use them for personal or professional purposes.

Introduction to Computer Vision

Learning Objectives

By the end of this chapter, you will be able to:

- Explain the impact of artificial intelligence and computer vision
- Deploy some of the basic computer vision algorithms
- Develop some of the basic machine learning algorithms
- Construct your first neural network

This chapter covers an introduction to computer vision followed by a few important basic computer vision and machine learning algorithms.

Introduction

Artificial Intelligence (**AI**) is changing everything. It tries to mimic human intelligence in order to achieve different tasks.

The section of AI that deals with images is called computer vision. Computer vision is an interdisciplinary scientific field that tries to mimic human eyes. It not only makes sense out of the pixels that are extracted from an image, but also gains a higher level of understanding from that specific image by performing automated tasks and using algorithms.

Some of these algorithms are better at object recognition, recognizing faces, classifying images, editing images, and even generating images.

This chapter will begin with an introduction to computer vision, starting with some of the most basic algorithms and an exercise to put them into practice. Later, an introduction to machine learning will be given, starting from the most basic algorithms to neural networks, involving several exercises to strengthen the knowledge acquired.

Basic Algorithms in Computer Vision

In this topic, we will be addressing how images are formed. We will introduce a library that is very useful for performing computer vision tasks and we will learn about the workings of some of these tasks and algorithms and how to code them.

Image Terminology

To understand computer vision, we first need to know how images work and how a computer interprets them.

A computer understands an image as a set of numbers grouped together. To be more specific, the image is seen as a two-dimensional array, a matrix that contains values from 0 to 255 (0 being for black and 255 for white in grayscale images) representing the values of the pixels of an image (**pixel values**), as shown in the following example:

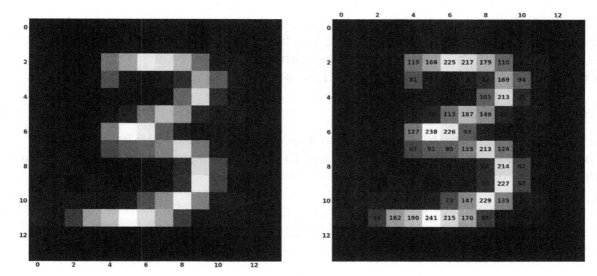

Figure 2.1: Image representation without and with pixel values

In the image on the left-hand side, the number 3 is shown in a low resolution. On the right-hand side, the same image is shown along with the value of every pixel. As this value rises, a brighter color is shown, and if the value decreases, the color gets darker.

This particular image is in grayscale, which means it is only a two-dimensional array of values from 0 to 255, but what about colored images? Colored images (or red/green/ blue (RGB) images) have three layers of two-dimensional arrays stacked together. Every layer represents one color each and putting them all together forms a colored image.

The preceding image has 14x14 pixels in its matrix. In grayscale, it is represented as 14x14x1, as it only has one matrix, and one channel. For the RGB format, the representation is 14x14x3 as it has 3 channels. From this, all that computers need to understand is that the images come from these pixels.

OpenCV

OpenCV is an open source computer vision library that has C++, Python, and Java interfaces and supports Windows, Linux, macOS, iOS, and Android.

For all the algorithms mentioned in this chapter, we will be using OpenCV. OpenCV helps us perform these algorithms using Python. If you want to practice one of these algorithms, we recommend using Google Colab. You will need to install Python 3.5 or above, OpenCV, and NumPy to carry on with this chapter. To display them on our screens, we will use Matplotlib. Both of these are great libraries for AI.

Basic Image Processing Algorithms

In order for a computer to understand an image, the image has to be processed first. There are many algorithms that can be used to process images and the output depends on the task at hand.

Some of the most basic algorithms are:

- Thresholding
- Morphological transformations
- Blurring

Thresholding

Thresholding is commonly used to simplify how an image is visualized by both the computer and the user in order to make analysis easier. It is based on a value that the user sets and every pixel is converted to white or black depending on whether the value of every pixel is higher or lower than the set value. If the image is in grayscale, the output image will be white and black, but if you choose to keep the RGB format for your image, the threshold will be applied for every channel, which means it will still output a colored image.

There are different methods for thresholding, and these are some of the most used ones:

1. **Simple Thresholding:** If the pixel value is lower than the threshold set by the user, this pixel will be assigned a 0 value (black), or 255 (white). There are also different styles of thresholding within simple thresholding:

   Threshold binary

   Threshold binary inverted

   Truncate

Threshold to zero

Threshold to zero inverted

The different types of thresholds are shown in figure 2.2

Figure 2.2: Different types of thresholds

Threshold binary inverted works like binary but the pixels that were black are white and vice versa. Global thresholding is another name given to binary thresholding under simple thresholding.

Truncate shows the exact value of the threshold if the pixel is above the threshold and the pixel value.

Threshold to zero outputs the pixel value (which is the actual value of the pixel) if the pixel value is above the threshold value, otherwise it will output a black image, whereas threshold to zero inverted does the exact opposite.

Note

The threshold value can be modified depending on the image or what the user wants to achieve.

2. **Adaptive Thresholding**: Simple thresholding uses a global value as the threshold. If the image has different lighting conditions in some parts, the algorithm does not perform that well. In such cases, adaptive thresholding automatically guesses different threshold values for different regions within the image, giving us a better overall result with varying lighting conditions.

There are two types of adaptive thresholding:

Adaptive mean thresholding

Adaptive Gaussian thresholding

The difference between the adaptive thresholding and simple thresholding is shown in figure 2.3

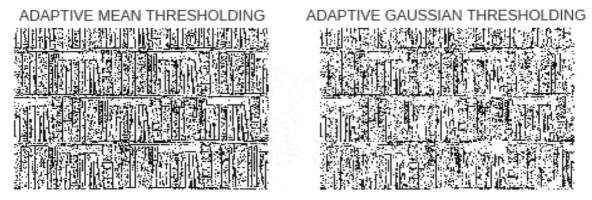

Figure 2.3: Difference between adaptive thresholding and simple thresholding

In adaptive mean thresholding, the threshold value is the mean of the neighborhood area, while in adaptive Gaussian thresholding, the threshold value is the weighted sum of the neighborhood values where weights are a Gaussian window.

3. **Otsu's Binarization:** In global thresholding, we used an arbitrary value to assign a threshold value. Consider a bimodal image (an image where the pixels are distributed over two dominant regions). How would you choose the correct value? Otsu's binarization automatically calculates a threshold value from the image histogram for a bimodal image. An **image histogram** is a type of histogram that acts as a graphical representation of the tonal distribution in a digital image:

Figure 2.4: Otsu's thresholding

Exercise 4: Applying Various Thresholds to an Image

NOTE

As we are training artificial neural networks on Google Colab, we should use the GPU that Google Colab provides us. In order to do that, we would have to go to `runtime > Change runtime type > Hardware accelerator: GPU > Save`.

All the exercises and activities will be primarily developed in Google Colab. It is recommended to keep a separate folder for different assignments, unless advised not to.

The **Dataset** folder is available on GitHub in the Lesson02 | Activity02 folder.

In this exercise, we will be loading an image of a subway, to which we will apply thresholding:

1. Open up your Google Colab interface.

2. Create a folder for the book, download the **Dataset** folder from GitHub, and upload it in the folder.

3. Import the drive and mount it as follows:

```
from google.colab import drive
drive.mount('/content/drive')
```

> **Note**
>
> Every time you use a new collaborator, mount the drive to the desired folder.

Once you have mounted your drive for the first time, you will have to enter the authorization code that you would get by clicking on the URL given by Google and pressing the **Enter** key on your keyboard:

```
[1]  from google.colab import drive
     drive.mount('/content/drive')

 ⌐•  Go to this URL in a browser: https://accounts.google.com/o/oauth2/auth?client_id=947318989803-6bn6qk8qdgf4n4g3pfee6491hc0brc4i.apps.googleusercontent.com/

     Enter your authorization code:
     ..........
     Mounted at /content/drive
```

Figure 2.5: Image displaying the Google Colab authorization step

4. Now that you have mounted the drive, you need to set the path of the directory:

```
cd /content/drive/My Drive/C13550/Lesson02/Exercise04/
```

> **Note**
>
> The path mentioned in step 5 may change as per your folder setup on Google Drive. The path will always begin with **cd /content/drive/My Drive/**.
>
> The **Dataset** folder must be present in the path you are setting up.

5. Now you need to import the corresponding dependencies: OpenCV **cv2** and Matplotlib:

```
import cv2
from matplotlib import pyplot as plt
```

6. Now type the code to load the **subway.jpg** image, which we are going to process in grayscale using OpenCV and show using Matplotlib:

> **Note**
>
> The **subway.jpg** image can be found on GitHub in the Lesson02 | Exercise04 folder.

```
img = cv2.imread('subway.jpg',0)
plt.imshow(img,cmap='gray')
plt.xticks([]),plt.yticks([])
plt.show()
```

Figure 2.6: Result of plotting the loaded subway image

7. Let's apply simple thresholding by using OpenCV methods.

The method for doing so in OpenCV is called **cv2.threshold** and it takes three parameters: **image** (grayscale), **threshold value** (used to classify the pixel values), and **maxVal**, which represents the value to be given if the pixel value is more than (sometimes less than) the threshold value:

```
_,thresh1 = cv2.threshold(img,107,255,cv2.THRESH_BINARY)
_,thresh2 = cv2.threshold(img,107,255,cv2.THRESH_BINARY_INV)
_,thresh3 = cv2.threshold(img,107,255,cv2.THRESH_TRUNC)
_,thresh4 = cv2.threshold(img,107,255,cv2.THRESH_TOZERO)
_,thresh5 = cv2.threshold(img,107,255,cv2.THRESH_TOZERO_INV)

titles = ['Original Image','BINARY', 'BINARY_INV',
'TRUNC','TOZERO','TOZERO_INV']
images = [img, thresh1, thresh2, thresh3, thresh4, thresh5]

for i in range(6):
    plt.subplot(2,3,i+1),plt.imshow(images[i],'gray')
    plt.title(titles[i])
    plt.xticks([]),plt.yticks([])
plt.show()
```

ORIGINAL IMAGE

THRESHOLD BINARY

THRESHOLD BINARY_INV

TRUNCATE

THRESHOLD TO ZERO

THRESHOLD TO ZERO_INV

Figure 2.7: Simple thresholding using OpenCV

8. We are going to do the same with adaptive thresholding.

   The method for doing so is **cv2.adaptiveThreshold** and it has three special input parameters and only one output argument. Adaptive method, block size (the size of the neighborhood area), and C (a constant that is subtracted from the mean or weighted mean calculated) are the inputs, whereas you only obtain the thresholded image as the output. This is unlike global thresholding, where there are two outputs:

```
th2=cv2.adaptiveThreshold(img,255,cv2.ADAPTIVE_THRESH_MEAN_C,cv2.THRESH_
BINARY,71,7)
th3=cv2.adaptiveThreshold(img,255,cv2.ADAPTIVE_THRESH_GAUSSIAN_C,cv2.
THRESH_BINARY,71,7)

titles = ['Adaptive Mean Thresholding', 'Adaptive Gaussian Thresholding']
images = [th2, th3]
for i in range(2):
    plt.subplot(1,2,i+1),plt.imshow(images[i],'gray')
    plt.title(titles[i])
    plt.xticks([]),plt.yticks([])

plt.show()
```

Figure 2.8: Adaptive thresholding using OpenCV

9. Finally, let's put Otsu's binarization into practice.

10. The method is the same as for simple thresholding, **cv2.threshold**, but with an extra flag, **cv2.THRESH_OTU**:

```
ret2,th=cv2.threshold(img,0,255,cv2.THRESH_BINARY+cv2.THRESH_OTSU)

titles = ['Otsu\'s Thresholding']
images = [th]
for i in range(1):
    plt.subplot(1,1,i+1),plt.imshow(images[i],'gray')
    plt.title(titles[i])
    plt.xticks([]),plt.yticks([])

plt.show()
```

Figure 2.9: Otsu's binarization using OpenCV

Now you are able to apply different thresholding transformations to any image.

Morphological Transformations

A morphological transformation consists of a set of simple image operations based on an image shape, and they are usually used on binary images. They are commonly used to differentiate text from the background or any other shapes. They need two inputs, one being the original image, and the other is called the **structuring element** or **kernel**, which decides the nature of the operation. The **kernel** is usually a matrix that slides through the image, multiplying its values by the values of the pixels of the image. Two basic morphological operators are erosion and dilation. Their variant forms are opening and closing. The one that should be used depends on the task at hand:

- **Erosion**: When given a binary image, it shrinks the thickness by one pixel both on the interior and the exterior of the image, which is represented by white pixels. This method can be applied several times. It can be used for different reasons, depending on what you want to achieve, but normally it is used with dilation (which is explained in figure 2.10) in order to get rid of holes or noise. An example of erosion is shown here with the same digit, 3:

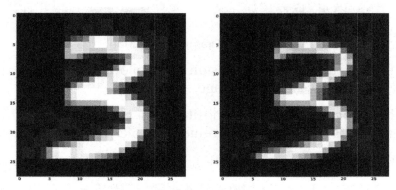

Figure 2.10: Example of erosion

- **Dilation**: This method does the opposite of erosion. It increases the thickness of the object in a binary image by one pixel both on the interior and the exterior. It can also be applied to an image several times. This method can be used for different reasons, depending on what you want to achieve, but normally it is implemented along with erosion in order to get rid of holes in an image or noise. An example of dilation is shown here (we have implemented dilation on the image several times):

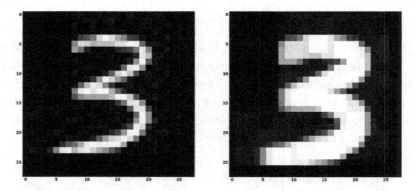

Figure 2.11: Example of dilation

- **Opening**: This method performs erosion first, followed by dilation, and it is usually used for removing noise from an image.

- **Closing**: This algorithm does the opposite of opening, as it performs dilation first before erosion. It is usually used for removing holes within an object:

Figure 2.12: Examples of opening and closing

As you can see, the opening method removes random noise from the image and the closing method works perfectly in fixing the small random holes within the image. In order to get rid of the holes of the output image from the opening method, a closing method could be applied.

There are more binary operations, but these are the basic ones.

Exercise 5: Applying the Various Morphological Transformations to an Image

In this exercise, we will be loading an image of a number, on which we will apply the morphological transformations that we have just learned about:

1. Open up your Google Colab interface.

2. Set the path of the directory:

```
cd /content/drive/My Drive/C13550/Lesson02/Exercise05/
```

> **Note**
>
> The path mentioned in step 2 may change, as per your folder setup on Google Drive.

3. Import the OpenCV, Matplotlib, and NumPy libraries. NumPy here is the fundamental package for scientific computing with Python and will help us create the kernels applied:

```
import cv2
import numpy as np
from matplotlib import pyplot as plt
```

4. Now type the code to load the **Dataset/three.png** image, which we are going to process in grayscale using OpenCV and show using Matplotlib:

> **Note**
>
> The **three.png** image can be found on GitHub in the Lesson02 | Exercise05 folder.

```
img = cv2.imread('Dataset/three.png',0)
plt.imshow(img,cmap='gray')
plt.xticks([]),plt.yticks([])
plt.savefig('ex2_1.jpg', bbox_inches='tight')
plt.show()
```

Figure 2.13: Result of plotting the loaded image

5. Let's apply erosion by using OpenCV methods.

   The method used here is **cv2.erode**, and it takes three parameters: the image, a kernel that slides through the image, and the number of iterations, which is the number of times that it is executed:

```
kernel = np.ones((2,2),np.uint8)
erosion = cv2.erode(img,kernel,iterations = 1)
plt.imshow(erosion,cmap='gray')
plt.xticks([]),plt.yticks([])
plt.savefig('ex2_2.jpg', bbox_inches='tight')
plt.show()
```

Figure 2.14: Output of the erosion method using OpenCV

As we can see, the thickness of the figure has decreased.

6. We are going to do the same with dilation.

   The method used here is **cv2.dilate**, and it takes three parameters: the image, the kernel, and the number of iterations:

```
kernel = np.ones((2,2),np.uint8)
dilation = cv2.dilate(img,kernel,iterations = 1)
plt.imshow(dilation,cmap='gray')
plt.xticks([]),plt.yticks([])
plt.savefig('ex2_3.jpg', bbox_inches='tight')
plt.show()
```

Figure 2.15: Output of the dilation method using OpenCV

As we can see, the thickness of the figure has increased.

7. Finally, let's put opening and closing into practice.

    The method used here is **cv2.morphologyEx**, and it takes three parameters: the image, the method applied, and the kernel:

```python
import random
random.seed(42)
def sp_noise(image,prob):
    '''
    Add salt and pepper noise to image
    prob: Probability of the noise
    '''
    output = np.zeros(image.shape,np.uint8)
    thres = 1 - prob
    for i in range(image.shape[0]):
        for j in range(image.shape[1]):
            rdn = random.random()
            if rdn < prob:
                output[i][j] = 0
            elif rdn > thres:
                output[i][j] = 255
            else:
                output[i][j] = image[i][j]
    return output


def sp_noise_on_figure(image,prob):
    '''
    Add salt and pepper noise to image
    prob: Probability of the noise
    '''
    output = np.zeros(image.shape,np.uint8)
    thres = 1 - prob
    for i in range(image.shape[0]):
        for j in range(image.shape[1]):
            rdn = random.random()
            if rdn < prob:
                if image[i][j] > 100:
                    output[i][j] = 0
            else:
                output[i][j] = image[i][j]
    return output

kernel = np.ones((2,2),np.uint8)
```

```python
# Create thicker figure to work with
dilation = cv2.dilate(img, kernel, iterations = 1)
# Create noisy image
noise_img = sp_noise(dilation,0.05)
# Create image with noise in the figure
noise_img_on_image = sp_noise_on_figure(dilation,0.15)
# Apply Opening to image with normal noise
opening = cv2.morphologyEx(noise_img, cv2.MORPH_OPEN, kernel)
# Apply Closing to image with noise in the figure
closing = cv2.morphologyEx(noise_img_on_image, cv2.MORPH_CLOSE, kernel)

images = [noise_img,opening,noise_img_on_image,closing]
for i in range(4):
    plt.subplot(1,4,i+1),plt.imshow(images[i],'gray')
    plt.xticks([]),plt.yticks([])
plt.savefig('ex2_4.jpg', bbox_inches='tight')
plt.show()
```

Figure 2.16: Output of the opening method (left) and closing method (right) using OpenCV

Note

The entire code file can be found on GitHub in the Lesson02 | Exercise05 folder.

Blurring (Smoothing)

Image blurring performs convolution over an image with a filter kernel, which in simpler terms is multiplying a matrix of specific values on every part of the image, in order to smooth it. It is useful for removing noise and edges:

- **Averaging**: In this method, we consider a box filter or kernel that takes the average of the pixels within the area of the kernel, replacing the central element by using convolution over the entire image.

- **Gaussian Blurring**: The kernel applied here is Gaussian, instead of the box filter. It is used for removing Gaussian noise in a particular image.

- **Median Blurring**: Similar to averaging, but this one replaces the central element with the median value of the pixels of the kernel. It actually has a very good effect on salt-and-pepper noise (that is, visible black or white spots in an image).

In Figure 2.17, we have applied the aforementioned methods:

Figure 2.17: Result of comparing different blurring methods

There are many more algorithms that could be applied, but these are the most important ones.

Exercise 6: Applying the Various Blurring Methods to an Image

In this exercise, we will be loading an image of a subway, to which we will apply the blurring method:

1. Open up your Google Colab interface.

2. Set the path of the directory:

```
cd /content/drive/My Drive/C13550/Lesson02/Exercise06/
```

> **Note**
>
> The path mentioned in step 2 may be different according to your folder setup on Google Drive.

3. Import the OpenCV, Matplotlib, and NumPy libraries:

```
import cv2
from matplotlib import pyplot as plt
import numpy as np
```

4. Type the code to load the **Dataset/subway.png** image that we are going to process in grayscale using OpenCV and show it using Matplotlib:

> **Note**
>
> The **subway.png** image can be found on GitHub in the Lesson02 | Exercise06 folder.

```
img = cv2.imread('Dataset/subway.jpg')
#Method to convert the image to RGB
img = cv2.cvtColor(img, cv2.COLOR_BGR2RGB)
plt.imshow(img)
plt.savefig('ex3_1.jpg', bbox_inches='tight')
plt.xticks([]),plt.yticks([])
plt.show()
```

Figure 2.18: Result of plotting the loaded subway image in RGB

5. Let's apply all the blurring methods:

The methods applied are **cv2.blur**, **cv2.GaussianBlur**, and **cv2.medianBlur**. All of them take an image as the first parameter. The first method takes only one argument, that is, the kernel. The second method takes the kernel and the standard deviation (sigmaX and sigmaY), and if both are given as zeros, they are calculated from the kernel size. The method mentioned last only takes one more argument, which is the kernel size:

```
blur = cv2.blur(img,(51,51)) # Apply normal Blurring
blurG = cv2.GaussianBlur(img,(51,51),0) # Gaussian Blurring
median = cv2.medianBlur(img,51) # Median Blurring

titles = ['Original Image','Averaging', 'Gaussian Blurring', 'Median
Blurring']
images = [img, blur, blurG, median]

for i in range(4):
    plt.subplot(2,2,i+1),plt.imshow(images[i])
    plt.title(titles[i])
    plt.xticks([]),plt.yticks([])
plt.savefig('ex3_2.jpg', bbox_inches='tight')
plt.show()
```

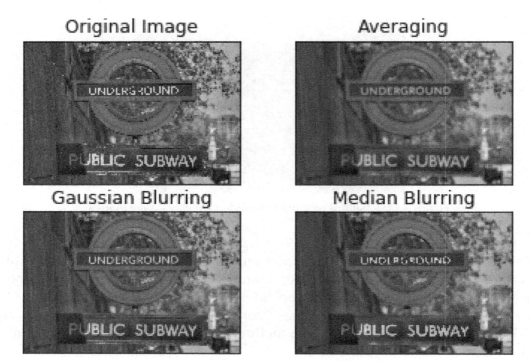

Figure 2.19: Blurring methods with OpenCV

Now you know how to apply several blurring techniques to any image.

Exercise 7: Loading an Image and Applying the Learned Methods

In this exercise, we will be loading an image of a number and we will apply the methods that we have learned so far.

> **Note**
>
> The entire code is available on GitHub in the Lesson02 | Exercise07-09 folder.

1. Open up a new Google Colab interface, and mount your drive as mentioned in *Exercise 4, Applying the Various Thresholds to an Image,* of this chapter.

2. Set the path of the directory:

```
cd /content/drive/My Drive/C13550/Lesson02/Exercise07/
```

> **Note**
>
> The path mentioned in step 2 may be different according to your folder setup on Google Drive.

3. Import the corresponding dependencies: NumPy, OpenCV, and Matplotlib:

```
import numpy as np   #Numpy
import cv2           #OpenCV
from matplotlib import pyplot as plt #Matplotlib
count = 0
```

4. Type the code to load the **Dataset/number.jpg** image, which we are going to process in grayscale using OpenCV and show using Matplotlib:

> **Note**
>
> The **number.jpg** image can be found on GitHub in the Lesson02 | Exercise07-09 | Dataset folder.

```
img = cv2.imread('Dataset/number.jpg',0)
plt.imshow(img,cmap='gray')
plt.xticks([]),plt.yticks([])
plt.show()
```

Figure 2.20: Result of loading the image with the number

5. If you want to recognize those digits using machine learning or any other algorithm, you need to simplify the visualization of them. Using thresholding seems to be the first logical step to proceed with this exercise. We have learned some thresholding methods, but the most commonly used one is Otsu's binarization, as it automatically calculates the threshold value without the user providing the details manually.

    Apply Otsu's binarization to the grayscale image and show it using Matplotlib:

    ```
    _,th1=cv2.threshold(img,0,255,cv2.THRESH_BINARY+cv2.THRESH_OTSU
    ```

    ```
    th1 = (255-th1)
    # This step changes the black with white and vice versa in order to have
    white figures
    plt.imshow(th1,cmap='gray')
    plt.xticks([]),plt.yticks([])
    plt.show()
    ```

    Figure 2.21: Using Otsu's binarization thresholding on the image

6. In order to get rid of the lines in the background, we need to do some morphological transformations. First, start by applying the closing method:

    ```
    open1 = cv2.morphologyEx(th1, cv2.MORPH_OPEN, np.ones((4, 4),np.uint8))
    plt.imshow(open1,cmap='gray')
    plt.xticks([]),plt.yticks([])
    plt.show()
    ```

    Figure 2.22: Applying the closing method

    Note

    The lines in the background have been removed completely. Now a number prediction will be much easier.

7. In order to fill the holes that are visible in these digits, we need to apply the opening method. Apply the opening method to the preceding image:

```
close1 = cv2.morphologyEx(open1, cv2.MORPH_CLOSE, np.ones((8, 8),
np.uint8))
plt.imshow(close1,cmap='gray')
plt.xticks([]),plt.yticks([])
plt.show()
```

Figure 2.23: Applying the opening method

8. There are still leftovers and imperfections around the digits. In order to remove these, a closing method with a bigger kernel would be the best choice. Now apply the corresponding method:

```
open2 = cv2.morphologyEx(close1, cv2.MORPH_OPEN,np.ones((7,12),np.uint8))
plt.imshow(open2,cmap='gray')
plt.xticks([]),plt.yticks([])
plt.show()
```

Figure 2.24: Applying the closing method with a kernel of a bigger size

Depending on the classifier that you use to predict the digits or the conditions of the given image, some other algorithms would be applied.

9. If you want to predict the numbers, you will need to predict them one by one. Thus, you should divide the numbers into smaller numbers.

Thankfully, OpenCV has a method to do this, and it's called **cv2.findContours**. In order to find contours, we need to invert blacks into whites. This piece of code is larger, but it is only required if you want to predict character by character:

```
_, contours, _ = cv2.findContours(open2, cv2.RETR_EXTERNAL, cv2.CHAIN_
APPROX_SIMPLE) #Find contours
cntsSorted = sorted(contours, key=lambda x: cv2.contourArea(x),
reverse=True) #Sort the contours
cntsLength = len(cntsSorted)
images = []

for idx in range(cntsLength): #Iterate over the contours
    x, y, w, h = cv2.boundingRect(contour_no) #Get its position and size
    ... # Rest of the code in Github
    images.append([x,sample_no]) #Add the image to the list of images
and the X position

images = sorted(images, key=lambda x: x[0]) #Sort the list of images using
the X position
{...}
```

> **Note**
>
> The entire code with added comments is available on GitHub in the Lesson02 | Exercise07-09 folder.

Figure 2.25: Extracted digits as the output

In the first part of the code, we are finding the **contours** of the image (the curve joining all the continuous points along the boundary and of the same color or intensity) to find every digit, which we then sort depending on the area of each contour (each digit).

After this, we loop over the contours, cropping the original image with the given contours, ending up with every number in a different image.

After this, we need to have all the images with the same shape, so we adapt the image to a given shape using NumPy and append the image to a list of images along with the X position.

Finally, we sort the list of images using the X position (from left to right, so they remain in order) and plot the results. We also save every single digit as an image so that we can use every digit separately afterward for any task we want.

Congratulations! You have successfully processed an image with text in it, obtained the text, and extracted every single character, and now the magic of machine learning can begin.

Introduction to Machine Learning

Machine learning (**ML**) is the science of making computers learn from data without stating any rules. ML is mostly based on models that are trained with a lot of data, such as images of digits or features of different objects, with their corresponding labels, such as the number of those digits or the type of the object. This is called **supervised learning**. There are other types of learning, such as **unsupervised learning** and **reinforcement learning**, but we will be focusing on supervised learning. The main difference between supervised learning and unsupervised learning is that the model learns clusters from the data (depending on how many clusters you specify), which are translated into classes. Reinforcement learning, on the other hand, is concerned with how software agents should take action in an environment in order to increase a reward that is given to the agent, which will be positive if the agent is performing the right actions and negative otherwise.

In this part of the chapter, we will gain an understanding of machine learning and check a variety of models and algorithms, going from the most basic models to explaining artificial neural networks.

Decision Trees and Boosting Algorithms

In this section, we will be explaining decision trees and boosting algorithms as some of the most basic machine learning algorithms.

Bagging (decision trees and random forests) and **boosting** (AdaBoost) will be explained in this topic.

Bagging:

<u>Decision trees</u> are perhaps the most basic machine learning algorithms, and are used for classification and regression, but on a basic level, they are used for teaching and performing tests.

In a decision tree, every node represents an attribute of the data that is being trained on (whether something is true or false), where every branch (line between nodes) represents a decision (if something is true, go this way; otherwise, the other way) and every leaf represents a final outcome (if all conditions are fulfilled, it's a sunflower or a daisy).

We are now going to use the Iris dataset. This dataset considers sepal width and length, along with petal width and length, in order to classify Iris flowers as setosa, versicolour, or virginica.

> **Note**
>
> The Iris dataset can be downloaded from scikit-learn using Python:
>
> https://scikit-learn.org/stable/modules/generated/sklearn.datasets.load_iris.html
>
> Scikit-learn is a library that provides useful tools for data mining and data analysis.

The following flowchart shows the learning representation of a decision tree trained on this dataset. X represents features from the dataset, X0 being sepal length, X1 being sepal width, X2 being petal length, and X3 petal width. The 'value' tag is how many samples of each category fall into each node. We can see that, in the first step, the decision tree already distinguishes setosa from the other two by only considering the X2 feature, petal length:

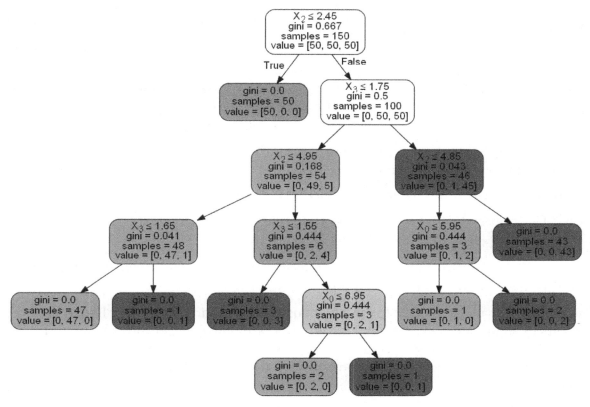

Figure 2.26: Graph of a decision tree for the Iris dataset

Decision trees can be implemented in Python using only a couple of lines thanks to scikit-learn:

```
from sklearn.tree import DecisionTreeClassifier
dtree=DecisionTreeClassifier()
dtree.fit(x,y)
```

x and **y** are the features and the labels of the training set, respectively.

x, apart from being only columns of data representing those lengths and widths, could also be every pixel of the image. In machine learning, when the input data is images, every pixel is treated as a feature.

Decision trees are trained for one specific task or dataset and cannot be transferred to another similar problem. Nevertheless, several decision trees can be combined in order to create bigger models and learn how to generalize. These are called **random forests**.

The name forest refers to an ensemble of many decision tree algorithms, following the **bagging** method, which states that the combination of several algorithms achieves the best result overall. The appearance of the word "random" refers to the randomness of the algorithm when selecting the features to take into account to split a node.

Thanks again to scikit-learn, we can implement the random forest algorithm with only a couple of lines, fairly similar to the previous lines:

```
from sklearn.ensemble import RandomForestClassifier

rndForest=RandomForestClassifier(n_estimators=10)

rndForest.fit(x,y)
```

n_estimators stands for the number of underlying decision trees. If you test the results with this method, the results will improve for sure.

There are other methods that follow the **boosting** methodology as well. Boosting consists of algorithms called **weak learners** that are put together into a weighted sum and generate a strong learner, which gives an output. These weak learners are trained sequentially, meaning each one of them tries to solve the mistakes made by its predecessor.

There are many algorithms that use this approach. The most famous ones are AdaBoost, gradient boosting, and XGBoost. We are only going to look at AdaBoost as it is the most well known and easy to understand.

Boosting

AdaBoost puts together weak learners in order to form a strong learner. The name AdaBoost stands for adaptive boosting, which means that this strategy would weigh differently at each point in time. Those examples that are incorrectly classified in a single iteration, get a higher weight than the next iteration, and vice versa.

The code for this method is as follows:

```
from sklearn.ensemble import AdaBoostClassifier

adaboost=AdaBoostClassifier(n_estimators=100)

adaboost.fit(x_train, y_train)
```

n_estimators is the maximum number of estimators once boosting is completed.

This method is initialized with a decision tree underneath; thus, the performance might not be as good as the random forest. But in order to make a better classifier, the random forest algorithm should be used instead:

```
AdaBoostClassifier(RandomForestClassifier(n_jobs=-1,n_estimators=500,max_
features='auto'),n_estimators=100)
```

Exercise 8: Predicting Numbers Using the Decision Tree, Random Forest, and AdaBoost Algorithms

In this exercise, we are going to use the digits obtained from the last exercise and the models that we have learned in this topic to correctly predict every number. To do that, we are going to extract several digits from some samples inside the **Dataset/numbers** folder, along with the MNIST dataset to have enough data, so the models learn properly. The MNIST dataset is a compound of handwritten digits, which go from 0 to 9 with a shape of 28 x 28 x 3, and it is mostly used for researchers to test their methods or to play around with. Nevertheless, it can help to predict some numbers even though they are not of the same kind. You can check out this dataset at http://yann.lecun.com/exdb/mnist/.

As the installation of Keras requires TensorFlow, we propose to use Google Colab, which is just like a Jupyter notebook but with the difference that your system is not being used. Instead, a remote virtual machine is used and everything for machine learning and Python is already installed.

Let's begin the exercise:

> **Note**
>
> We will be continuing the code from Exercise 7, here in the same notebook.

1. Head to the interface on Google Colab, where you executed the code for *Exercise 7, Loading an Image and Applying the Learned Methods*.

2. Import the libraries:

    ```
    import numpy as np
    import random
    from sklearn import metrics
    from sklearn.ensemble import RandomForestClassifier, AdaBoostClassifier
    from sklearn.tree import DecisionTreeClassifier
    from sklearn.utils import shuffle
    from matplotlib import pyplot as plt
    import cv2
    ```

```
import os
import re
random.seed(42)
```

> **Note**
>
> We are setting the seed of the random method to 42, which is for reproducibility: all random steps have the same randomness and always give the same output. It could be set to any number that does not vary.

3. Now we are going to import the MNIST dataset:

```
from keras.datasets import mnist

(x_train, y_train), (x_test, y_test) = mnist.load_data()
```

In the last line of the code, we are loading the data in **x_train**, which is the training set (60,000 examples of digits), **y_train**, which are the labels of those digits, **x_test**, which is the testing set, and **y_test**, which are the corresponding labels. These are in NumPy format.

4. Let's show some of those digits using Matplotlib:

```
for idx in range(5):
    rnd_index = random.randint(0, 59999)
    plt.subplot(1,5,idx+1),plt.imshow(x_train[idx],'gray')
    plt.xticks([]),plt.yticks([])
plt.show()
```

Figure 2.27: MNIST dataset

> **Note**
>
> These digits do not look like the ones that we extracted in the previous exercise. In order to make the models properly predict the digits from the image processed in the first exercise, we will need to add some of those digits to this dataset.

Here's the process for adding new digits that look like the ones we want to predict:

Add a Dataset folder with subfolders numbered from 0 to 9 (already done).

Get the code from the previous exercise.

Use the code to extract all the digits from the images that are stored in 'Dataset/numbers/' (already done).

Paste the generated digits to the corresponding folders with the name that corresponds to the digit generated (already done).

Add those images to the original dataset (step 5 in this exercise).

5. To add those images to your training set, these two methods should be declared:

```python
# ------------------------------------------------------------
def list_files(directory, ext=None):
    return [os.path.join(directory, f) for f in os.listdir(directory)
            if os.path.isfile(os.path.join(directory, f)) and ( ext==None
or re.match('([\w_-]+\.(?:' + ext + '))', f) )]
    # ------------------------------------------------------
def load_images(path,label):
    X = []
    Y = []
    label = str(label)
    for fname in list_files( path, ext='jpg' ):
        img = cv2.imread(fname,0)
        img = cv2.resize(img, (28, 28))
        X.append(img)
        Y.append(label)

    if maximum != -1 :
        X = X[:maximum]
        Y = Y[:maximum]

    X = np.asarray(X)
    Y = np.asarray(Y)
    return X, Y
```

The first method, **list_files()**, lists all the files within a folder with the specified extension, which in this case is **jpg**.

In the main method, **load_images()**, we are loading the images from those folders, which are from the digit folder, with its corresponding label. If the maximum is different to –1, we establish a limit to the quantity that is loaded for every digit. We do this because there should be similar samples for every digit. Finally, we convert the lists to NumPy arrays.

6. Now we need to add these arrays to the training set so that our models can learn how to recognize the extracted digits:

```
print(x_train.shape)
print(x_test.shape)
X, Y = load_images('Dataset/%d'%(0),0,9)
for digit in range(1,10):
  X_aux, Y_aux = load_images('Dataset/%d'%(digit),digit,9)
  print(X_aux.shape)
  X = np.concatenate((X, X_aux), axis=0)
  Y = np.concatenate((Y, Y_aux), axis=0)
```

After adding those digits using the method declared in the preceding code, we concatenate those arrays to the sets created before the for loop mentioned:

```
from sklearn.model_selection import train_test_split
x_tr, x_te, y_tr, y_te = train_test_split(X, Y, test_size=0.2)
```

After this, the **train_test_split** method from **sklearn** is used in order to separate those digits – 20% for testing and the rest for training:

```
x_train = np.concatenate((x_train, x_tr), axis=0)
y_train = np.concatenate((y_train, y_tr), axis=0)
x_test = np.concatenate((x_test, x_te), axis=0)
y_test = np.concatenate((y_test, y_te), axis=0)

print(x_train.shape)
print(x_test.shape)
```

Once done, we concatenate those to the original training and testing sets. We have printed the shape of x_train and x_test before and after so those extra 60 digits can be seen. It goes from shape (60,000, 28, and 28) and (10,000, 28, and 28) to shape (60,072, 28, and 28) and (10,018, 28, and 28).

7. For the models imported from sklearn that we are going to use in this exercise, we need to format the arrays to the shape (n samples and array), and now we have (n samples, array_height, and array_width):

```
x_train = x_train.reshape(x_train.shape[0],x_train.shape[1]*x_train.
shape[2])
x_test = x_test.reshape(x_test.shape[0],x_test.shape[1]*x_test.shape[2])
print(x_train.shape)
print(x_test.shape)
```

We multiply the height and the width of the array in order to get the total length of the array, but only in one dimension: (28*28) = (784).

8. Now we are ready to feed the data into the models. We will start training a decision tree:

```
print ("Applying Decision Tree...")
dtc = DecisionTreeClassifier()
dtc.fit(x_train, y_train)
```

In order to see how well this model performs, metric accuracy is used. This represents the number of samples from **x_test** that have been predicted, which we have already imported from the **metrics** module and from sklearn. Now we will be using **accuracy_score()** from that module to calculate the accuracy of the model. We need to predict the results from **x_test** using the **predict()** function from the model and see whether the output matches the **y_test** labels:

```
y_pred = dtc.predict(x_test)
accuracy = metrics.accuracy_score(y_test, y_pred)
print(accuracy*100)
```

After that, the accuracy is calculated and printed. The resulting accuracy percentage is **87.92%**, which is not a bad result for a decision tree. It can be improved though.

9. Let's try the random forest algorithm:

```
print ("Applying RandomForest...")
rfc = RandomForestClassifier(n_estimators=100)
rfc.fit(x_train, y_train)
```

Following the same methodology to calculate the accuracy, the accuracy obtained is **94.75%**, which is way better and could be classified as a good model.

10. Now, we will try AdaBoost initialized with random forest:

```
print ("Applying Adaboost...")
adaboost = AdaBoostClassifier(rfc,n_estimators=10)
adaboost.fit(x_train, y_train)
```

The accuracy obtained using AdaBoost is **95.67%**. This algorithm takes much more time than the previous ones but gets better results.

11. We are now going to apply random forest to the digits that were obtained in the last exercise. We apply this algorithm because it takes much less time than AdaBoost and gives better results. Before checking the following code, you need to run the code from the exercise one for the image stored in the **Dataset/number. jpg** folder, which is the one used in the first exercise, and for the other two images that are extracted for testing in the **Dataset/testing/** folder. Once you have done that, you should have five images of digits in your directory for every image, ready to be loaded. Here's the code:

```
for number in range(5):
    imgLoaded = cv2.imread('number%d.jpg'%(number),0)
    img = cv2.resize(imgLoaded, (28, 28))
    img = img.flatten()
    img = img.reshape(1,-1)
    plt.subplot(1,5,number+1),
    plt.imshow(imgLoaded,'gray')
    plt.title(rfc.predict(img)[0])
    plt.xticks([]),plt.yticks([])
plt.show()
```

Figure 2.28: Random forest prediction for the digits 1, 6, 2, 1, and 6

Here, we are applying the **predict()** function of the random forest model, passing every image to it. Random forest seems to perform pretty well, as it has predicted all of the numbers correctly. Let's try another number that has not been used (there is a folder with some images for testing inside the **Dataset** folder):

Figure 2.29: Random forest prediction for the digits 1, 5, 8, 3, and 4

It is still performing well with the rest of the digits. Let's try another number:

Figure 2.30: Random forest prediction for the digits 1, 9, 4, 7, and 9

With the number 7, it seems to be having problems. It is probably because we have not introduced enough samples, and due to the simplicity of the model.

> **Note**
>
> The entire code for this exercise is available on GitHub in the Lesson02 | Exercise07-09 folder.

Now, in the next topic, we are going to explore the world of artificial neural networks, which are far more capable of achieving these tasks.

Artificial Neural Networks (ANNs)

Artificial neural networks (ANNs) are information processing systems that are modeled on and inspired by the human brain, which they try to mimic by learning how to recognize patterns in data. They accomplish tasks by having a well structured architecture. This architecture is composed of several small processing units called neurons, which are interconnected in order to solve major problems.

ANNs learn by having enough examples in the dataset that they are processing, and enough examples means thousands of examples, or even millions. The amount of data here can be a disadvantage, since if you do not have this data, you will have to create it yourself, and that means that you will probably need a lot of money to gather sufficient data.

Another disadvantage of these algorithms is that they need to be trained on specific hardware and software. They are well trained on high-performance GPUs, which are expensive. You can still do certain things using a GPU that does not cost that much, but the data will take much longer to be trained. You also need to have specific software, such as **TensorFlow**, **Keras**, **PyTorch**, or **Fast.AI**. For this book, we will be using TensorFlow and Keras, which runs on top of TensorFlow.

These algorithms work by taking all of the data as input, in which the first layer of neurons acts as the input. After that, every entry is passed to the next layer of neurons, where these are multiplied by some value and processed by an activation function, which makes "decisions" and passes those values to the next layer. The layers in the middle of the network are called hidden layers. This process keeps going until the last layer, where the output is given. When introducing the MNIST images as input to the neural network, the end of the network should have 10 neurons, each neuron representing each digit, and if the neural network guesses that an image is a specific digit, then the corresponding neuron will be activated. The ANN checks whether it has succeeded for the decision, and if not, it performs a correction process called **backpropagation**, where every pass of the network is checked and corrected, adjusting the weights of the neurons. In Figure 2.31, backpropagation is shown:

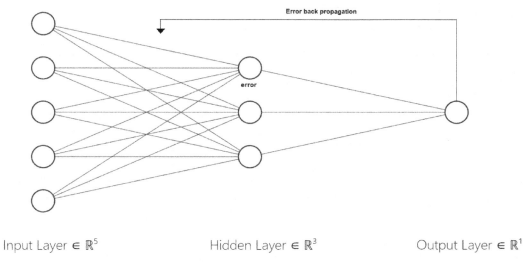

Input Layer $\in \mathbb{R}^5$ Hidden Layer $\in \mathbb{R}^3$ Output Layer $\in \mathbb{R}^1$

Figure 2.31: Backpropagation process

Here is a graphical representation of an ANN:

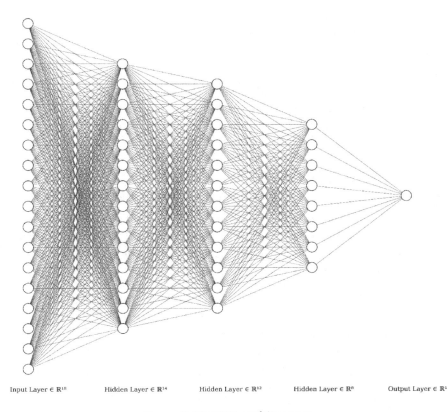

Input Layer $\in \mathbb{R}^{18}$ Hidden Layer $\in \mathbb{R}^{14}$ Hidden Layer $\in \mathbb{R}^{12}$ Hidden Layer $\in \mathbb{R}^8$ Output Layer $\in \mathbb{R}^1$

Figure 2.32: ANN architecture

In the preceding diagram, we can see the neurons, which is where all the processing occurs, and the connections between them, which are the weights of the network.

We are going to gain an understanding of how to create one of these neural networks, but first, we need to take a look at the data that we have.

In the previous exercise, we had the shapes (60,072 and 784) and (10,018 and 784) as integer types, and 0 to 255 as pixel values, for training and testing, respectively. ANNs perform better and faster with **normalized data**, but what is that?

Having normalized data means converting that 0-255 range of values to a range of 0-1. The values must be adapted to fit between 0 and 1, which means they will be float numbers, because there is no other way to fit a higher range of numbers into a shorter range So, first we need to convert the data to a float and then normalize it. Here's the code for doing so:

```
x_train = (x_train.astype(np.float32))/255.0 #Converts to float and then
normalize

x_test = (x_test.astype(np.float32))/255.0 #Same for the test set

x_train = x_train.reshape(x_train.shape[0], 28, 28, 1)

x_test = x_test.reshape(x_test.shape[0], 28, 28, 1)
```

For the labels, we also need to change the format to one-hot encoding.

In order to do that, we need to use a function from Keras, from its **utils** package (the name has changed to **np_utils**), called **to_categorical()**, which transforms the number of the digit of every label to **one-hot encoding**. Here's the code:

```
y_train = np_utils.to_categorical(y_train, 10)

y_test = np_utils.to_categorical(y_test, 10)
```

If we print the first label of **y_train**, 5, and then we print the first value of **y_train** after the conversion, it will output [0. 0. 0. 0. 0. 1. 0. 0. 0. 0.]. This format puts a 1 in the sixth place of an array of 10 positions (because there are 10 numbers) for the number 5 (in the sixth place because the first one is for the 0, and not for the 1). Now we are ready to go ahead with the architecture of the neural network.

For a basic neural network, dense layers (or **fully connected layers**) are employed. These neural networks are also called **fully connected neural networks**. These contain a series of neurons that represent the neurons of the human brain. They need an activation function to be specified. An activation function is a function that takes the input and calculates a weighted sum of it, adding a bias and deciding whether it should be activated or not (outputs 1 and 0, respectively).

The two most used activation functions are sigmoid and ReLU, but ReLU has demonstrated better performance overall. They are represented on the following chart:

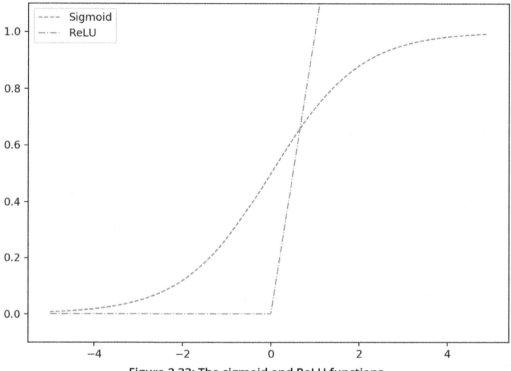

Figure 2.33: The sigmoid and ReLU functions

The sigmoid and ReLU functions calculate the weighted sum and add the bias. They then output a value depending on the value of that calculation. The sigmoid function will give different values depending on the value of the calculation, from 0 to 1. But ReLU will give 0 for negative values or return the value of the calculation for positive values.

Toward the end of a neural network, normally the **softmax** activation function takes place, which will output a non-probabilistic number for every class, which is higher for the class that has the highest chance of corresponding to the input image. There are other activation functions, but this one is the best for the output of a network for multi-classification problems.

In **Keras**, a neural network could be coded as follows:

```
model = Sequential()
model.add(Dense(16, input_shape=input_shape))
model.add(Activation('relu'))


model.add(Dense(8))
model.add(Activation('relu'))


model.add(Flatten())
model.add(Dense(10, activation="softmax"))
```

The model is created as **Sequential()** as the layers are created sequentially. First, we add a dense layer with 16 neurons and the shape of the input is passed so that the neural network knows the shape of the input. After which, the **ReLU** activation function is applied. We use this function because it generally gives good results. We stack another layer with eight neurons and the same activation function.

At the end, we use the **Flatten** function to convert the array to one dimension and then the last dense layer is stacked, where the number of classes should represent the number of neurons (in this case, there would be 10 classes for the MNIST dataset). The softmax function is applied in order to get the results as a one-hot encoder, as we have mentioned before.

Now we have to compile the model. In order to do that, we use the **compile** method as follows:

```
model.compile(loss='categorical_crossentropy', optimizer=Adadelta(),
metrics=['accuracy'])
```

We pass the loss function, which is used to calculate the error for the backpropagation process. For this problem, we will be using categorial cross-entropy as the loss function, as this is a categorical problem. The optimizer used is **Adadelta**, which performs very well in most situations. We establish accuracy as the main metric to be considered in the model.

We are going to use what is called a callback in Keras. These are called in every epoch during training. We will be using the **Checkpoint** function in order to save our model with the best validation result on every epoch:

```
ckpt = ModelCheckpoint('model.h5', save_best_only=True,monitor='val_loss',
mode='min', save_weights_only=False)
```

The function to train this model is called **fit()** and is implemented as follows:

```
model.fit(x_train, y_train, batch_size=64, epochs=10, verbose=1, validation_
data=(x_test, y_test),callbacks=[ckpt])
```

We pass the training set with its labels, and we establish a batch size of 64 (these are the images that are passed on every step of every epoch), out of which we choose to have 10 training epochs (on every epoch the data is processed). The validation set is also passed in order to see how the model performs on unseen data, and at the end, we set the callback that we created before.

All these parameters have to be adjusted according to the problem that we are facing. In order to put all of this into practice, we are going to perform an exercise – the same exercise that we did with decision trees, but with neural networks.

Exercise 9: Building Your First Neural Network

> **Note**
>
> We will be continuing the code from Exercise 8 here.
>
> The entire code for this exercise can be found on GitHub in the Lesson02 | Exercise07-09 folder.

1. Head to the interface on Google Colab where you executed the code for *Exercise 8, Predicting Numbers Using the Decision Tree, Random Forest, and AdaBoost Algorithms.*

2. Now import the packages from the Keras library:

```
from keras.callbacks import ModelCheckpoint
from keras.layers import Dense, Flatten, Activation, BatchNormalization,
Dropout
from keras.models import Sequential
from keras.optimizers import Adadelta
from keras import utils as np_utils
```

3. We normalize the data as we explained in this part of the chapter. We also declare the **input_shape** instance that will be passed to the neural network, and we print it:

```
x_train = (x_train.astype(np.float32))/255.0
x_test = (x_test.astype(np.float32))/255.0
x_train = x_train.reshape(x_train.shape[0], 28, 28, 1)
x_test = x_test.reshape(x_test.shape[0], 28, 28, 1)
y_train = np_utils.to_categorical(y_train, 10)
y_test = np_utils.to_categorical(y_test, 10)
input_shape = x_train.shape[1:]
print(input_shape)
print(x_train.shape)
```

The output is as follows:

(28, 28, 1)

(60072, 28, 28, 1)

Figure 2.34: Data output when passed for normalization using neural networks

4. Now we are going to declare the model. The model that we built before was never going to perform well enough on this problem, so we have created a deeper model with more neurons and with a couple of new methods:

```
def DenseNN(input_shape):
    model = Sequential()

    model.add(Dense(512, input_shape=input_shape))
    model.add(Activation('relu'))
    model.add(BatchNormalization())
    model.add(Dropout(0.2))

    model.add(Dense(512))
    model.add(Activation('relu'))
    model.add(BatchNormalization())
    model.add(Dropout(0.2))

    model.add(Dense(256))
    model.add(Activation('relu'))
    model.add(BatchNormalization())
    model.add(Dropout(0.2))

    model.add(Flatten())
```

```
model.add(Dense(256))
model.add(Activation('relu'))
model.add(BatchNormalization())
model.add(Dropout(0.2))

model.add(Dense(10, activation="softmax"))
```

We have added a **BatchNormalization()** method, which helps the network converge faster and may give better results overall.

We have also added the **Dropout()** method, which helps the network to avoid **overfitting** (the accuracy of the training set is much higher than the accuracy of the validation set). It does that by disconnecting some neurons during training (0.2 -> 20% of neurons), which allows better generalization of the problem (better classification of unseen data).

Furthermore, the number of neurons has increased drastically. Also, the number of layers has increased. The more layers and neurons are added, the deeper the understanding is and more complex features are learned.

5. Now we compile the model using categorical cross-entropy, as there are several classes, and we use Adadelta, which is great overall for these kinds of tasks. Also, we use accuracy as the main metric:

```
model.compile(loss='categorical_crossentropy', optimizer=Adadelta(),
metrics=['accuracy'])
```

6. Let's create the **Checkpoint** callback, where the model will be stored in the **Models** folder with the name **model.h5**. We will be using validation loss as the main method to be tracked and the model will be saved in its entirety:

```
ckpt = ModelCheckpoint('Models/model.h5', save_best_
only=True,monitor='val_loss', mode='min', save_weights_only=False)
```

7. Start to train the network with the **fit()** function, just like we explained before. We use 64 as the batch size, 10 epochs (which is enough as every epoch is going to last a very long time and between epochs it will not improve that much), and we will introduce the Checkpoint callback:

```
model.fit(x_train, y_train,
          batch_size=64,
          epochs=10,
          verbose=1,
          validation_data=(x_test, y_test),
          callbacks=[ckpt])
```

This is going to take a while.

The output should look like this:

```
Train on 60072 samples, validate on 10018 samples
Epoch 1/10
60072/60072 [==============================] - 261s 4ms/step - loss: 0.2079 - acc: 0.9383 - val_loss: 0.1066 - val_acc: 0.9689
Epoch 2/10
60072/60072 [==============================] - 257s 4ms/step - loss: 0.1001 - acc: 0.9708 - val_loss: 0.0808 - val_acc: 0.9752
Epoch 3/10
60072/60072 [==============================] - 257s 4ms/step - loss: 0.0694 - acc: 0.9791 - val_loss: 0.0849 - val_acc: 0.9727
Epoch 4/10
60072/60072 [==============================] - 257s 4ms/step - loss: 0.0497 - acc: 0.9849 - val_loss: 0.0778 - val_acc: 0.9761
Epoch 5/10
60072/60072 [==============================] - 257s 4ms/step - loss: 0.0361 - acc: 0.9889 - val_loss: 0.0804 - val_acc: 0.9748
Epoch 6/10
60072/60072 [==============================] - 257s 4ms/step - loss: 0.0268 - acc: 0.9922 - val_loss: 0.0788 - val_acc: 0.9771
Epoch 7/10
60072/60072 [==============================] - 257s 4ms/step - loss: 0.0211 - acc: 0.9938 - val_loss: 0.0939 - val_acc: 0.9731
Epoch 8/10
60072/60072 [==============================] - 257s 4ms/step - loss: 0.0166 - acc: 0.9955 - val_loss: 0.0901 - val_acc: 0.9766
Epoch 9/10
60072/60072 [==============================] - 257s 4ms/step - loss: 0.0150 - acc: 0.9959 - val_loss: 0.0821 - val_acc: 0.9764
Epoch 10/10
60072/60072 [==============================] - 257s 4ms/step - loss: 0.0129 - acc: 0.9963 - val_loss: 0.0802 - val_acc: 0.9783
```

Figure 2.35: Neural network output

The final accuracy of the model corresponds to the last **val_acc**, which is **97.83%**. This is a better result than we got using AdaBoost or random forest.

8. Now let's make some predictions:

```
for number in range(5):
    imgLoaded = cv2.imread('number%d.jpg'%(number),0)
    img = cv2.resize(imgLoaded, (28, 28))
    img = (img.astype(np.float32))/255.0
    img = img.reshape(1, 28, 28, 1)
    plt.subplot(1,5,number+1),plt.imshow(imgLoaded,'gray')
    plt.title(np.argmax(model.predict(img)[0]))
    plt.xticks([]),plt.yticks([])
plt.show()
```

The code looks similar to the code used in the last exercise but has some minor differences. One is that, as we changed the input format, we have to change the format of the input image too (float and normalize). The other is that the prediction is in one-hot encoding, so we use the **argmax()** NumPy function in order to get the position of the maximum value of the one-hot output vector, which would be the predicted digit.

Let's see the output of the last number that we tried using random forest:

Figure 2.36: Prediction of numbers using neural networks

The output has been successful – even the 7 that the random forest model struggled with.

> **Note**
>
> The entire code can be found on GitHub in the Lesson02 | Exercise07-09 folder.

If you try the other numbers, it will classify them all very well – it has learned how to.

Congratulations! You have built your first neural network and you have applied it to a real-world problem! Now you are ready to go through the activity for this chapter.

Activity 2: Classify 10 Types of Clothes from the Fashion-MNIST Database

Now you are going to face a similar problem to the previous one but with types of clothes. This database is very similar to the original MNIST. It has 60,000 images – 28x28 in grayscale – for training and 10,000 for testing. You will have to follow the steps mentioned in the first exercise as this activity is not focused on the real world. You will have to put into practice the abilities learned in the last exercise by building a neural network on your own. For this, you will have to open a Google Colab notebook. The following steps will guide you in the right direction:

1. Load the dataset from Keras:

   ```
   from keras.datasets import fashion_mnist
   (x_train, y_train), (x_test, y_test) = fashion_mnist.load_data()
   ```

> **Note**
>
> The data is preprocessed like MNIST, so the next steps should be similar to *Exercise 5, Applying the Various Morphological Transformations to an Image*.

2. Import **random** and set the seed to 42. Import **matplotlib** and plot five random samples of the dataset, just as we did in the last exercise.

3. Now normalize the data and reshape it to fit properly into the neural network and convert the labels to one–hot encoder.

4. Start to build the architecture of the neural network by using dense layers. You have to build it inside a method that will return the model.

> **Note**
>
> We recommend starting off by building a very small, easy architecture and improving it by testing it with the given dataset.

5. Compile the model with the appropriate parameters and start training the neural network.

6. Once trained, we should make some predictions in order to test the model. We have uploaded some images into the same **testing** folder inside the **Dataset** folder of the last exercise. Make predictions using those images, just as we did in the last exercise.

> **Note**
>
> You have to consider that the images that were fed into the neural network had a black background and the clothes were white, so you should make corresponding adjustments to make the image look like those. If needed, you should invert white as black and vice versa. NumPy has a method that does that: **image = np.invert(image)**.

7. Check the results:

T-shirt	Trouser	Pullover	Dress	Coat	Sandal	Shirt	Sneaker	Bag	Ankle boot
0	1	2	3	4	5	6	7	8	9

Figure 2.37: The output of the prediction is the index of the position in this list

Note

The solution for this activity is available on page 302.

Summary

Computer vision is a big field within AI. By understanding this field, you can achieve results such as extracting information from an image or generating images that look just like they do in real life, for example. This chapter has covered image preprocessing for feature extraction using the OpenCV library, which allows easy training and prediction for machine learning models. Some basic machine learning models have also been covered, such as decision trees and boosting algorithms. These served as an introduction to machine learning and were mostly used to play around. Finally, neural networks were introduced and coded using Keras and TensorFlow as a backend. Normalization was explained and put into practice, along with dense layers, though convolutional layers are known to work better with images than dense layers do, and they will be explained later in the book.

Concepts for avoiding overfitting were also covered, and toward the end, we used the model to make predictions and put it into practice using real-world images.

In the next chapter, the fundamentals of **natural language processing (NLP)** will be introduced, along with the most widely used techniques for extracting information from a corpus in order to create basic models for language prediction.

3

Fundamentals of Natural Language Processing

Learning Objectives

By the end of this chapter, you will be able to:

- Classify different areas of natural language processing
- Analyze basic natural language processing libraries in Python
- Predict the topics in a set of texts
- Develop a simple language model

This chapter covers different fundamentals and areas of natural language processing, along with its libraries in Python.

Introduction

Natural Language Processing (**NLP**) is an area of **Artificial Intelligence** (**AI**) with the goal of enabling computers to understand and manipulate human language in order to perform useful tasks. Within this area, there are two sections: **Natural Language Understanding** (**NLU**) and **Natural Language Generation** (**NLG**).

In recent years, AI has changed the way machines interact with humans. AI helps people solve complex equations by performing tasks such as recommending a movie according to your tastes (recommender systems). Thanks to the high performance of GPUs and the huge amount of data available, it's possible to create intelligent systems that are capable of learning and behaving like humans.

There are many libraries that aim to help with the creation of these systems. In this chapter, we will review the most famous Python libraries to extract and clean information from raw text. You may consider this task complex, but a complete understanding and interpretation of the language is a difficult task in itself. For example, the sentence "Cristiano Ronaldo scores three goals" would be hard for a machine to understand because it would not know who Cristiano Ronaldo is or what is meant by the number of goals.

One of the most popular topics in NLP is **Question Answering** (**QA**). This discipline also consists of **Information Retrieval** (**IR**). These systems construct answers by querying a database for knowledge or information, but they are capable of extracting answers from a collection of natural language documents. That is how a search engine such as Google works.

In the industry today, NLP is becoming more and more popular. The latest NLP trends are online advertisement matching, sentiment analysis, automated translation, and chatbots.

Conversational agents, popularly known as chatbots, are the next challenge for NLP. They can hold real conversation and many companies use them to get feedback about their products or to create a new advertising campaign, by analyzing the behavior and opinions of clients through the chatbot. Virtual assistants are a great example of NLP and they have already been introduced to the market. The most famous are Siri, Amazon's Alexa, and Google Home. In this book, we will create a chatbot to control a virtual robot that is able to understand what we want the robot to do.

Natural Language Processing

As mentioned before, NLP is an AI field that takes care of understanding and processing human language. NLP is located at the intersection between AI, computer science, and linguistics. The main aim of this area is to make computers understand statements or words written in human languages:

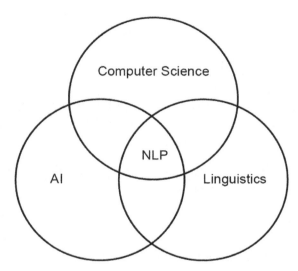

Figure 3.1: Representation of NLP within AI, linguistics, and computer science

Linguistic science focuses on the study of human language, trying to characterize and explain the different approaches of language.

A language can be defined as a set of rules and a set of symbols. Symbols are combined and used to broadcast information and are structured by rules. Human language is special. We cannot simply picture it as naturally formed symbols and rules; depending on the context, the meaning of words can change.

NLP is becoming more popular and can solve many difficult problems. The amount of text data available is very large, and it is impossible for a human to process all that data. In Wikipedia, the average number of new articles per day is 547, and in total, there are more than 5,000,000 articles. As you can imagine, a human cannot read all that information.

There are three challenges faced by NLP. The first challenge is collecting all the data, the second is classifying it, and the final one is extracting the relevant information.

NLP solves many tedious tasks, such as spam detection in emails, **part-of-speech (POS)** tagging, and named entity recognition. With deep learning, NLP can also solve voice-to-text problems. Although NLP shows a lot of power, there are some cases such as working without having a good solution from the dialog between a human and a machine, QA systems summarization and machine translation.

Parts of NLP

As mentioned before, NLP can be divided into two groups: NLU and NLG.

Natural Language Understanding

This section of NLP relates to the understanding and analysis of human language. It focusses on the comprehension of text data, and processing it to extract relevant information. NLU provides direct human-computer interaction and performs tasks related to the comprehension of language.

NLU covers the hardest of AI challenges, and that is the interpretation of text. The main challenge of NLU is understanding dialog.

> **Note**
>
> NLP uses a set of methods for generating, processing, and understanding language. NLU uses functions to understand the meaning of a text.

Previously, a conversation was represented as a tree, but this approach cannot cover many dialog cases. To cover more cases, more trees would be required, one for each context of the conversation, leading to the repeating of many sentences:

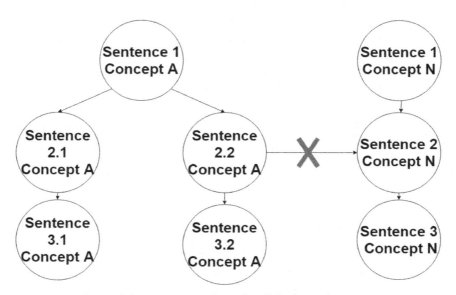

Figure 3.2: Representation of a dialogue using trees

This approach is outdated and inefficient because is based on fixed rules; it's essentially an if-else structure. But now, NLU has contributed another approach. A conversation can be represented as a Venn diagram where each set is a context of the conversation:

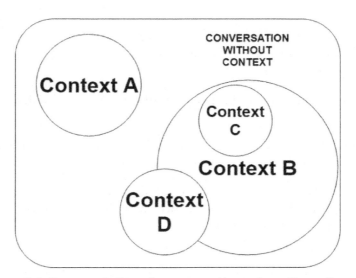

Figure 3.3: Representation of a conversation using a Venn diagram

As you can see in the previous figures, the NLU approach improves the structure of understanding a conversation, because it is not a fixed structure that contains if-else conditions. The main goal of NLU is to interpret the meaning of human language and deal with the contexts of a conversation, solving ambiguities and managing data.

Natural Language Generation

NLG is the process of producing phrases, sentences, and paragraphs with meaning and structure. It is an area of NLP that does not deal with understanding text.

To generate natural language, NLG methods need relevant data.

NLG has three components:

- **Generator**: Responsible for including the text within an intent to have it related with the context of the situation

- **Components and levels of representations**: Gives structure to the generated text

- **Application**: Saves relevant data from the conversation to follow a logical thread

Generated text must be in a human-readable format. The advantages of NLG are that you can make your data accessible and you can create summaries of reports rapidly.

Levels of NLP

Human language has different levels of representation. Each representation level is more complex than the previous level. As we ascend through the levels, it gets more difficult to understand the language.

The two first levels depend on the data type (audio or text), in which we have the following:

- **Phonological analysis**: If the data is speech, first, we need to analyze the audio to have sentences.

- **OCR/tokenization**: If we have text, we need to recognize the characters and form words using computer vision (OCR). If not, we will need to tokenize the text (that is, split the sentence into units of text).

> **Note**
>
> The OCR process is the identification of characters in an image. Once it generates words, they are processed as raw text.

- **Morphological analysis**: Focused on the words of a sentence and analyzing its morphemes.

- **Syntactic analysis**: This level focuses on the grammatical structure of a sentence. That means understanding different parts of a sentence, such as the subject or the predicate.

- **Semantic representation**: A program does not understand a single word; it can know the meaning of a word by knowing how the word is used in a sentence. For example, "cat" and "dog" could mean the same for an algorithm because they can be used in the same way. Understanding sentences in this way is called word-level meaning.

- **Discourse processing**: Analyzing and identifying connected sentences in a text and their relationships. By doing this, an algorithm could understand what the topic of the text is.

NLP shows great potential in today's industry, but there are some exceptions. Using deep learning concepts, we can work with some of these exceptions to get better results. Some of these problems will be reviewed in *Chapter 4*, *Neural Networks with NLP*. The advantage of text processing techniques and the improvement of recurrent neural networks are the reasons why NLP is becoming increasingly important.

NLP in Python

Python has become very popular in recent years, by combining the power of general-purpose programming languages with the use of specific domain languages, such as MATLAB and R (designed for mathematics and statistics). It has different libraries for data loading, visualization, NLP, image processing, statistics, and more. Python has the most powerful libraries for text processing and machine learning algorithms.

Natural Language Toolkit (NLTK)

NLTK is the most common kit of tools for working with human language data in Python. It includes a set of libraries and programs for processing natural language and statistics. NLTK is commonly used as a learning tool and for carrying out research.

This library provides interfaces and methods for over 50 corpora and lexical resources. NLTK is capable of classifying text and performing other functions, such as tokenization, stemming (extracting the stem of a word), tagging (identifying the tag of a word, such as person, city...), and parsing (syntax analysis).

Exercise 10: Introduction to NLTK

In this exercise, we will review the most basic concepts about the NLTK library. As we said before, this library is one of the most widely used tools for NLP. It can be used to analyze and study text, disregarding useless information. These techniques can be applied to any text data, for example, to extract the most important keywords from a set of tweets or to analyze an article in a newspaper:

> **Note**
>
> All the exercises in this chapter will be executed in Google Colab.

1. Open up your Google Colab interface.

2. Create a folder for the book.

3. Here, we are going to process a sentence with basic methods of the NLTK library. First of all, let's import the necessary methods (**stopwords**, **word_tokenize**, and **sent_tokenize**):

```
from nltk.corpus import stopwords
from nltk.tokenize import word_tokenize
from nltk.tokenize import sent_tokenize
import nltk
nltk.download('punkt')
```

4. Now we create a sentence and apply the methods:

```
example_sentence = "This course is great. I'm going to learn deep
learning; Artificial Intelligence is amazing and I love robotics..."

sent_tokenize(example_sentence) # Divide the text into sentences
```

```
['This course is great.',
 "I'm going to learn deep learning; Artificial Intelligence is amazing and I love robotics..."]
```

Figure 3.4: Sentence divided into a sub-sentence

```
word_tokenize(example_sentence)
```

```
['This',
 'course',
 'is',
 'great',
 '.',
 'I',
 "'m",
 'going',
 'to',
 'learn',
 'deep',
 'learning',
 ';',
 'Artificial',
 'Intelligence',
 'is',
 'amazing',
 'and',
 'I',
 'love',
 'robotics',
 '...']
```

Figure 3.5: Tokenizing a sentence into words

> **Note**
>
> **Sent_tokenize** returns a list of different sentences. One of the disadvantages of NLTK is that **sent_tokenize** does not analyze the semantic structure of the whole text; it just splits the text by the dots.

5. With the sentence tokenized sentence by words, let's subtract the stop words. The stop words are a set of words without relevant information about the text. Before using **stopwords**, we will need to download it:

```
nltk.download('stopwords')
```

6. Now, we set the language of our **stopwords** as English:

```
stop_words = set(stopwords.words("english"))
print(stop_words)
```

The output is as follows:

```
{'too', 'your', 'has', 'needn', "isn't", 'shan', 'below', 'the', 'if', 'not', 'itself', 'out', 'don', 'to', 'before', 'is', 'on
ce', "didn't", 'hasn', 'into', 'there', 'yours', 'or', "you'll", 'will', 're', 'ourselves', 'weren', "she's", 'couldn', 'on',
'off', 'an', 'again', 'while', 'where', "needn't", 'her', 'nor', 'but', 'was', 'been', 'a', 'wouldn', 'with', 'you', 'further',
'all', 'them', 'those', 'up', 'ours', "you're", 'they', "shan't", 'mustn', 'then', "couldn't", "that'll", 'of', 'i', 'as', 's',
'll', 'd', 'y', 'their', 'being', 'few', 'did', 'how', 'be', 'doing', 'both', 't', 'from', "you've", 'more', 'who', 'himself',
'whom', 'doesn', 'are', 'after', 'now', "doesn't", "shouldn't", 'haven', 'were', 'what', 'this', "haven't", 'by', 'yourselves',
'he', 'his', "should've", 'most', 'should', 'won', 'why', "mustn't", 'just', 'other', 'at', 'myself', "you'd", 'herself', 'her
s', 'so', "don't", 'hadn', "mightn't", 'no', 'about', 'does', 'my', 'until', 'in', 'which', 'through', 'any', 'and', 'am', 'is
n', 'only', 'these', 'me', 'ain', 'some', 'for', 'each', 'm', 'we', "it's", "wouldn't", 'had', 'o', "hadn't", 'between', "has
n't", 'yourself', 'theirs', 've', 'aren', 'same', 'during', 'when', 'wasn', 'its', 'very', 'down', 'it', 'mightn', 'such', "was
n't", "won't", "aren't", 'own', 'him', 'ma', 'she', 'over', 'having', 'have', "weren't", 'above', 'against', 'our', 'do', 'did
n', 'here', 'themselves', 'that', 'than', 'because', 'under', 'shouldn', 'can'}
```

Figure 3.6: Stopwords set as English

7. Process the sentence, deleting **stopwords**:

```
print(word_tokenize(example_sentence))
print([w for w in word_tokenize(example_sentence.lower()) if w not in
stop_words])
```

The output is as follows:

```
['This', 'course', 'is', 'great', '.', 'I', "'m", 'going', 'to', 'learn', 'deep', 'learning', ';', 'Artificial', 'Intelligenc
e', 'is', 'amazing', 'and', 'I', 'love', 'robotics', '...']
['course', 'great', '.', "'m", 'going', 'learn', 'deep', 'learning', ';', 'artificial', 'intelligence', 'amazing', 'love', 'rob
otics', '...']
```

Figure 3.7: Sentence without stop words

8. We can now modify the set of **stopwords** and check the output:

```
stop_words = stop_words - set(('this', 'i', 'and'))
print([w for w in word_tokenize(example_sentence.lower()) if w not in
```

```
['this', 'course', 'great', '.', 'i', "'m", 'going', 'learn', 'deep', 'learning', ';', 'artificial', 'intelligence', 'amazing',
'and', 'i', 'love', 'robotics', '...']
```

Figure 3.8: Setting stop words

9. Stemmers remove morphological affixes from words. Let's define a stemmer and process our sentence. **Porter stemmer** is an algorithm for performing this task:

```
from nltk.stem.porter import *     # importing a stemmer
stemmer = PorterStemmer()     # importing a stemmer
print([stemmer.stem(w) for w in  word_tokenize(example_sentence)])
```

The output is as follows:

```
['thi', 'cours', 'is', 'great', '.', 'I', "'m", 'go', 'to', 'learn', 'deep', 'learn', ';', 'artifici', 'intellig', 'is', 'ama
z', 'and', 'I', 'love', 'robot', '...']
```

Figure 3.9: Setting stop words

10. Finally, let's classify each word by its type. To do this, we will use a POS tagger:

```
nltk.download('averaged_perceptron_tagger')
t = nltk.pos_tag(word_tokenize(example_sentence)) #words with each tag
t
```

The output is as follows:

```
[('This', 'DT'),
 ('course', 'NN'),
 ('is', 'VBZ'),
 ('great', 'JJ'),
 ('.', '.'),
 ('I', 'PRP'),
 ("'m", 'VBP'),
 ('going', 'VBG'),
 ('to', 'TO'),
 ('learn', 'VB'),
 ('deep', 'JJ'),
 ('learning', 'NN'),
 (';', ':'),
 ('Artificial', 'NNP'),
 ('Intelligence', 'NNP'),
 ('is', 'VBZ'),
 ('amazing', 'JJ'),
 ('and', 'CC'),
 ('I', 'PRP'),
 ('love', 'VBP'),
 ('robotics', 'NNS'),
 ('...', ':')]
```

Figure 3.10: POS tagger

> **Note**
>
> The averaged perceptron tagger is an algorithm trained to predict the category of a word.

As you may have noticed in this exercise, NLTK can easily process a sentence. Also, it can analyze a huge set of text documents without any problem. It supports many languages and the tokenization process is faster than that for similar libraries, and it has many methods for each NLP problem.

spaCy

spaCy is another library for NLP in Python. It does look similar to NLTK, but you will see some differences in the way it works.

spaCy was developed by Matt Honnibal and is designed for data scientists to clean and normalize text easily. It's the quickest library in terms of preparing text data for a machine learning model. It includes built-in word vectors and some methods for comparing the similarity between two or more texts (these methods are trained with neural networks).

Its API is easy to use and more intuitive than NLTK. Often, in NLP, spaCy is compared to NumPy. It provides methods and functions for performing tokenization, lemmatization, POS tagging, NER, dependency parsing, sentence and document similarity, text classification, and more.

As well as having linguistic features, it also has statistical models. This means you can predict some linguistic annotations, such as whether a word is a verb or a noun. Depending on the language you want to make predictions in, you will need to change a module. Within this section are Word2Vec models, which we will discuss in *Chapter 4, Neural Networks with NLP*.

spaCy has many advantages, as we said before, but there are some cons too; for instance, it supports only 8 languages (NLTK supports 17 languages), the tokenization process is slow (and this time-consuming process could be critical on a long corpus), and overall, it is not flexible (that is, it just provides API methods without the possibility of modifying any parameters).

Before starting with the exercise, let's review the architecture of spaCy. The most important data structures of spaCy are the Doc and the Vocab.

The Doc structure is the text you are loading; it is not a string. It is composed of a sequence of tokens and their annotations. The Vocab structure is a set of lookup tables, but what are lookup tables and why is the structure important? Well, a lookup table in computation is an array indexing an operation that replaces a runtime. spaCy centralizes information that is available across documents. This means that it is more efficient, as this saves memory. Without these structures, the computational speed of spaCy would be slower.

However, the structure of Doc is different to Vocab because Doc is a container of data. A Doc object owns the data and is composed of a sequence of tokens or spans. There are also a few lexemes, which are related to the Vocab structure because they do not have context (unlike the token container).

> **Note**
>
> A lexeme is a unit of lexical meaning without having inflectional endings. The area of study for this is morphological analysis.

The figure 3.11 shows us the spaCy architecture.

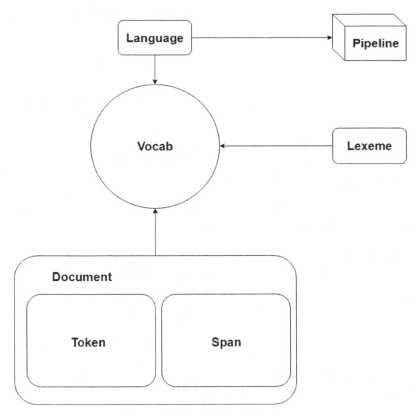

Figure 3.11: spaCy architecture

Depending on the language model you are loading, you will have a different pipeline and a different Vocab.

Exercise 11: Introduction to spaCy

In this exercise, we will do the same transformations that we performed in *Exercise 10, Introduction to NLTK*, and to the same sentence as in that exercise but with the spaCy API. This exercise will help you to understand and learn about the differences between these libraries:

1. Open up your Google Colab interface.

2. Create a folder for the book.

3. Then, import the package to use all its features:

    ```
    import spacy
    ```

4. Now we are going to initialize our **nlp** object. This object is a part of the spaCy methods. By executing this line of code, we are loading the model inside the parenthesis:

    ```
    import en_core_web_sm
    nlp = spacy.load('en')
    ```

5. Let's take the same sentence as in *Exercise 10, Introduction to NLTK*, and create the Doc container:

    ```
    example_sentence = "This course is great. I'm going to learn deep
    learning; Artificial Intelligence is amazing and I love robotics..."
    doc1 = nlp(example_sentence)
    ```

6. Now, print **doc1**, its format, the 5th and 11th token, and a span between the 5th and the 11th token. You will see this:

    ```
    print("Doc structure: {}".format(doc1))
    print("Type of doc1:{}".format(type(doc1)))
    print("5th and 10th Token of the Doc: {}, {}".format(doc1[5], doc1[11]))
    print("Span between the 5th token and the 10th: {}".format(doc1[5:11]))
    ```

    The output is as follows:

    ```
    Doc structure: This course is great. I'm going to learn deep learning; Artifici
    al Intelligence is amazing and I love robotics...
    Type of doc1:<class 'spacy.tokens.doc.Doc'>
    5th and 10th Token of the Doc: I, learning
    Span between the 5th token and the 10th: I'm going to learn deep
    ```

    Figure 3.12: Output of a spaCy document

7. As we saw in Figure 3.5, documents are composed of tokens and spans. First, we are going to see the spans of **doc1**, and then its tokens.

Print the spans:

```
for s in doc1.sents:
    print(s)
```

The output is as follows:

```
This course is great.

I'm going to learn deep learning; Artificial Intelligence is amazing
and I love robotics...
```

Figure 3.13: Printing the spans of doc1

Print the tokens:

```
for i in doc1:
    print(i)
```

The output is as follows:

```
This
course
is
great
.
I
'm
going
to
learn
deep
learning
;
Artificial
Intelligence
is
amazing
and
I
love
robotics

...
```

Figure 3.14: Printing the tokens of doc1

8. Once we have the document divided into tokens, the stop words can be removed.

    First, we need to import them:

    ```
    from spacy.lang.en.stop_words import STOP_WORDS
    print("Some stopwords of spaCy: {}".format(list(STOP_WORDS)[:10]))
    type(STOP_WORDS)
    ```

    The output is as follows:

    ```
    Some stopwords of spaCy: ['within', 'put', 'may', 'part', 'amongst', 'into', 'a
    t', 'everyone', 'often', 'though']
    ```

    Figure 3.15: 10 stop words in spaCy

    But the token container has the **is_stop** attribute:

    ```
    for i in doc1[0:5]:
        print("Token: {} | Stop word: {}".format(i, i.is_stop))
    ```

    The output is as follows:

    ```
    Token: This | Stop word: False
    Token: course | Stop word: False
    Token: is | Stop word: True
    Token: great | Stop word: False
    Token: . | Stop word: False
    ```

    Figure 3.16: The is_stop attribute of tokens

9. To add new stop words, we must modify the **vocab** container:

    ```
    nlp.vocab["This"].is_stop = True
    doc1[0].is_stop
    ```

    The output here would be as follows:

    True

10. To perform speech tagging, we initialize the token container:

    ```
    for i in doc1[0:5]:
        print("Token: {} | Tag: {}".format(i.text, i.pos_))
    ```

The output is as follows:

```
Token: This | Tag: DET
Token: course | Tag: NOUN
Token: is | Tag: VERB
Token: great | Tag: ADJ
Token: . | Tag: PUNCT
```

Figure 3.17: The .pos_ attribute of tokens

11. The document container has the **ents** attribute, with the entity of the tokens. To have more entities in our document, let's declare a new one:

```
doc2 = nlp("I live in Madrid and I am working in Google from 10th of
December.")
for i in doc2.ents:
    print("Word: {} | Entity: {}".format(i.text, i.label_))
```

The output is as follows:

```
Word: Madrid | Entity: GPE
Word: Google | Entity: GPE
Word: 10th | Entity: ORDINAL
Word: December | Entity: DATE
```

Figure 3.18: The .label_ attribute of tokens

> **Note**
>
> As you can see in this exercise, spaCy is much easier to use than NLTK, but NLTK provides more methods to perform different operations on text. spaCy is perfect for production. That means, in the least amount of time, you can perform basic processes on text.

The exercise has ended! You can now pre-process a text using NLTK or spaCy. Depending on the task you want to perform, you will be able to choose one of these libraries to clean your data.

Topic Modeling

Within NLU, which is a part of NLP, one of the many tasks that can be performed is extracting the meaning of a sentence, a paragraph, or a whole document. One approach to understanding a document is through its topics. For example, if a set of documents is from a newspaper, the topics might be politics or sports. With topic modeling techniques, we can obtain a bunch of words representing various topics. Depending on your set of documents, you will then have different topics represented by different words. The goal of these techniques is to know the different types of documents in your corpus.

Term Frequency – Inverse Document Frequency (TF-IDF)

TF-IDF is a commonly used NLP model for extracting the most important words from a document. To perform this classification, the algorithm will assign a weight to each word. The idea of this method is to ignore words without relevance to the meaning of a global concept, (which means the overall topic of a text), so those terms will be down-weighted (which means that they will be ignored). Down-weighing them will allow us to find the keywords of that document (the words with the greatest weights).

Mathematically, the algorithm to find the weight of a term in a document is as follows:

$$w_{i,j} = tf_{i,j} * \log\left(\frac{N}{df_i}\right)$$

Figure 3.19: TF-IDF formula

- $W_{i,j}$: Weight of the term, i, in the document, j
- $tf_{i,j}$: Number of occurrences of i in j
- $df_{i,j}$: Number of documents containing i
- N: Total number of documents

The result is the number of times a term appears in that document, multiplied by the log of the total number of documents, divided by the number of documents that contain the term.

Latent Semantic Analysis (LSA)

LSA is one of the foundational techniques of topic modeling. It analyzes the relationship between a set of documents and their terms, and produces a set of concepts related to them.

LSA is a step ahead when compared to TF-IDF. In a large set of documents, the TF-IDF matrix has very noisy information and many redundant dimensions, so the LSA algorithm performs dimensionality reduction.

This reduction is performed with Singular Value Decomposition (SVD). SVD factorizes a matrix, M, into the product of three separate matrices:

$$A_{m\,n} = U_{m\,r}\,S_{r\,r}(V_{n\,r})^{T}$$

Figure 3.20: Singular Value Decomposition

- A: This is the input data matrix.
- m: This is the number of documents.
- n: This is the number of terms.
- U: Left singular vectors. Our document-topic matrix.
- S: Singular values. Represents the strength of each concept. This is a diagonal matrix.
- V: Right singular vectors. Represents terms' vectors in terms of topics.

> **Note**
>
> This method is more efficient on a large set of documents, but there are better algorithms to perform this task such as LDA or PLSA.

Exercise 12: Topic Modeling in Python

In this exercise, TF-IDF and LSA will be coded in Python using a specific library. By the end of this exercise, you will be able to perform these techniques to extract the weights of a term in a document:

1. Open up your Google Colab interface.

2. Create a folder for the book.

3. To generate the TF-IDF matrix, we could code the formula in Figure 3.19, but we are going to use one of the most famous libraries for machine learning algorithms in Python, scikit-learn:

    ```
    from sklearn.feature_extraction.text import TfidfVectorizer
    from sklearn.decomposition import TruncatedSVD
    ```

4. The corpus we are going to use for this exercise will be simple, with just four sentences:

    ```
    corpus = [
            'My cat is white',
            'I am the major of this city',
            'I love eating toasted cheese',
            'The lazy cat is sleeping',
    ]
    ```

5. With the **TfidfVectorizer** method, we can convert the collection of documents in our corpus to a matrix of TF-IDF features:

    ```
    vectorizer = TfidfVectorizer()
    X = vectorizer.fit_transform(corpus)
    ```

6. The **get_feature_names()** method shows the extracted features.

> **Note**
>
> To understand the **TfidfVectorizer** function better, visit the Scikit Learn documentation - https://bit.ly/2S6lwWP

```
vectorizer.get_feature_names()
```

The output is as follows:

```
['am',
 'cat',
 'cheese',
 'city',
 'eating',
 'is',
 'lazy',
 'love',
 'major',
 'my',
 'of',
 'sleeping',
 'the',
 'this',
 'toasted',
 'white']
```

Figure 3.21: Feature names of the corpus

7. X is a sparse matrix. To see its content, we can use the **todense()** function:

```
X.todense()
```

The output is as follows:

```
matrix([[0.        , 0.43779123, 0.        , 0.        , 0.        ,
         0.43779123, 0.        , 0.        , 0.        , 0.55528266,
         0.        , 0.        , 0.        , 0.        , 0.        ,
         0.55528266],
        [0.42176478, 0.        , 0.        , 0.42176478, 0.        ,
         0.        , 0.        , 0.        , 0.42176478, 0.        ,
         0.42176478, 0.        , 0.3325242 , 0.42176478, 0.        ,
         0.        ],
        [0.        , 0.        , 0.5       , 0.        , 0.5       ,
         0.        , 0.        , 0.5       , 0.        , 0.        ,
         0.        , 0.        , 0.        , 0.        , 0.5       ,
         0.        ],
        [0.        , 0.40104275, 0.        , 0.        , 0.        ,
         0.40104275, 0.50867187, 0.        , 0.        , 0.        ,
         0.        , 0.50867187, 0.40104275, 0.        , 0.        ,
         0.        ]])
```

Figure 3.22: TF-IDF matrix of the corpus

8. Now let's perform dimensionality reduction with LSA. The **TruncatedSVD** method uses SVD to transform the input matrix. In this exercise, we'll use **n_components=10**. From now on, you have to use **n_components=100** (it has better results in larger corpuses):

```
lsa = TruncatedSVD(n_components=10,algorithm='randomized',n_
iter=10,random_state=0)
lsa.fit_transform(X)
```

The output is as follows:

```
array([[ 7.75313171e-01,  0.00000000e+00, -3.55033830e-01,
        -5.22341331e-01],
       [ 2.94444444e-01, -1.58085674e-16,  9.34853453e-01,
        -1.98372101e-01],
       [ 1.77654527e-16,  1.00000000e+00,  1.47786938e-16,
        5.69692241e-17],
       [ 8.29341934e-01, -1.58085674e-16, -3.33066907e-16,
        5.58741404e-01]])
```

Figure 23: Dimensionality reduction with LSA

9. **attribute** **.components_** shows the weight of each **vectorizer.get_feature_names()**. Notice that the LSA matrix has a range of 4x16, we have 4 documents in our corpus (concepts), and the vectorizer has 16 features (terms):

```
lsa.components_
```

The output is as follows:

```
array([[ 9.02768569e-02,  4.88527927e-01,  4.16333634e-16,
         9.02768569e-02,  3.74700271e-16,  4.88527927e-01,
         3.06671984e-01,  3.74700271e-16,  9.02768569e-02,
         3.12963746e-01,  9.02768569e-02,  3.06671984e-01,
         3.12959025e-01,  9.02768569e-02,  3.74700271e-16,
         3.12963746e-01],
       [-3.40005801e-16, -1.94289029e-16,  5.00000000e-01,
        -2.77555756e-16,  5.00000000e-01, -1.87350135e-16,
        -3.81639165e-16,  5.00000000e-01, -2.77555756e-16,
         1.31838984e-16, -2.77555756e-16, -3.81639165e-16,
        -5.13478149e-16, -2.77555756e-16,  5.00000000e-01,
         1.31838984e-16],
       [ 3.94288263e-01, -1.55430698e-01,  2.70616862e-16,
         3.94288263e-01,  2.91433544e-16, -1.55430698e-01,
        -2.49800181e-16,  2.91433544e-16,  3.94288263e-01,
        -1.97144132e-01,  3.94288263e-01, -2.49800181e-16,
         3.10861395e-01,  3.94288263e-01,  2.91433544e-16,
        -1.97144132e-01],
       [-1.33998273e-01, -7.36288530e-03,  1.68918698e-16,
        -1.33998273e-01,  1.96891115e-16, -7.36288530e-03,
         4.55194360e-01,  1.96891115e-16, -1.33998273e-01,
        -4.64533246e-01, -1.33998273e-01,  4.55194360e-01,
         2.53234685e-01, -1.33998273e-01,  1.96891115e-16,
        -4.64533246e-01]])
```

Figure 3.24: The desired TF-IDF matrix output

The exercise has ended successfully! This was a preparatory exercise for *Activity 3, Process a Corpus*. Do check the seventh step of the exercise – it will give you the key to complete the activity ahead. I encourage you to read the scikit-learn documentation and learn how to see the potential of these two methods. Now you know how to create the TF-IDF matrix. This matrix could be huge, so to manage the data better, the LSA algorithm performs dimensionality reduction on the weight of each term in the document.

Activity 3: Process a Corpus

In this activity, we will process a really small corpus to clean the data and extract the keywords and concepts using LSA.

Imagine this scenario: the newspaper vendor in your town has published a competition. It consists of predicting the category of an article. This newspaper does not have a structural database, which means it has only raw data. They provide a small set of documents, and they need to know whether the article is political, scientific, or sports-related:

> **Note**
>
> You can choose between spaCy and the NLTK library to do the activity. Both solutions will be valid if the keywords are related at the end of the LSA algorithm.

1. Load the corpus documents and store them in a list.

> **Note**
>
> The corpus documents can be found on GitHub, https://github.com/
> PacktPublishing/Artificial-Vision-and-Language-Processing-for-Robotics/tree/
> master/Lesson03/Activity03/dataset

2. Pre-process the text with spaCy or NLTK.
3. Apply the LSA algorithm.
4. Show the first five keywords related to each concept:

    Keywords: moon, apollo, earth, space, nasa

    Keywords: yard, touchdown, cowboys, prescott, left

    Keywords: facebook, privacy, tech, consumer, data

> **Note**
>
> The output keywords probably will not be the same as yours. If your keywords are not related then check the solution.

The output is as follows:

	Terms	Components
1845	moon	0.338403
272	apollo	0.315843
958	earth	0.180482
2558	space	0.157921
1879	nasa	0.135361

Figure 3.25: Output example of the most relevant words in a concept (f1)

Note

The solution for this activity is available on page 306.

Language Modeling

So far, we have reviewed the most basic techniques for pre-processing text data. Now we are going to dive deep into the structure of natural language – language models. We can consider this topic an introduction to machine learning in NLP.

Introduction to Language Models

A statistical **Language Model** (**LM**) is the probability distribution of a sequence of words, which means, to assign a probability to a particular sentence. For example, LMs could be used to calculate the probability of an upcoming word in a sentence. This involves making some assumptions about the structure of the LM and how it will be formed. An LM is never totally correct with its output, but using one is often necessary.

LMs are used in many more NLP tasks. For example, in machine translation, it is important to know what sentence precedes the next. LMs are also used for speech recognition, to avoid ambiguity, for spelling corrections, and for summarization.

Let's see how an LM is mathematically represented:

- $P(W) = P(w1, w2,w3,w4,...wn)$

P(W) is our LM and wi are the words included in W, and as we mentioned before, we can use it to compute the probability of an upcoming word in this way:

- P(w5|w1,w2,w3,w4)

This (w1, w2, w3, w4) states what the probability of $w5$ (the upcoming word) could be in a given sequence of words.

Looking at this example, P (w5|w1, w2, w3, w4), we can assume this:

- P(actual word | previous words)

Depending on the number of previous words we are looking at to obtain the probability of the actual word, there are different models we can use. So, now we are going to introduce some important concepts regarding such models.

The Bigram Model

The bigram model is a sequence of two consecutive words. For example, in the sentence "My cat is white," there are these bigrams:

My cat

Cat is

Is white

Mathematically, a bigram has this form:

- Bigram model: P(wi|wi-1)

N-gram Model

If we change the length of the previous word, we obtain the N-gram model. It works just like the bigram model but considers more words than the previous set.

Using the previous example of "My cat is white," this is what we can obtain:

- **Trigram**

  My cat is

  Cat is white

- **4-gram**
- My cat is white

N-Gram Problem

At this point, you could think the n-gram model is more accurate than the bigram model because the n-gram model has access to additional "previous knowledge." However, n-gram models are limited to a certain extent, because of long-distance dependencies. An example would be, "After thinking about it a lot, I bought a television," which we compute as:

- P(television| after thinking about it a lot, I bought a)

The sentence "After thinking about it a lot, I bought a television" is probably the only sequence of words with this structure in our corpus. If we change the word "television" for another word, for example "computer," the sentence "After thinking about it a lot, I bought a computer" is also valid, but in our model, the following would be the case:

- P(computer| after thinking about it a lot, I bought a) = 0

This sentence is valid, but our model is not accurate, so we need to be careful with the use of n-gram models.

Calculating Probabilities

Unigram Probability

The unigram is the simplest case for calculating probabilities. It counts the number of times a word appears in a set of documents. Here is the formula for this:

$$P(w_i) = \frac{c(w_i)}{size(Corpus)}$$

Figure 3.27: Unigram probability estimation

- $c(wi)$ is the number of times
- wi appears in the whole corpus. The size of the corpus is just how many tokens are in it.

Bigram Probability

To estimate bigram probability, we are going to use maximum likelihood estimation:

$$P(w_i|w_{i-1}) = \frac{c(w_{i-1}, w_i)}{c(w_{i-1})}$$

Figure 3.27: Bigram probability estimation

To understand this formula better, let's look at an example.

Imagine our corpus is composed of these three sentences:

My name is Charles.

Charles is my name.

My dog plays with the ball.

The size of the corpus is 14 words, and now we are going to estimate the probability of the sequence "my name":

$$P(name|my) = \frac{c(my, name)}{c(my)} = \frac{2}{3} = 0.67$$

Figure 3.28: Example of bigram estimation

The Chain Rule

Now we know the concepts of bigrams and n-grams, we need to know how we can obtain those probabilities.

If you have basic statistics knowledge, you might think the best option is to apply the chain rule and join each probability. For example, in the sentence "My cat is white," the probability is as follows:

- P(my cat is white) = p(white|my cat is) p(is|my cat) p(cat|my) p(my)

It seems to be possible with this sentence, but if we had a much longer sentence, long-distance dependency problems would appear and the result of the n-gram model could be incorrect.

Smoothing

So far, we have a probabilistic model, and if we want to estimate the parameters of our model, we can use the maximum likelihood of estimation.

One of the big problems of LMs is insufficient data. Our data is limited, so there will be many unknown events. What does this mean? It means we'll end up with an LM that gives a probability of 0 to unseen words.

To solve this problem, we are going to use a smoothing method. With this smoothing method, every probability estimation result will be greater than zero. The method we are going to use is add-one smoothing:

$$P(w_i|w_{i-1}) = \frac{c(w_{i-1}, w_i) + 1}{|V| + c(w_{i-1})}$$

Figure 3.29: Add-one smoothing in bigram estimation

V is the number of distinct tokens in our corpus.

> **Note**
>
> There are more smoothing methods with better performance; this is the most basic method.

Markov Assumption

Markov assumption is very useful for estimating the probabilities of a long sentence. With this method, we can solve the problem of long-distance dependencies. Markov assumption simplifies the chain rule to estimate long sequences of words. Each estimation only depends on the previous step:

$$P(w_i|w_{i-1}, w_{i-2}, \dots, w_1) = P(w_i|w_{i-1})$$

Figure 3.30: Markov assumption

We can also have a second-order Markov assumption, which depends on two previous terms, but we are going to use first-order Markov assumption:

$$P(white|my\ cat\ is) = P(white|is)$$

Figure 3.31: Example of Markov

If we apply this to the whole sentence, we get this:

$$P\ (my\ cat\ is\ white) = P\ (white|is)P(is|cat)P(cat|my)P(my)$$

Figure 3.32: Example of Markov for a whole sentence

Decomposing the sequence of words in the aforementioned way will output the probabilities more accurately.

Exercise 13: Create a Bigram Model

In this exercise, we are going to create a simple LM with unigrams and bigrams. Also, we will compare the results of creating the LM both without add-one smoothing and with it. One application of the n-gram is, for example, in keyboard apps. They can predict your next word. That prediction could be done with a bigram model:

1. Open up your Google Colab interface.

2. Create a folder for the book.

3. Declare a small, easy training corpus:

    ```
    import numpy as np
    corpus = [
            'My cat is white',
            'I am the major of this city',
            'I love eating toasted cheese',
            'The lazy cat is sleeping',
    ]
    ```

4. Import the required libraries and load the model:

    ```
    import spacy
    import en_core_web_sm
    from spacy.lang.en.stop_words import STOP_WORDS
    nlp = en_core_web_sm.load()
    ```

5. Tokenize it with spaCy. To be faster in doing the smoothing and the bigrams, we are going to create three lists:

Tokens: All tokens of the corpus

Tokens_doc: List of lists with the tokens of each corpus

`Distinc_tokens`: All tokens removing duplicates:

```
tokens = []
tokens_doc = []
distinc_tokens = []
```

Let's create a first loop to iterate over the sentences in our corpus. The **doc** variable will contain a sequence of the sentences' tokens:

```
for c in corpus:
    doc = nlp(c)
    tokens_aux = []
```

Now we are going to create a second loop to iterate through the tokens to push them into the corresponding list. The **t** variable will be each token of the sentence:

```
for t in doc:
    tokens_aux.append(t.text)
    if t.text not in tokens:
        distinc_tokens.append(t.text) # without duplicates
    tokens.append(t.text)
tokens_doc.append(tokens_aux)
tokens_aux = []
print(tokens)
print(distinc_tokens)
print(tokens_doc)
```

6. Create the unigram model and test it:

```
def unigram_model(word):
    return tokens.count(word)/len(tokens)
unigram_model("cat")
```

Result = 0.1388888888888889

7. Add the smoothing and test it with the same word:

```
def unigram_model_smoothing(word):
    return (tokens.count(word) + 1)/(len(tokens) + len(distinc_tokens))
unigram_model_smoothing("cat")
```

Result = 0.1111111111111111

> **Note**
>
> The problem with this smoothing method is that every unseen word has the same probability.

8. Create the bigram model:

```
def bigram_model(word1, word2):
    hit = 0
```

9. We need to iterate through all of the tokens in the documents to try to find the number of times that **word1** and **word2** appear together:

```
for d in tokens_doc:
    for t,i in zip(d, range(len(d))): # i is the length of d
        if i <= len(d)-2:
            if word1 == d[i] and word2 == d[i+1]:
                hit += 1
    print("Hits: ",hit)
    return hit/tokens.count(word1)
bigram_model("I","am")
```

The output is as follows:

```
Hits:   1
0.5
```

Figure 3.33: Output showing the times word1 and word2 appear together in the document

10. Add the smoothing to the bigram model:

```
def bigram_model_smoothing(word1, word2):
    hit = 0
    for d in tokens_doc:
        for t,i in zip(d, range(len(d))):
            if i <= len(d)-2:
                if word1 == d[i] and word2 == d[i+1]:
                    hit += 1
    return (hit+1)/(tokens.count(word1)+len(distinc_tokens))
bigram_model("I","am")
```

The output is as follows:

$$0.1$$

Figure 3.34: Output after adding smoothing to the model

Congratulations! You have completed the last exercise of this chapter. In the next chapter, you will see that this LM approach is a fundamental deep NLP approach. You can now take a huge corpus and create your own LM.

> **Note**
>
> Applying the Markov assumption, the final probability will round the 0. I recommend using log() and adding each component. Also, check the precision bits of your code (float16 < float32 < float64).

Summary

NLP is becoming more and more important in AI. Industries analyze huge quantities of raw text data, which is unstructured. To understand this data, we use many libraries to process it. NLP is divided into two groups of methods and functions: NLG to generate natural language, and NLU to understand it.

Firstly, it is important to clean text data, since there will be a lot of useless, irrelevant information. Once the data is ready to be processed, through a mathematical algorithm such as TF-IDF or LSA, a huge set of documents can be understood. Libraries such as NLTK and spaCy are useful for doing this task. They provide methods to remove the noise in data. A document can be represented as a matrix. First, TF-IDF can give a global representation of a document, but when a corpus is big, the better option is to perform dimensionality reduction with LSA and SVD. scikit-learn provides algorithms for processing documents, but if documents are not pre-processed, the result will not be accurate. Finally, the use of language models could be necessary, but they need to be formed of a valid training set of documents. If the set of documents is good, the language model should be able to generate language.

In the next chapter, we will introduce **Recurrent Neural Networks (RNNs)**. We will be looking at some advanced models of these RNNs and will accordingly be one step ahead in building our robot.

Neural Networks with NLP

Learning Objectives

By the end of this chapter, you will be able to:

- Explain what a Recurrent Neural Network is
- Design and build a Recurrent Neural Network
- Evaluate non-numeric data
- Evaluate the different state-of-the-art language models with RNNs
- Predict a value with a temporal sequence of data

This chapter covers various aspects of RNNs. it deals with explaining, designing, and building the various RNN models.

Introduction

As mentioned in the previous chapter, Natural Language Processing (NLP) is an area of Artificial Intelligence (AI) that covers how computers can understand and manipulate human language in order to perform useful tasks. Now, with the growth of deep learning techniques, deep NLP has become a new area of research.

So, what is deep NLP? It is a combination of NLP techniques and deep learning. The result of the combination of these techniques are advances in the following areas:

- Linguistics: Speech to text

- Tools: POS tagging, entity recognition, and sentence parsing

- Applications: Sentiment analysis, question answering, dialogue agents, and machine translation

One of the most important approaches of deep NLP is the representation of words and sentences. Words can be represented as a vector located in a plane full of other words. Depending on the similarity of each word to another word, its distance in the plane would be accordingly set as greater or smaller.

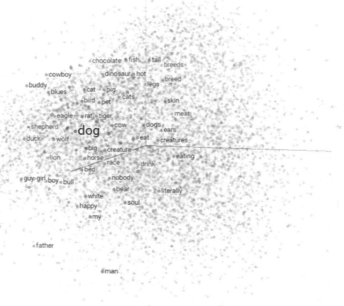

Figure 4.1: Representation of words in multiple dimensions

The previous figure shows an example of word embedding. **Word embedding** is a collection of techniques and methods that map words and sentences from a corpus into vectors or real numbers. It generates a representation of each word in terms of the context in which a word appears. Then, word embedding can find the similarities between words. For example, the nearest words to dog are as follows:

1. Dogs
2. Cat
3. Cow
4. Rat
5. Bird

There are different ways to generate embeddings, such as Word2Vec, which will be covered in *Chapter 7, Build a Conversational Agent to Manage the Robot*.

This is not the only big change deep learning brings to NLP on a morphological level. With deep learning, a word can be represented as a combination of vectors.

Each morpheme is a vector, and a word is the result of combining several morpheme vectors.

This technique of combining vectors is also used on a semantic level, but for the creation of words and for the creation of a sentence. Each phrase is formed by a combination of many word vectors, so a sentence can be represented as one vector.

Another improvement is in parsing sentences. This task is hard because it is ambiguous. Neural networks can accurately determine the grammatical structure of a sentence.

In full application terms, the areas are as follows:

- **Sentiment analysis**: Traditionally, this consists of a bag of words labeled with positive or negative sentiments. Then, combining these words returns the sentiment of the whole sentence. Now, using deep learning and word representation models, the results are better.

- **Question answering**: To find the answer to a question, vector representations can match a document, a paragraph, or a sentence with an input question.

- **Dialogue agents**: With neural language models, a model can understand a query and create a response.

- **<u>Machine translation</u>**: Machine translation is one of the hardest tasks in NLP. A lot of approaches and models have been tried. Traditional models are very large and complex, but deep learning neural machine translation has solved that problem. Sentences are encoded with vectors, and the output is decoded.

The vector representation of words is fundamental to deep NLP. Creating a plane, many tasks can be completed. Before analyzing deep NLP techniques, we are going to review what a recurrent neural network (RNN) is, what its applications are within deep learning, and how to create our first RNN.

Our future conversational agent will detect the intention of a conversation and respond with a predefined answer. But with a good dataset of conversations, we could create a Recurrent Neural Network to train a language model (LM) capable of generating a response to a given topic in a conversation. This task can be performed by other neural network architectures, such as seq2seq models.

Recurrent Neural Networks

In this section, we are going to review **<u>Recurrent Neural Networks</u>** (**<u>RNNs</u>**). This topic will first look at the theory of RNNs. It will review many architectures within this model and help you to work out which model to use to solve a certain problem, and it will also look at several types of RNN and their pros and cons. Also, we will look at how to create a simple RNN, train it, and make predictions.

Introduction to Recurrent Neural Networks (RNN)

Human behavior shows a variety of serially ordered action sequences. A human is capable of learning dynamic paths based on a set of previous actions or sequences. This means that people do not start learning from scratch; we have some previous knowledge, which helps us. For example you could not understand a word if you did not understand the previous word in a sentence!

Traditionally, neural networks cannot solve these types of problem because they cannot learn previous information. But what happens with problems that cannot be solved with just current information?

In 1986, Michael I. Jordan proposed a model that deals with the classical problem of temporal organization. This model is capable of learning the trajectories of a dynamic object by studying its previous movements. Jordan created the first RNN.

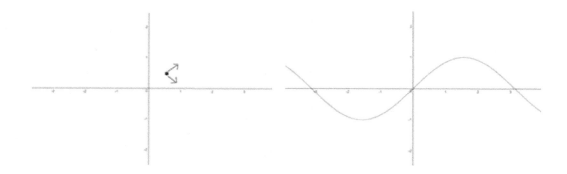

Figure 4.2: Example of non-previous information versus temporal sequences

In the previous figure, the image on the left shows us that, without any information, we cannot know what the next action of the black point will be, but if we suppose its previous movements are recorded as the red line on the right-hand side of the graph we can predict what its next action will be.

Inside Recurrent Neural Networks

So far, we have seen that RNNs are different to neural networks (NNs). RNN neurons are like normal neurons, but with loops within them, allowing them to store a time state. Storing the state of a certain moment in time, they can make predictions based on previous state of time.

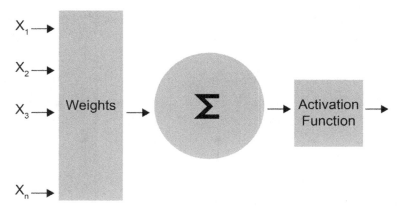

Figure 4.3: Traditional neuron

The preceding figure shows a traditional neuron, used in an NN. X_n are the inputs of the neuron, and after the activation function, it generates a response. The schema of an RNN neuron is different:

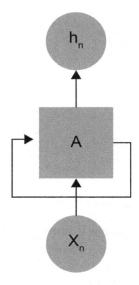

Figure 4.4: Recurrent neuron

The loop in the previous figure allows the neuron to store the time state. h_n is the output of the input, X_n, and the previous state. The neuron changes and evolves over time.

If the input of the neuron is a sequence, an unrolled RNN would be like this:

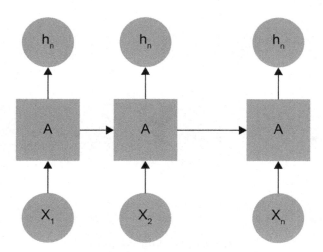

Figure 4.5: Unrolled recurrent neuron

The chain-like schema in figure 4.5 shows that RNNs are closely related to sequences and lists. So, we have as many neurons as inputs, and each neuron passes its state to the next.

RNN architectures

Depending on the quantity of inputs and outputs in the RNN, there are many architectures with different numbers of neurons. Each architecture is specialized for a certain task. So far, there are many types of network:

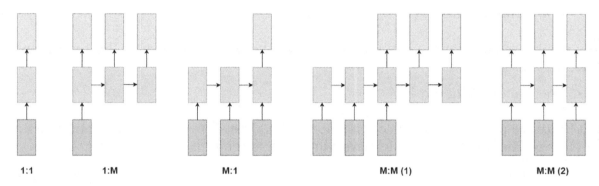

1:1   1:M   M:1   M:M (1)   M:M (2)

Figure 4.6: Structures of RNNs

The previous figure shows the various classifications of RNNs. Earlier in this book, we reviewed the one-to-one architecture. In this chapter, we will learn about the many-to-one architecture.

- **One-to-one**: Classification or regression tasks from one input (image classification).

- **One-to-many**: Image captioning tasks. These are hard tasks in deep learning. For example, a model that passes an image as an input could describe the elements that are in the picture.

- **Many-to-one**: Temporal series, sentiment analysis... every task with just one output but based in a sequence of different inputs.

- **Many-to-many**: Machine automated translation systems.

- **Synchronized many-to-many**: Video classification.

Long-Dependency Problem

In some tasks, it is only necessary to use the most recent information to predict the next step of a model. With a temporal series, it is necessary to check older elements to learn or predict the next element or word in a sentence. For example, take a look at this sentence:

- The clouds are in the sky.

Now imagine this sentence:

- The clouds are in the [?]

You would assume that the required word would be sky, and you know this because of the previous information:

- The clouds are in the

But there are other tasks in which the model would need previous information to obtain a better prediction. For example, have a look at this sentence:

- I was born in Italy, but when I was 3, I moved to France... that's the reason why I speak [?]

To predict the word, the model needs to take the information from the beginning of the sentence, and that could be a problem. This is a problem with RNNs: when the distance to the information is large, it is more difficult to learn. This problem is called the **vanishing gradient**.

The vanishing gradient problem

Information travels through time in an RNN so that information from previous steps is used as input in the next step. At each step, the model calculates the cost function, so each time, the model may obtain an error measure. While propagating the error calculated through the network, and trying to minimize that error when updating the weights, the result of that operation is a number closer to zero (if you multiply two small numbers, the result is a smaller number). This means the gradient of the model becomes less and less with each multiplication. The problem here is that the network will not train properly. A solution to this problem with RNNs is to use Long Short-Term Memory (LSTM).

Exercise 14: Predict House Prices with an RNN

We are going to create our first RNN using Keras. This exercise is not a time-series problem. We are going to use a regression dataset to introduce RNNs.

We can use several methods included in the Keras library as a model or a type of layer:

- Keras models: These let us use the different available models in Keras. We are going to use the Sequential model.

- Keras layers: We can add different types of layers to our neural network. In this exercise, we are going to use LSTM and a Dense layer. A dense layer is a regular layer of neurons in a neural network. Each neuron receives input from all the neurons in the previous layer, but they are densely connected.

The main objective of this exercise is to predict the value of a house in Boston, so our dataset will contain information on each house, such as the total area of the property or the number of rooms:

1. Import the dataset of Boston house prices from **sklearn** and take a look at the data:

```
from sklearn.datasets import load_boston
boston = load_boston()
boston.data
```

```
array([[6.3200e-03, 1.8000e+01, 2.3100e+00, ..., 1.5300e+01, 3.9690e+02,
        4.9800e+00],
       [2.7310e-02, 0.0000e+00, 7.0700e+00, ..., 1.7800e+01, 3.9690e+02,
        9.1400e+00],
       [2.7290e-02, 0.0000e+00, 7.0700e+00, ..., 1.7800e+01, 3.9283e+02,
        4.0300e+00],
       ...,
       [6.0760e-02, 0.0000e+00, 1.1930e+01, ..., 2.1000e+01, 3.9690e+02,
        5.6400e+00],
       [1.0959e-01, 0.0000e+00, 1.1930e+01, ..., 2.1000e+01, 3.9345e+02,
        6.4800e+00],
       [4.7410e-02, 0.0000e+00, 1.1930e+01, ..., 2.1000e+01, 3.9690e+02,
        7.8800e+00]])
```

Figure 4.7: Boston house prices data

2. You can see the data has high values, so the best thing to do is to normalize the data. With the **MinMaxScaler** function of **sklearn**, we are going to transform our data into values between 0 and 1:

```
from sklearn.preprocessing import MinMaxScaler
import numpy as np

scaler = MinMaxScaler()
x = scaler.fit_transform(boston.data)

aux = boston.target.reshape(boston.target.shape[0], 1)
y = scaler.fit_transform(aux)
```

3. Divide the data into train and test sets. A good percentage for the test set is 20% of the data:

```
from sklearn.model_selection import train_test_split

x_train, x_test, y_train, y_test = train_test_split(x, y, test_size=0.2,
shuffle=False)
print('Shape of x_train {}'.format(x_train.shape))
print('Shape of y_train {}'.format(y_train.shape))
print('Shape of x_test {}'.format(x_test.shape))
print('Shape of y_test {}'.format(y_test.shape))
```

```
Shape of x_train (404, 13)
Shape of y_train (404, 1)
Shape of x_test (102, 13)
Shape of y_test (102, 1)
```

Figure 4.8: Shape of the train and test data

4. Import the Keras libraries and set a seed to initialize the weights:

```
import tensorflow as tf
from keras.models import Sequential
from keras.layers import Dense
tf.set_random_seed(1)
```

5. Create a simple model. The dense layer is just a set of neurons. The last dense layer has only one neuron to return the output:

```
model = Sequential()

model.add(Dense(64, activation='relu'))
model.add(Dense(32, activation='relu'))
model.add(Dense(1))

model.compile(loss='mean_squared_error', optimizer='adam')
```

6. Train the network:

```
history = model.fit(x_train, y_train, batch_size=32, epochs=5, verbose=2)
```

```
Epoch 1/5
 - 1s - loss: 0.1098
Epoch 2/5
 - 0s - loss: 0.0569
Epoch 3/5
 - 0s - loss: 0.0364
Epoch 4/5
 - 0s - loss: 0.0277
Epoch 5/5
 - 0s - loss: 0.0241
```

Figure 4.9: Training the network

7. Compute the error of the model:

```
error = model.evaluate(x_test, y_test)
print('MSE: {:.5f}'.format(error))
```

```
102/102 [==============================] - 0s 353us/step
MSE: 0.01253
```

Figure 4.10: Computing the error of the model

8. Plot the predictions:

```
import matplotlib.pyplot as plt

prediction = model.predict(x_test)
print('Prediction shape: {}'.format(prediction.shape))

plt.plot(range(len(x_test)), prediction.reshape(prediction.shape[0]),
'--r')
plt.plot(range(len(y_test)), y_test)
plt.show()
```

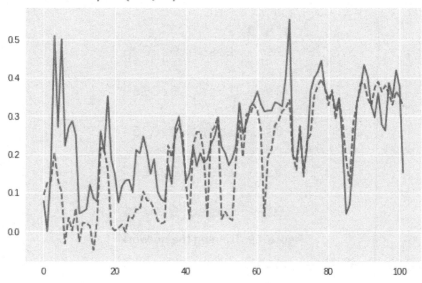

Figure 4.11: Predictions of our model

Now you have an RNN for a regression problem! You can try to modify the parameters, add more layers, or change the number of neurons to see what happens. In the next exercise, we will solve time-series problems with LSTM layers.

Long Short-Term Memory

LSTM is a type of RNN that's designed to solve the long-dependency problem. It can remember values for long or short time periods. The principal way it differs from traditional RNNs is that they include a cell or a loop to store the memory internally.

This type of neural network was created in 1997 by Hochreiter and Schmidhuber. This is the basic schema of an LSTM neuron:

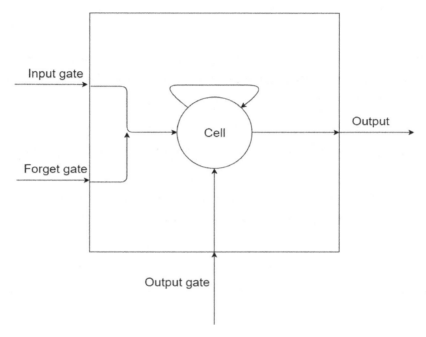

Figure 4.12: LSTM neuron structure

As you can see in the previous figure, the schema of an LSTM neuron is complex. It has three types of gate:

- Input gate: Allows us to control the input values to update the state of the memory cell.

- Forget gate: Allows us to erase the content of the memory cell.

- Output gate: Allows us to control the returned values of the input and cell memory content.

An LSTM model in Keras has a three-dimensional input:

- Sample: Is the amount of data you have (quantity of sequences).

- Time step: Is the memory of your network. In other words, it stores previous information in order to make better predictions.

- Features: Is the number of features in every time step. For example, if you are processing pictures, the features are the number of pixels.

> **Note**
>
> This complex design causes another type of network to be formed. This new type of neural network is a **Gated Recurrent Unit (GRU)**, and it solves the vanishing gradient problem.

Exercise 15: Predict the Next Solution of a Mathematical Function

In this exercise, we are going to build an LSTM to predict the values of a sine function. In this exercise, you will learn how to train and predict a model with Keras, using the LSTM model. Also, this exercise will cover data generation and how to split data into training samples and test samples:

1. With Keras, we can create an RNN using the Sequential class, and we can create an LSTM to add new recurrent neurons. Import the Keras libraries for LSTM models, NumPy for setting up the data, and matplotlib to print the graphs:

```
import tensorflow as tf
from keras.models import Sequential
from keras.layers import LSTM, Dense
import numpy as np
import matplotlib.pyplot as plt
```

2. Create the dataset to train and evaluate the model. We are going to generate an array of 1,000 values as a result of the sine function:

```
serie = 1000
x_aux = [] #Natural numbers until serie
x_aux = np.arange(serie)
serie = (np.sin(2 * np.pi * 4 * x_aux / serie) + 1) / 2
```

3. To see if the data is good, let's plot it:

```
plt.plot(x_aux, serie)
plt.show()
```

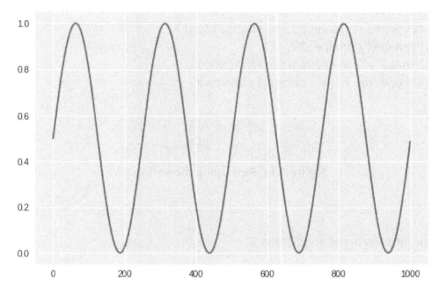

Figure 4.13: Output with the plotted data

4. As this chapter explains, RNN works with sequences of data, so we need to split our data into sequences. In our case, the maximum length of the sequences will be 5. This is necessary because the RNNs need sequences as input.

This model will be **many-to-one** because the input is a sequence and the output is just a value. To see why we are going to create an RNN using the many-to-one structure, we just need to know the dimensions of our input and output data:

```
#Prepare input data
maxlen = 5
seq = []
res = []
for i in range(0, len(serie) - maxlen):
    seq.append(serie[i:maxlen+i])
    res.append(serie[maxlen+i])
print(seq[:5])
print(res[:5])
```

5. Prepare the data to introduce it to the LSTM model. Pay attention to the shape of the **x** and **y** variables. RNNs need a three-dimensional vector as input and a two-dimensional vector as output. That's why we will reshape the variables:

```
x = np.array(seq)
y = np.array(res)
x = x.reshape(x.shape[0], x.shape[1], 1)
y = y.reshape(y.shape[0], 1)
print('Shape of x {}'.format(x.shape))
print('Shape of y {}'.format(y.shape))
```

```
Shape of x (995, 5, 1)
Shape of y (995, 1)
```

Figure 4.14: Reshaping the variables

> **Note**
>
> The input dimension of an LSTM is 3.

6. Split the data into train and test sets:

```
from sklearn.model_selection import train_test_split

x_train, x_test, y_train, y_test = train_test_split(x, y, test_size=0.2, shuffle=False)
print('Shape of x_train {}'.format(x_train.shape))
print('Shape of y_train {}'.format(y_train.shape))
print('Shape of x_test {}'.format(x_test.shape))
print('Shape of y_test {}'.format(y_test.shape))
```

```
Shape of x_train (796, 5, 1)
Shape of y_train (796, 1)
Shape of x_test (199, 5, 1)
Shape of y_test (199, 1)
```

Figure 4.15: Splitting data into train and test sets

7. Build a simple model with one LSTM unit and one dense layer with one neuron and linear activation. The dense layer is just a regular layer of neurons receiving the input from the previous layer and generating many neurons as output. Because of that, our dense layer has only one neuron because we need a scalar value as the output:

```
tf.set_random_seed(1)
model = Sequential()
model.add(LSTM(1, input_shape=(maxlen, 1)))
model.add(Dense(1, activation='linear'))
model.compile(loss='mse', optimizer='rmsprop')
```

8. Train the model for 5 epochs (one epoch is when the entire dataset is processed by the neural network) and a batch size of 32 and evaluate it:

```
history = model.fit(x_train, y_train, batch_size=32, epochs=5, verbose=2)
error = model.evaluate(x_test, y_test)
print('MSE: {:.5f}'.format(error))
```

```
Epoch 1/5
 - 1s - loss: 0.4022
Epoch 2/5
 - 0s - loss: 0.3674
Epoch 3/5
 - 0s - loss: 0.3383
Epoch 4/5
 - 0s - loss: 0.3115
Epoch 5/5
 - 0s - loss: 0.2868
199/199 [==============================] - 0s 579us/step
MSE: 0.21822
```

Figure 4.16: Training with 5 epochs with a batch size of 32

9. Plot the test predictions to see if it works well:

```
prediction = model.predict(x_test)
print('Prediction shape: {}'.format(prediction.shape))
plt.plot(range(len(x_test)), prediction.reshape(prediction.shape[0]),
'--r')
plt.plot(range(len(y_test)), y_test)
plt.show()
```

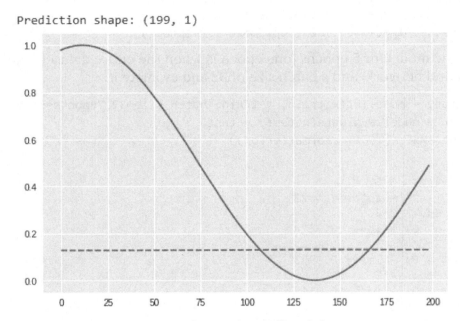

Figure 4.17: Plotting the predicted shape

10. Let's improve our model. Create a new one with four units in the LSTM layer and one dense layer with one neuron, but with the sigmoid activation:

```
model2 = Sequential()
model2.add(LSTM(4,input_shape=(maxlen,1)))
model2.add(Dense(1, activation='sigmoid'))
model2.compile(loss='mse', optimizer='rmsprop')
```

11. Train and evaluate it for 25 epochs and with a batch size of 8:

```
history = model2.fit(x_train, y_train,
                     batch_size=8,
                     epochs=25,
                     verbose=1)
error = model2.evaluate(x_test, y_test)
print('MSE: {:.5f}'.format(error))
```

```
Epoch 3/25
796/796 [==============================] - 0s 510us/step - loss: 0.0336
Epoch 4/25
796/796 [==============================] - 0s 505us/step - loss: 0.0129
Epoch 5/25
796/796 [==============================] - 0s 498us/step - loss: 0.0078
Epoch 6/25
796/796 [==============================] - 0s 463us/step - loss: 0.0067
Epoch 7/25
796/796 [==============================] - 0s 479us/step - loss: 0.0060
Epoch 8/25
796/796 [==============================] - 0s 477us/step - loss: 0.0054
Epoch 9/25
796/796 [==============================] - 0s 450us/step - loss: 0.0050
Epoch 10/25
796/796 [==============================] - 0s 450us/step - loss: 0.0046
Epoch 11/25
796/796 [==============================] - 0s 424us/step - loss: 0.0043
Epoch 12/25
796/796 [==============================] - 0s 401us/step - loss: 0.0040
Epoch 13/25
796/796 [==============================] - 0s 388us/step - loss: 0.0038
Epoch 14/25
796/796 [==============================] - 0s 386us/step - loss: 0.0035
Epoch 15/25
796/796 [==============================] - 0s 413us/step - loss: 0.0033
Epoch 16/25
796/796 [==============================] - 0s 388us/step - loss: 0.0031
Epoch 17/25
796/796 [==============================] - 0s 444us/step - loss: 0.0028
Epoch 18/25
796/796 [==============================] - 0s 459us/step - loss: 0.0026
Epoch 19/25
796/796 [==============================] - 0s 476us/step - loss: 0.0024
Epoch 20/25
796/796 [==============================] - 0s 429us/step - loss: 0.0022
Epoch 21/25
796/796 [==============================] - 0s 433us/step - loss: 0.0020
Epoch 22/25
796/796 [==============================] - 0s 428us/step - loss: 0.0018
Epoch 23/25
796/796 [==============================] - 0s 434us/step - loss: 0.0016
Epoch 24/25
796/796 [==============================] - 0s 445us/step - loss: 0.0014
Epoch 25/25
796/796 [==============================] - 0s 467us/step - loss: 0.0012
199/199 [==============================] - 0s 1ms/step
MSE: 0.00123
```

Figure 4.18: Training for 25 epochs with a batch size of 8

12. Plot the predictions of the model:

```
predict_2 = model2.predict(x_test)
predict_2 = predict_2.reshape(predict_2.shape[0])
print(x_test.shape)
plt.plot(range(len(x_test)),predict_2, '--r')
plt.plot(range(len(y_test)), y_test)
plt.show()
```

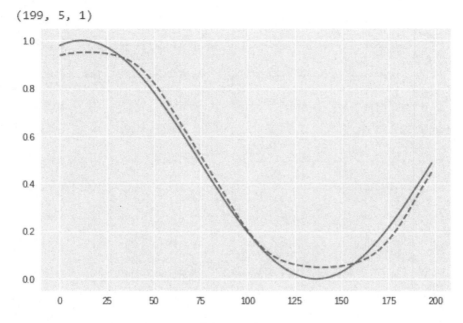

Figure 4.19: Predictions of our neural network

You can now compare the plots of each model, and we can see that the second model is better. With this exercise, you have learned the basics of LSTM, how to train and evaluate the model you have created, and also how to determine whether it is good or not.

Neural Language Models

Chapter 3, *Fundamentals of Natural Language Processing* introduced us to statistical language models (LMs), which are the probability distribution for a sequence of words. We know LMs can be used to predict the next word in a sentence, or to compute the probability distribution of the next word.

$$P(x_{t+1}) = (w_j | x_t, ..., x_1)$$

Figure 4.20: LM formula to compute the probability distribution of an upcoming word

The sequence of words is $x1$, $x2$ ... and the next word is x_{t+1}. w_j is a word in the vocabulary. V is the vocabulary and j is a position of a word in that vocabulary. w_j is the word located in position j within V.

You use LMs every day. The keyboards on cell phones use this technology to predict the next word of a sentence, and search engines such as Google use it to predict what you want to search in their search for engine.

We talked about the n-gram model and bigrams counting the words in a corpus, but that solution has some limitations, such as long dependencies. Deep NLP and neural LMs will help to get around these limitations.

Introduction to Neural Language Models

Neural LMs follow the same structure as statistical LMs. They aim to predict the next word in a sentence, but in a different way. A neural LM is motivated by an RNN because of the use of sequences as inputs.

Exercise 15, Predict the Next Solution of a Mathematical Function predicts the next result of the sine function from a sequence of five previous steps. In this case, instead of sequences of sine function results, the data is words, and the model will predict the next word.

These neural LMs emerged from the necessity to improve the statistical approach. Newer models can work around some of the limitations and problems of traditional LMs.

Problems of statistical LMs

In the previous chapter, we reviewed LMs and the concepts of N-grams, bigrams, and the Markov model. These methods are executed by counting occurrences in the text. That's why these methods are called statistical LMs.

The main problem with LMs is data limitation. What can we do if the probability distribution of the sentence we want to compute does not exist in the data? A partial solution here is the smoothing method, but that is insufficient.

Another solution is to use the Markov Assumption (each probability only depends on the previous step, simplifying the Chain Rule) to simplify the sentence, but that will not give a good prediction. What this means is, we could simplify our model using 3-grams.

A solution to this problem is to increase the size of the corpus, but the corpus will end up being to large. These limitations in n-gram models are called **sparsity problems**.

Window-Based Neural Model

A first approximation of this new model was the use of a sliding window to compute the probabilities of the next word. The concept of this solution comes from window classification.

In terms of words, it is hard to understand the meaning of a single word without any context. There are many problems if that word is not in a sentence or in a paragraph, for example, ambiguity between two similar words or auto-antonyms. Auto-antonyms are words with multiple meanings. The word handicap, depending on its context, can mean an advantage (for example, in sport) or a disadvantage (sometimes offensive, a physical problem).

Window classification classifies a word in the context (created by the window) of its neighboring words. The approach of a sliding window can be used to generate an LM. Here is a graphical example:

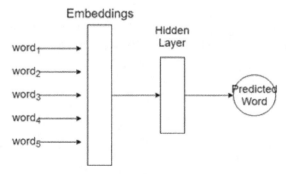

Figure 4.21: Window-based neural LM

In the previous figure, there is an example of how a window-based neural model works. The window size is 5 (word1 to word5). It creates a vector joining the embedding vector of each word, and computes this in a hidden layer:

$$h = f(Weights_{embedding} + bias_1)$$

Figure 4.22: Hidden layer formula

And finally, to predict a word, the model returns a value that can be used to classify the probability of the word:

$$output = softmax(Uh + bias_2)$$

Figure 4.23: Softmax function

Then, the word with the highest value will be the predicted word.

> **Note**
>
> We are not going to go deeper into these terms because we will use an LSTM to create the LM.

The benefits of this approach over the traditional one are as follows:

- Less computational work. Window-based neural models need less computational resources because they don't need to iterate through the corpus computing probabilities.

- It avoids the problem of changing the dimension of the N-gram to find a good probability distribution.

- The generated text will have more sense in terms of meaning because this approach solves the sparsity problem.

But there are some problems:

- Window limitations: The size of the window cannot be large, so the meaning of some words could be wrong.

- Each window has its own weight value, so it can cause ambiguity.

- If the window grows in size, the model grows too.

Analyzing the problems with the window model, an RNN can improve its performance.

RNN Language Model

An RNN is able to compute the probabilities of an upcoming word in a sequence of previous steps. The core idea of this approach is to apply the same weights repeatedly throughout the process of training.

There are some advantages of using an RNN LM over a window-based model:

- This architecture can process any length sentence; it does not have a fixed size, unlike the window-based approach.

- The model is the same for every input size. It will not grow if the input is larger.

- Depending on the NN architecture, it can use information from the previous steps and from the steps ahead.

- The weights are shared across the timesteps.

So far, we have talked about different ways to improve the statistical LM and the pros and cons of each one. Before developing an RNN LM, we need to know how to introduce a sentence as input in the NN.

One-hot encoding

Neural networks and machine learning are about numbers. As we have seen throughout this book, input elements are numbers and outputs are codified labels. But if a neural network has a sentence or a set of characters as input, how can it transform this into numerical values?

One-hot encoding is a numerical representation of discrete variables. It assumes a feature vector with the same size for different values within a discrete set of variables. This means that if there is a corpus of size 10, each word will be codified as a vector of length 10. So, each dimension corresponds to a unique element of the set.

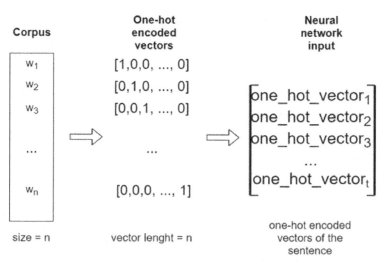

Figure 4.24: RNN pre-processing data flow

The previous figure shows how one-hot encoding works. It is important to understand the shapes of each vector because the neural network needs to understand what input data we have and what output we want to obtain. Next, *Exercise 16*, *Encoding a small Corpus* will help you examine the fundamentals of one-hot encoding in more detail.

Exercise 16: Encoding a Small Corpus

In this exercise, we are going to learn how to encode a set of words using one-hot encoding. It is the most basic encoding method, and it gives us a representation of discrete variables.

This exercise will cover different ways of performing this task. One way is to manually perform encoding, while another way is to use libraries. After finishing the exercise, we will obtain a vector representation of each word, ready to use as the input for a neural network:

1. Define a corpus. This corpus is the same one that we used in *Chapter 3, Fundamentals of Natural Language Processing*:

```
corpus = [
    'My cat is white',
    'I am the major of this city',
    'I love eating toasted cheese',
    'The lazy cat is sleeping',
]
```

2. Tokenize it using **spaCy**. We are not going to use the stop-words (erasing useless words, such as articles) method because we have a small corpus. We want all the tokens:

```
import spacy
import en_core_web_sm
nlp = en_core_web_sm.load()

corpus_tokens = []
for c in corpus:
    doc = nlp(c)
    tokens = []
    for t in doc:
        tokens.append(t.text)
    corpus_tokens.append(tokens)
corpus_tokens
```

3. Create a list with every unique token in the corpus:

```
processed_corpus = [t for sentence in corpus_tokens for t in sentence]
processed_corpus = set(processed_corpus)
processed_corpus
```

```
[['My', 'cat', 'is', 'white'],
 ['I', 'am', 'the', 'major', 'of', 'this', 'city'],
 ['I', 'love', 'eating', 'toasted', 'cheese'],
 ['The', 'lazy', 'cat', 'is', 'sleeping']]
```

Figure 4.25: List with each unique token in the corpus

4. Create a dictionary with each word in the corpus as the key and a unique number as the value. This dictionary will look like {word:value}, and this value will have the index of 1 in the one-hot encoded vector:

```
word2int = dict([(tok, pos) for pos, tok in enumerate(processed_corpus)])
word2int
```

```
{'I',
 'My',
 'The',
 'am',
 'cat',
 'cheese',
 'city',
 'eating',
 'is',
 'lazy',
 'love',
 'major',
 'of',
 'sleeping',
 'the',
 'this',
 'toasted',
 'white'}
```

Figure 4.26: Each word as a key and a unique number as a value

5. Encode a sentence. This way of performing encoding is manual. There are some libraries, such as sklearn, that provide automatic encoding methods:

```
Import numpy as np
sentence = 'My cat is lazy'
tokenized_sentence = sentence.split()
encoded_sentence = np.zeros([len(tokenized_sentence),len(processed_
corpus)])
encoded_sentence
for i,c in enumerate(sentence.split()):
    encoded_sentence[i][ word2int[c] ] = 1
encoded_sentence
```

```
array([[0., 0., 0., 0., 0., 0., 0., 0., 0., 0., 0., 0., 0., 0., 0.,
        1., 0.],
       [0., 0., 0., 0., 0., 0., 0., 1., 0., 0., 0., 0., 0., 0., 0., 0.,
        0., 0.],
       [0., 0., 0., 0., 0., 0., 1., 0., 0., 0., 0., 0., 0., 0., 0., 0.,
        0., 0.],
       [0., 1., 0., 0., 0., 0., 0., 0., 0., 0., 0., 0., 0., 0., 0., 0.,
        0., 0.]])
```

Figure 4.27: Manual one-hot encoded vectors.

```
print("Shape of the encoded sentence:", encoded_sentence.shape)
```

6. Import the **sklearn** methods. sklearn first encodes each unique token in the corpus with **LabelEncoder**, and then uses **OneHotEncoder** to create the vectors:

```
from sklearn.preprocessing import LabelEncoder
from sklearn.preprocessing import OneHotEncoder
Declare the LabelEncoder() class.
le = LabelEncoder()
Encode the corpus with this class.
labeled_corpus = le.fit_transform(list(processed_corpus))
labeled_corpus
```

```
array([10,  9,  5, 13,  0, 14,  6,  7, 16, 15, 11,  2, 12,  1,  8,  3, 17,
        4])
```

Figure 4.28: Vectors created with OneHotEncoder

7. Now, take the same sentence that we encoded before and apply the **LabelEncoder** transform method we created:

```
sentence = 'My cat is lazy'
tokenized_sentence = sentence.split()
integer_encoded = le.transform(tokenized_sentence)
integer_encoded
```

```
array([1, 4, 8, 9])
```

Figure 4.29: LabelEncoder transform applied

8. We can decode **LabelEncoder** in the initial sentence:

```
le.inverse_transform(integer_encoded)
```

```
array(['My', 'cat', 'is', 'lazy'], dtype='<U8')
```

Figure 4.30: Decoded LabelEncoder

9. Declare **OneHotEncoder** with **sparse=False** (if you do not specify this, it will return a sparse matrix):

```
onehot_encoder = OneHotEncoder(sparse=False)
```

10. To encode our sentence with the label encoder that we have created, we need to reshape our labeled corpus to fit it into the **onehot_encoder** method:

```
labeled_corpus = labeled_corpus.reshape(len(labeled_corpus), 1)
onehot_encoded = onehot_encoder.fit(labeled_corpus)
```

11. Finally, we can transform our sentence (encoded with LabelEncoder) into a one-hot vector. The results of this way of encoding and manual encoding will not be the same, but they will have the same shape:

```
sentence_encoded = onehot_encoded.transform(integer_encoded.
reshape(len(integer_encoded), 1))
print(sentence_encoded)
```

```
[[0. 1. 0. 0. 0. 0. 0. 0. 0. 0. 0. 0. 0. 0. 0. 0. 0. 0.]
 [0. 0. 0. 0. 1. 0. 0. 0. 0. 0. 0. 0. 0. 0. 0. 0. 0. 0.]
 [0. 0. 0. 0. 0. 0. 0. 0. 1. 0. 0. 0. 0. 0. 0. 0. 0. 0.]
 [0. 0. 0. 0. 0. 0. 0. 0. 0. 1. 0. 0. 0. 0. 0. 0. 0. 0.]]
```

Figure 4.31: One-hot encoded vectors using Sklearn methods

Note

This exercise is really important. If you do not understand the shapes of the matrices, it will be very hard to understand the inputs of RNNs.

Good job! You have finished *Exercise 16*. Now you can encode discrete variables into vectors. This is part of pre-processing data to train and evaluate a neural network. Next, we have the activity of the chapter, the objective of which is to create an LM using RNNs and one-hot encoding.

Note

For larger corpuses, one-hot encoding is not very useful because it would create huge vectors for the words. Instead, it is normal to use an embedding vector. This concept will be covered later in this chapter.

The Input Dimensions of RNNs

Before getting started with the RNN activity, you may not understand input dimensions. In this section, we will focus on understanding the shape of the n-dimensional arrays, and how we can add a new dimension or erase one.

Sequence data format

We've mentioned the many-to-one architecture, where each sample consists of a fixed sequence and a label. That label corresponds with the upcoming value in the sequence. It is something like this:

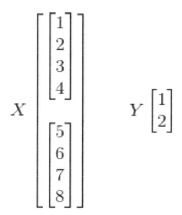

Figure 4.32: Format of sequence data

In this example, we have two sequences in matrix X, and the two output labels in Y. So, the shapes are as follows:

X = (2, 4)

Y = (2)

But if you tried to insert this data into an RNN, it wouldn't work because it does not have the correct dimensions.

RNN data format

To implement an RNN with temporal sequences in Keras, the model will need an input vector with three dimensions and, as output, one vector with two dimensions.

So, for the X matrix, we will have the following:

- Number of samples
- Sequence length
- Value length

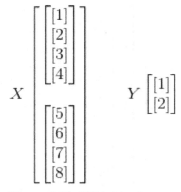

Figure 4.33: RNN data format

The shapes here are as follows:

X = (2, 4, 1)

Y = (2, 1)

One-hot format

With one-hot encoding, we have the same dimensions as input, but the value length changes. In the preceding figure, we can see the values ([1], [2], ...) with one-dimensionality. But with one-hot encoding, these values will change to vectors, so the shape would be as follows:

$$X \begin{bmatrix} \begin{bmatrix} [1, 0, 0] \\ [0, 1, 0] \\ [0, 1, 0] \\ [1, 0, 0] \end{bmatrix} \\ \begin{bmatrix} [0, 0, 1] \\ [1, 0, 0] \\ [0, 1, 0] \\ [1, 0, 0] \end{bmatrix} \end{bmatrix} \qquad Y \begin{bmatrix} [1, 0, 0] \\ [0, 0, 1] \end{bmatrix}$$

Figure 4.34: One-hot format

X = (2, 4, 3)

Y = (2, 3)

To perform all these changes to the dimensions, the **reshape** method from the NumPy library will be used.

> **Note**
>
> With this knowledge of dimensions, you can start the activity, and remember, the input dimension of an LSTM is three and the output dimension is two. So, if you create two LSTM layers continuously, how can you add the third dimension to the output of the first layer? Change the return state to True.

Activity 4: Predict the Next Character in a Sequence

In this activity, we will predict the upcoming character in a long sequence. The activity has to be performed using one-hot encoding to create the input and output vectors. The architecture of the model will be an LSTM, as we saw in *Exercise 14, Predict Houses Prices with an RNN*.

Scenario: You work in a global company as the security manager. One morning, you notice a hacker has discovered and changed all the passwords for the company's databases. You and your team of engineers start trying to decode the hacker's passwords to enter the system and fix everything. After analyzing all the new passwords, you see a common structure.

You only need to decode one more character in the password, but you don't know what the character is and you only have one more opportunity to get the correct password.

Then, you decide to create a program that analyzes long sequences of data and the five characters of the password you already know. With this information, it can predict the last character of the password.

The first five characters of the password are: tyuio. What will the last character be?

> **Note**
>
> You have to use one-hot encoding and LSTM. You will train your model with one-hot encoded vectors.

1. This is the sequence of data: qwertyuiopasdfghjklñzxcvbnm

    > **Note**
    >
    > This sequence is repeated 100 times, so do this: sequence = 'qwertyuiopasdfghjklñzxcvbnm' * 100.

2. Divide the data into sequences of five characters and prepare the output data.

3. Encode the input and the output sequences as one-hot encoded vectors.

4. Set the train and test data.

5. Design the model.

    > **Note**
    >
    > The output has many zeroes, so it is hard to achieve an exact result. Use the LeakyRelu activation function with an alpha of 0.01, and when you do the prediction, round off the value of that vector.

6. Train and evaluate it.

7. Create a function that, when given five characters, predicts the next one in order to work out the last character of the password.

    > **Note**
    >
    > The solution for this activity can be found on page 308.

Summary

AI and deep learning are making huge advances in terms of images and artificial vision thanks to convolutional networks. But RNNs also have a lot of power.

In this chapter, we reviewed how a neural network would can to predict the values of a sine function using temporal sequences. If you change the training data, this architecture can learn about stock movements for each distribution. Also, there are many architectures for RNNs, each of which is optimized for a certain task. But RNNs have a problem with vanishing gradients. A solution to this problem is a new model, called LSTM, which changes the structure of a neuron to memorize timesteps.

Focusing on linguistics, statistical LMs have many problems related with computational load and distribution probabilities. To solve the sparsity problem, the size of the n-gram model was lowered to 4 or 3 grams, but that was an insufficient number of steps back to predict an upcoming word. If we use this approach, the sparsity problem appears. A neural LM with a fixed window size can prevent the sparsity problem, but there are still problems with the limited size of the window and the weights. With RNNs, these problems do not arise, and depending on the architecture, it can obtain better results, looking many steps back and forward. But deep learning is about vectors and numbers. When you want to predict words, you need to encode the data to train the model. There are various different methods, such as the one-hot encoder or the label encoder. You can now generate text from a trained corpus and an RNN.

In the next chapter, we will talk about Convolutional Neural Networks (CNNs). We will review the fundamental techniques and architectures of CNNs, and also look at more complex implementations, such as transfer learning.

5

Convolutional Neural Networks for Computer Vision

Learning Objectives

By the end of this chapter, you will be able to:

- Explain how convolutional neural networks work
- Construct a convolutional neural network
- Improve the constructed model by using data augmentation
- Use state-of-the-art models by implementing transfer learning

In this chapter, we will learn how to use probability distributions as a form of unsupervised learning.

Introduction

In the previous chapter, we learned about how a neural network can be trained to predict values and how a **recurrent neural network (RNN)**, based on its architecture, can prove to be useful in many scenarios. In this chapter, we will discuss and observe how **convolutional neural networks (CNNs)** work in a similar way to dense neural networks (also called fully-connected neural networks, as mentioned in *Chapter 2, Introduction to Computer Vision*).

CNNs have neurons with weights and biases that are updated during training time. CNNs are mainly used for image processing. Images are interpreted as pixels and the network outputs the class it thinks the image belongs to, along with loss functions that state the errors with every classification and every output.

These types of networks make an assumption that the input is an image or works like an image, allowing them to work more efficiently (CNNs are faster and better than deep neural networks). In the following sections, you will learn more about CNNs.

Fundamentals of CNNs

In this topic, we will see how CNNs work and explain the process of convolving an image.

We know that images are made up of pixels, and if the image is in RGB, for example, it will have three channels where each letter/color (Red-Green-Blue) has its own channel with a set of pixels of the same size. Fully-connected neural networks do not represent this depth in an image in every layer. Instead, they have a single dimension to represent this depth, which is not enough. Furthermore, they connect every single neuron of one layer to every single neuron of the next layer, and so on. This in turn results in lower performance, meaning you would have to train a network for longer and would still not get good results.

CNNs are a category of neural networks that has ended up being very effective for tasks such as classification and image recognition. Although, they also work very well for sound and text data. CNNs consist of an input, hidden layers, and an output layer, just like normal neural networks. The input and hidden layers are commonly formed by **convolutional layers**, **pooling layers** (layers that reduce the spatial size of the input), and **fully-connected layers** (fully-connected layers are explained in *Chapter 2, Introduction to Computer Vision*). Convolutional layers and pooling layers will be explained later on in this chapter.

CNNs give depth to every layer, starting from the original depth of the image to deeper hidden layers as well. The following figure shows how a CNN works and what one looks like:

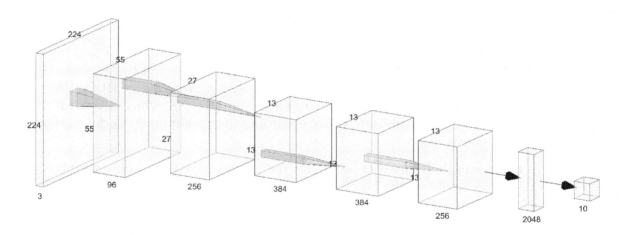

Figure 5.1: Representation of a CNN

In the preceding figure, the CNN takes an input image of 224 x 224 x 3, which by convolutional processes is transformed into the next layer, which compresses the size but has more depth to it (we will explain how these processes work later on). These operations continue over and over until the graphical representation is flattened and these dense layers are used to end up with the corresponding classes of the dataset as output.

Convolutional Layers: Convolutional layers consist of a set of **filters** of fixed size (typically a small size), which are matrices with certain values/weights, that are applied all over the input (an image, for example), by computing the scalar product between the filters and the input, which is called convolution. Each of these filters produces a two-dimensional activation map, which is stacked along the depth of the input. These activation maps look for features in the input and will determine how well the network learns. The more filters you have, the deeper the layer is, thus, the more your network learns, but the slower it gets at training time. For instance, in a particular image say, you would like to have 3 filters in the first layer, 96 filters in the next layer, 256 in the next, and so on. Note that, at the beginning of the network, there are usually fewer filters than at the end or in the middle of the network. This is because the middle and the end of the network have more potential features to extract, thus we need more filters, of a smaller size, toward the end of the network. This is because the deeper we advance into the network, the more we look at little details within an image, therefore we want to extract more features from those details to get a good understanding of the image.

The sizes of the filters of convolutional layers often go from 2x2 to 7x7, for example, depending on whether you are at the beginning of the network (higher sizes) or toward the end (smaller sizes).

In Figure 5.1, we can see convolution being applied using filters (in light blue) and the output would be a single value that goes to the next step/layer.

After performing convolution, and before another convolution is applied, a max pooling (**pooling layer**) layer is normally applied in order to reduce the size of the input so that the network can get a deeper understanding of the image. Nevertheless, lately, there is a tendency to avoid max pooling and instead encourage strides, which are naturally applied when performing convolution, so we are going to explain image reduction by naturally applying convolution.

Strides: This is the length, defined in pixels, for the steps of the filter being applied over the entire image. If a stride of one is selected, the filter will be applied, but one pixel at a time. Similarly, if a stride of two is selected, then the filter will be applied two pixels at a time, the output size is smaller than the input, and so on.

Let's look at an example. Firstly, Figure 5.2 will be used as the filter to convolve the image, which is a 2x2 matrix:

Figure 5.2: Convolution filter

And the following could be the image (matrix) we are convolving:

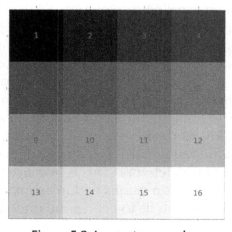

Figure 5.3: Image to convolve

Of course, this is not a real image, but for the sake of simplicity, we are taking a matrix of 4x4 with random values to demonstrate how convolution works.

Now, if we want to apply convolution with stride equal to 1, this would be the process, graphically:

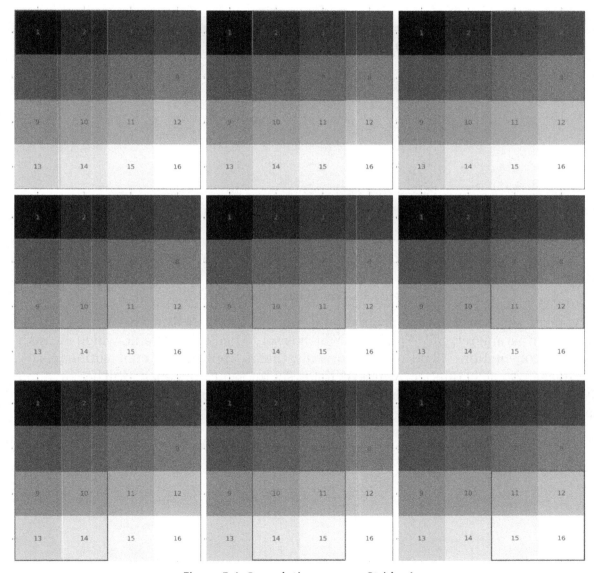

Figure 5.4: Convolution process Stride=1

The preceding Figure shows a 2x2 filter being applied to the input image, pixel by pixel. The process goes from left to right and from top to bottom.

The filter multiplies every value of every position in its matrix to every value of every position of the zone (matrix) where it's being applied. For instance, in the first part of the process, the filter is being applied to the first 2x2 part of the image [1 2; 5 6] and the filter we have is [2 1; -1 2], so it would be 1*2 + 2*1 + 5*(-1) + 6*2 = 11.

The resulting image, after applying the filter matrix, would be as shown here:

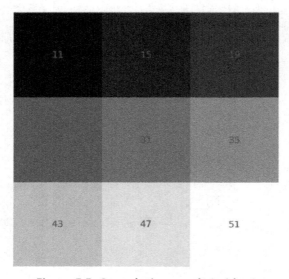

Figure 5.5: Convolution result Stride=1

As you can see, the resulting image is now one dimension smaller. This is because there is another parameter, called **padding**, which is set to "valid" by default, which means that the convolution will be applied normally; that is, applying the convolution makes the image one pixel thinner by nature. If it is set to "same," the image will be surrounded by one line of pixels with a value equal to zero, thus the output matrix will have the same size as the input matrix.

Now, we are going to apply a stride of 2, to reduce the size by 2 (just like a max pooling layer of 2x2 would do). Remember that we are using a padding equal to "valid."

The process would have fewer steps, just like in the following figure:

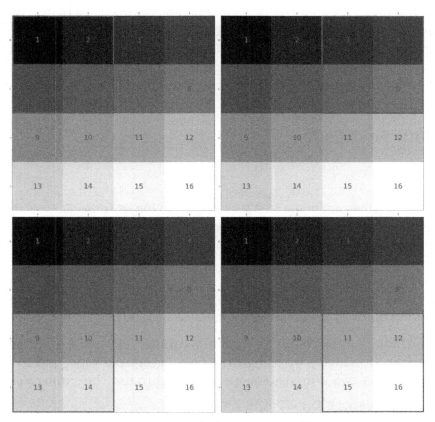

Figure 5.6: Convolution process Stride=2

And the output image/matrix would look like this:

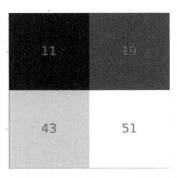

Figure 5.7: Convolution result Stride=2

The resulting image would be an image of 2x2 pixels. This is due to the natural process of convolution with stride equal to 2.

These filters, which are applied on every convolutional layer, have weights that the neural network adjusts so that the outputs of those filters help the neural network learn valuable features. These weights, as explained, are updated by the process of backpropagation. As a reminder, backpropagation is the process where the network's loss (or the amount of errors) of the predictions made versus the expected results in a training step of the network is calculated, updating all the weights of the neurons of the network that have contributed to that error so that they do not make the same mistake again.

Building Your First CNN

> **Note**
>
> For this chapter, we are going to still use Keras on top of TensorFlow as the backend, as mentioned in *Chapter 2, Introduction to Computer Vision* of this book. Also, we will still use Google Colab to train our network.

Keras is a very good library for implementing convolutional layers, as it abstracts the user so that layers do not have to be implemented by hand.

In *Chapter 2, Introduction to Computer Vision*, we imported the Dense, Dropout, and BatchNormalization layers by using the **keras.layers** package, and to declare convolutional layers of two dimensions, we are going to use the same package:

```
from keras.layers import Conv2D
```

The **Conv2D** module is just like the other modules: you have to declare a sequential model, which was explained in *Chapter 2, Introduction to Computer Vision* of this book, and we also add **Conv2D**:

```
model = Sequential()

model.add(Conv2D(32, kernel_size=(3, 3), padding='same', strides=(2,2),
input_shape=input_shape))
```

For the first layer, the input shape has to be specified, but after that, it is no longer needed.

The first parameter that must be specified is the **number of filters** that the network is going to learn in that layer. As mentioned before, in the earlier layers, we will filter few layers which will be learned, rather than the layers deeper in the network.

The second parameter that must be specified is the **kernel size**, which is the size of the filter applied to the input data. Usually, a kernel of size 3x3 is set, or even 2x2, but sometimes when the image is large, a bigger kernel size is set.

The third parameter is **padding**, which is set to "valid" by default, but it needs to be set to "same," as we want to preserve the size of the input in order to understand the behavior of down-sampling the input.

The fourth parameter is **strides**, which, by default, is set to (1, 1). We will be setting it to (2, 2), since there are two numbers here and it has to be set for both the x and y axes.

After the first layer, we will apply the same methodology as was mentioned in *Chapter 2, Introduction to Computer Vision*:

```
model.add(BatchNormalization())
model.add(Activation('relu'))
model.add(Dropout(0.2))
```

As a reminder, the **BatchNormalization** layer is used to normalize the inputs of each layer, which helps the network converge faster and may give better results overall.

The **Activation** layer is where the activation function is applied, and an `activation` function is a function that takes the input and calculates a weighted sum of it, adding a bias and deciding whether it should be activated or not (outputting 1 and 0, respectively).

The **Dropout** layer helps the network avoid overfitting, which is when the accuracy of the training set is much higher than the accuracy of the validation set, by switching off a percentage of neurons.

We could apply more sets of layers like this, varying the parameters, depending on the size of the problem to solve.

The last layers remain the same as those of dense neural networks, depending on the problem.

Exercise 17: Building a CNN

> **Note**
>
> This exercise uses the same packages and libraries as *Chapter 2, Introduction to Computer Vision*. These libraries are Keras, Numpy, OpenCV, and Matplotlib.

In this exercise, we are going to take the same problem as *Chapter 2, Activity 2, Classify 10 Types of Clothes of the Fashion-MNIST Database*.

Remember that, in that activity, the neural network that was built was not capable of generalizing well enough to classify the unseen data that we passed to it.

As a reminder, this problem is a classification problem, where the model has to classify 10 types of clothes correctly:

1. Open up your Google Colab interface.

2. Create a folder for the book and download the **Datasets** folder from GitHub and upload it in the folder in your drive.

3. Import drive and mount it as follows:

    ```
    from google.colab import drive
    drive.mount('/content/drive')
    ```

> **Note**
>
> Every time you use a new collaborator, mount the drive to the desired folder.

4. Once you have mounted your drive for the first time, you will have to enter the authorization code mentioned by clicking on the URL given by Google and press the **Enter** key on your keyboard:

```
[1]  from google.colab import drive
     drive.mount('/content/drive')

 ⤷   Go to this URL in a browser: https://accounts.google.com/o/oauth2/auth?client_id=947318989803-6bn6qk8qdgf4n4g3pfee6491hc0brc4i.apps.googleusercontent.com

     Enter your authorization code:
     ..........
     Mounted at /content/drive
```

Figure 5.8: Mounting on Google Collab

5. Now that you have mounted the drive, you need to set the path of the directory:

```
cd /content/drive/My Drive/C13550/Lesson05/
```

> **Note**
>
> The path mentioned in step 5 may change as per your folder setup on Google Drive. The path will always begin with **cd /content/drive/My Drive/**.

6. First, let's import the data from Keras and initialize the random seed to 42 for reproducibility:

```
from keras.datasets import fashion_mnist
(x_train, y_train), (x_test, y_test) =fashion_mnist.load_data()
import random
random.seed(42)
```

7. We import NumPy in order to pre-process the data and Keras utils to one-hot encode the labels:

```
import numpy as np
from keras import utils as np_utils
x_train = (x_train.astype(np.float32))/255.0
x_test = (x_test.astype(np.float32))/255.0
x_train = x_train.reshape(x_train.shape[0], 28, 28, 1)
x_test = x_test.reshape(x_test.shape[0], 28, 28, 1)
y_train = np_utils.to_categorical(y_train, 10)
y_test = np_utils.to_categorical(y_test, 10)
input_shape = x_train.shape[1:]
```

8. We declare the **Sequential** function to make a sequential model in Keras, the callbacks, and, of course, the layers:

```
from keras.models import Sequential
from keras.callbacks import EarlyStopping, ModelCheckpoint
from keras.layers import Input, Dense, Dropout, Flatten
from keras.layers import Conv2D, Activation, BatchNormalization
```

> **Note**
>
> We have imported a callback called **EarlyStopping**. What this callback does is stop the training after a number of epochs, where the metric that you choose (for example, validation accuracy) has dropped. You can set that number with the number of epochs that you want.

9. Now, we are going to build our first CNN. First, let's declare the model as **Sequential** and add the first **Conv2D**:

```
def CNN(input_shape):
    model = Sequential()
    model.add(Conv2D(32, kernel_size=(3, 3), padding='same',
strides=(2,2), input_shape=input_shape))
```

We add 32 filters as is the first layer, and a filter size of 3x3. Padding is set to **"same"** and the strides are set to 2 to naturally reduce the dimensionality of the **Conv2D** module.

10. We follow this layer by adding **Activation** and **BatchNormalization** layers:

```
    model.add(Activation('relu'))
    model.add(BatchNormalization())
```

11. We are going to add another three layers with the same characteristics as before, applying dropout and jumping to another block:

```
    model.add(Conv2D(32, kernel_size=(3, 3), padding='same',
strides=(2,2)))
    model.add(Activation('relu'))
    model.add(BatchNormalization())
```

12. Now, we apply dropout of 20%, which turns off 20% of the neurons in the network:

```
    model.add(Dropout(0.2))
```

13. We are going to do the same procedure one more time but with 64 filters:

```
model.add(Conv2D(64, kernel_size=(3, 3), padding='same',
strides=(2,2)))
    model.add(Activation('relu'))
    model.add(BatchNormalization())
    model.add(Conv2D(64, kernel_size=(3, 3), padding='same',
strides=(2,2)))
    model.add(Activation('relu'))
    model.add(BatchNormalization())
    model.add(Dropout(0.2))
```

14. For the end of the network, we apply the **Flatten** layer to make the output of the last layer one-dimensional. We apply a **Dense** layer with 512 neurons. Where the logistics of the network occur, we apply the **Activation** layer and the **BatchNormalization** layer, before applying a **Dropout** of 50%:

```
model.add(Flatten())
model.add(Dense(512))
model.add(Activation('relu'))
model.add(BatchNormalization())
model.add(Dropout(0.5))
```

15. And, finally, we declare the last layer as a **dense** layer with 10 neurons, which is the number of classes of the dataset, and a **Softmax** activation function, which establishes which class the image is more likely to be, and we return the model:

```
model.add(Dense(10, activation="softmax"))
return model
```

16. Let's declare the model along with the callbacks and compile it:

```
model = CNN(input_shape)

model.compile(loss='categorical_crossentropy', optimizer='Adadelta',
metrics=['accuracy'])

ckpt = ModelCheckpoint('Models/model.h5', save_best_
only=True,monitor='val_loss', mode='min', save_weights_only=False)
earlyStopping = EarlyStopping(monitor='val_loss', patience=5,
verbose=0,mode='min')
```

For compiling, we are using the same optimizer. For declaring the checkpoint, we are using the same parameters. For declaring **EarlyStopping**, we are using the validation loss as the main metric and we set a patience of five epochs.

17. Let the training begin!

```
model.fit(x_train, y_train, batch_size=128, epochs=100, verbose=1,
validation_data=(x_test, y_test), callbacks=[ckpt,earlyStopping])
```

We set the batch size to 128 because there are enough images and because this way, it will take less time to train. The number of epochs is set to 100, as **EarlyStopping** will take care of stopping the training.

The accuracy obtained is better than in the exercise in *Chapter 2, Introduction to Computer Vision* – we have obtained an accuracy of **92.72%**.

Take a look at the following output:

```
Epoch 12/100
60000/60000 [==============================] - 14s 235us/step - loss: 0.1283 - acc: 0.9516 - val_loss: 0
.2217 - val_acc: 0.9313
Epoch 13/100
60000/60000 [==============================] - 14s 234us/step - loss: 0.1197 - acc: 0.9564 - val_loss: 0
.2610 - val_acc: 0.9240
```

Figure 5.9: val_acc shown as 0.9240, which is 92.72%

> **Note**
>
> The entire code for this exercise is available on GitHub: https://github.com/
> PacktPublishing/Artificial-Vision-and-Language-Processing-for-Robotics/blob/
> master/Lesson05/Exercise17/Exercise17.ipynb.

18. Let's try with the same examples that we tried in *Activity 2, Classify 10 Types of Clothes of the Fashion-MNIST Database* of *Chapter 2*, which is located in **Dataset/ testing/**:

```
import cv2

images = ['ankle-boot.jpg', 'bag.jpg', 'trousers.jpg', 't-shirt.jpg']

for number in range(len(images)):
    imgLoaded = cv2.imread('Dataset/testing/%s'%(images[number]),0)
    img = cv2.resize(imgLoaded, (28, 28))
    img = np.invert(img)
    img = (img.astype(np.float32))/255.0
    img = img.reshape(1, 28, 28, 1)
```

```
        plt.subplot(1,5,number+1),plt.imshow(imgLoaded,'gray')
        plt.title(np.argmax(model.predict(img)[0]))
        plt.xticks([]),plt.yticks([])
    plt.show()
```

Here's the output:

Figure 5.10: Prediction of clothes using CNNs

As a reminder, here is the table with the number of corresponding clothes:

T-shirt	Trouser	Pullover	Dress	Coat	Sandal	Shirt	Sneaker	Bag	Ankle boot
0	1	2	3	4	5	6	7	8	9

Figure 5.11: The table with the number of corresponding clothes

We can see that the model has predicted all the pictures well, so we can state that the model is far better than one with only dense layers.

Improving Your Model - Data Augmentation

There are situations, at times, where you would not be able to improve the accuracy of your model by building a better model. Sometimes, the problem is not the model but the data. One of the most important things to consider when working with machine learning is that the data you work with has to be good enough for a potential model to generalize that data.

Data can represent real-life things, but it can also include incorrect data that may perform badly. This can happen when you have incomplete data or data that does not represent the classes well. For those cases, data augmentation has become one of the most popular approaches.

Data augmentation actually increases the number of samples of the original dataset. For computer vision, this could mean increasing the number of images in a dataset. There are several data augmentation techniques, and you may want to use a specific technique, depending on the dataset. Some of these techniques are mentioned here:

- **Rotation**: The user sets the degree of rotation for images in the dataset.
- **Flip**: To flip the images horizontally or vertically.
- **Crop**: Crop a section from the images randomly.
- **Change color**: Change or vary the color of the images.
- **Add Noise**: To add noise to images.

Applying these or other techniques, you end up generating new images that vary from the original ones.

In order to implement this in code, Keras has a module called **ImageDataGenerator**, where you declare transformations that you want to apply to your dataset. You can import that module using this line of code:

```
from keras.preprocessing.image import ImageDataGenerator
```

In order to declare the variable that is going to apply all those changes to your dataset, you have to declare it as in the following code snippet:

```
datagen = ImageDataGenerator(
        rotation_range=20,
        zoom_range = 0.2,
        width_shift_range=0.1,
        height_shift_range=0.1,
        horizontal_flip=True
        )
```

> **Note**
>
> You can see what attributes you can pass to **ImageDataGenerator** by looking at this documentation from Keras: https://keras.io/preprocessing/image/.

After declaring **datagen**, you have to compute some calculations for feature-wise normalization by using the following:

```
datagen.fit(x_train)
```

Here, **x_train** is your training set.

In order to train the model using data augmentation, the following code should be used:

```
model.fit_generator(datagen.flow(x_train, y_train,
                                 batch_size=batch_size),
                    epochs=epochs,
                    validation_data=(x_test, y_test),
                    callbacks=callbacks,
                    steps_per_epoch=len(x_train) // batch_size)
```

Datagen.flow() is used so that data augmentation can be applied. As Keras does not know when to stop applying data augmentation in the given data, **Steps_per_epoch** is the parameter that sets that limit, which should be the length of the training set divided by the batch size.

Now we are going to jump right into the second exercise of this chapter to observe the output. Data augmentation promises better results and better accuracy. Let's find out whether that is true or not.

Exercise 18: Improving Models Using Data Augmentation

In this exercise, we are going to use the The Oxford - III Pet dataset, which is RGB images, of varying sizes and several classes, of different cat/dog breeds. In this case, we will separate the dataset into two classes: cats and dogs, for simplicity. There are 1,000 images for each class, which is not much, but it will increment the effect of data augmentation. This dataset is stored in the **Dataset/dogs-cats/** folder, added on GitHub.

We will build a CNN and train it with and without data augmentation, and we will compare the results:

> **Note**
>
> For this exercise, we are going to open another Google Colab notebook.
>
> The entire code for this exercise can be found on GitHub: https://github.com/PacktPublishing/Artificial-Vision-and-Language-Processing-for-Robotics/blob/master/Lesson05/Exercise18/Exercise18.ipynb.

1. Open up your Google Colab interface.

2. Create a folder for the book and download the **Datasets** folder from GitHub and upload it in the folder in your drive.

3. Import drive and mount it as follows:

```
from google.colab import drive
drive.mount('/content/drive')
```

> **Note**
>
> Every time you use a new collaborator, mount the drive to the desired folder.

4. Once you have mounted your drive for the first time, you have to enter the authorization code mentioned by clicking on the URL given by Google.

5. Now that you have mounted the drive, you need to set the path of the directory:

```
cd /content/drive/My Drive/C13550/Lesson5/Dataset
```

> **Note**
>
> The path mentioned in step 5 may change as per your folder setup on Google Drive. The path will always begin with **cd /content/drive/My Drive/**.

6. First, let's use these two methods, which we have already used before, to load the data from disk:

```
import re, os, cv2
import numpy as np
rows,cols = 128,128

//{…}##the detailed code can be found on Github##
```

```
def list_files(directory, ext=None):

//{…}##the detailed code can be found on Github##

def load_images(path,label):
//{…}
    for fname in list_files( path, ext='jpg' ):
        img = cv2.imread(fname)
        img = cv2.resize(img, (rows, cols))
//{…}##the detailed code can be found on Github##
```

Note

The size of the image is specified as 128x128. This size is larger than the sizes used before, because we need more detail in these images, as the classes are more difficult to differentiate and the subjects are presented in varying positions, which makes the work even more difficult.

7. We load the corresponding images of dogs and cats as **X** for the images and **y** for the labels, and we print the shape of those:

```
X, y = load_images('Dataset/dogs-cats/dogs',0)
X_aux, y_aux = load_images('Dataset/dogs-cats/cats',1)
X = np.concatenate((X, X_aux), axis=0)
y = np.concatenate((y, y_aux), axis=0)
print(X.shape)
print(y.shape)
```

```
(2000, 128, 128, 3)
(2000,)
```

Figure 5.12: Dogs-cats data shape

8. Now we will import **random**, set the seed, and show some samples of the data:

```
import random
random.seed(42)
from matplotlib import pyplot as plt

for idx in range(5):
    rnd_index = random.randint(0, X.shape[0]-1)
    plt.subplot(1,5,idx+1)
    plt.imshow(cv2.cvtColor(X[rnd_index],cv2.COLOR_BGR2RGB))
    plt.xticks([]),plt.yticks([])
plt.show()
```

Figure 5.13: Image samples of the Oxford Pet dataset

9. To pre-process the data, we are going to use the same procedure as in *Exercise 17: Building a CNN*:

```
from keras import utils as np_utils
X = (X.astype(np.float32))/255.0
X = X.reshape(X.shape[0], rows, cols, 3)
y = np_utils.to_categorical(y, 2)
input_shape = X.shape[1:]
```

10. Now, we separate **X** and **y** into **x_train** and **y_train** for the training set, and **x_test** and **y_test** for the testing set, and we print the shapes:

```
from sklearn.model_selection import train_test_split
x_train, x_test, y_train, y_test = train_test_split(X, y, test_size=0.2)
print(x_train.shape)
print(y_train.shape)
print(x_test.shape)
print(y_test.shape)
```

```
(1600, 128, 128, 3)
(1600, 2)
(400, 128, 128, 3)
(400, 2)
```

Figure 5.14: Training and testing set shapes

11. We import the corresponding data to build, compile, and train the model:

```
from keras.models import Sequential
from keras.callbacks import EarlyStopping, ModelCheckpoint
from keras.layers import Input, Dense, Dropout, Flatten
from keras.layers import Conv2D, Activation, BatchNormalization
```

12. Let's build the model:

```
def CNN(input_shape):
    model = Sequential()

    model.add(Conv2D(16, kernel_size=(5, 5), padding='same',
strides=(2,2), input_shape=input_shape))
    model.add(Activation('relu'))
    model.add(BatchNormalization())
    model.add(Conv2D(16, kernel_size=(3, 3), padding='same',
strides=(2,2)))
    model.add(Activation('relu'))
    model.add(BatchNormalization())
    model.add(Dropout(0.2))

//{…}##the detailed code can be found on Github##

    model.add(Conv2D(128, kernel_size=(2, 2), padding='same',
strides=(2,2)))
    model.add(Activation('relu'))
```

```
model.add(BatchNormalization())
model.add(Dropout(0.2))

model.add(Flatten())
model.add(Dense(512))
model.add(Activation('relu'))
model.add(BatchNormalization())
model.add(Dropout(0.5))

model.add(Dense(2, activation="softmax"))

return model
```

The model goes from 16 filters in the very first layer to 128 filters at the end, doubling the size in every 2 layers.

Because this problem is harder (we have bigger images with 3 channels and 128x128 images), we have made the model deeper, adding another couple of layers with 16 filters at the beginning (the first layer having a kernel size of 5x5, which is better in the very first stages) and another couple of layers with 128 filters at the end of the model.

13. Now, let's compile the model:

```
model = CNN(input_shape)

model.compile(loss='categorical_crossentropy', optimizer='Adadelta',
metrics=['accuracy'])

ckpt = ModelCheckpoint('Models/model_dogs-cats.h5', save_best_
only=True,monitor='val_loss', mode='min', save_weights_only=False)

earlyStopping = EarlyStopping(monitor='val_loss', patience=15,
verbose=0,mode='min')
```

We have set the patience to 15 epochs for the EarlyStopping callback because it takes more epochs for the model to converge to the sweet spot, and the validation loss can vary a lot until then.

14. Then, we train the model:

```
model.fit(x_train, y_train,
          batch_size=8,
          epochs=100,
          verbose=1,
          validation_data=(x_test, y_test),
          callbacks=[ckpt,earlyStopping])
```

The batch size is also low as we do not have much data, but it could be increased to 16 easily.

15. Then, evaluate the model:

```
from sklearn import metrics
model.load_weights('Models/model_dogs-cats.h5')
y_pred = model.predict(x_test, batch_size=8, verbose=0)
y_pred = np.argmax(y_pred, axis=1)
y_test_aux = y_test.copy()
y_test_pred = list()
for i in y_test_aux:
    y_test_pred.append(np.argmax(i))

print (y_pred)

# Evaluate the prediction
accuracy = metrics.accuracy_score(y_test_pred, y_pred)
precision, recall, f1, support = metrics.precision_recall_fscore_
support(y_test_pred, y_pred, average=None)
print('\nFinal results...')
print(metrics.classification_report(y_test_pred, y_pred))
print('Acc      : %.4f' % accuracy)
print('Precision: %.4f' % np.average(precision))
print('Recall   : %.4f' % np.average(recall))
print('F1       : %.4f' % np.average(f1))
print('Support  :', np.sum(support))
```

You should see the following output:

```
Final results...
                precision    recall    f1-score    support

            0      0.67       0.70       0.68        204
            1      0.67       0.65       0.66        196

    micro avg      0.67       0.67       0.67        400
    macro avg      0.67       0.67       0.67        400
 weighted avg      0.67       0.67       0.67        400

Acc       : 0.6725
Precision: 0.6725
Recall    : 0.6720
F1        : 0.6720
Support   : 400
```

Figure 5.15: Output showing the accuracy of the model

As you can see from the preceding figure, the accuracy achieved in this dataset with this model is **67.25%**.

16. We are going to apply data augmentation to this process. We have to import ImageDataGenerator from Keras and declare it with transformations that we are going to make:

```
from keras.preprocessing.image import ImageDataGenerator
datagen = ImageDataGenerator(
        rotation_range=15,
        width_shift_range=0.2,
        height_shift_range=0.2,
        horizontal_flip=True,
        zoom_range=0.3
        )
```

The following transformations have been applied:

We have set a rotation range of 15 degrees because dogs and cats within images can be positioned in slightly different ways (feel free to tweak this parameter).

We have set the width shift range and height shift range to 0.2 to shift the image horizontally and vertically, as an animal could be anywhere within the image (also tweakable).

We have set the horizontal flip property to **True** because these animals can be flipped in the dataset (horizontally; with vertical flipping, it is much more difficult to find an animal).

Finally, we set zoom range to 0.3 to make random zooms on the images as the dogs and cats may be farther in the image or closer.

17. We fit the **datagen** instance declared with the training data in order to compute quantities for feature-wise normalization and declare and compile the model again to make sure we are not using the previous one:

```
datagen.fit(x_train)

model = CNN(input_shape)

model.compile(loss='categorical_crossentropy', optimizer='Adadelta',
metrics=['accuracy'])

ckpt = ModelCheckpoint('Models/model_dogs-cats.h5', save_best_
only=True,monitor='val_loss', mode='min', save_weights_only=False)
```

18. Finally, we train the model with the **fit_generator** method of the model and the **flow()** method of the **datagen** instance generated:

```
model.fit_generator(
            datagen.flow(x_train, y_train, batch_size=8),
            epochs=100,
            verbose=1,
            validation_data=(x_test, y_test),
            callbacks=[ckpt,earlyStopping],
            steps_per_epoch=len(x_train) // 8,
            workers=4)
```

We set the **steps_per_epoch** parameter equal to the length of the training set divided by the batch size (8).

We also set the number of workers to 4 to take advantage of the 4 cores of the processor:

```
from sklearn import metrics
# Make a prediction
print ("Making predictions...")
model.load_weights('Models/model_dogs-cats.h5')
#y_pred = model.predict(x_test)
y_pred = model.predict(x_test, batch_size=8, verbose=0)
y_pred = np.argmax(y_pred, axis=1)
```

```
y_test_aux = y_test.copy()
y_test_pred = list()
for i in y_test_aux:
    y_test_pred.append(np.argmax(i))

print (y_pred)

# Evaluate the prediction
accuracy = metrics.accuracy_score(y_test_pred, y_pred)
precision, recall, f1, support = metrics.precision_recall_fscore_
support(y_test_pred, y_pred, average=None)
print('\nFinal results...')
print(metrics.classification_report(y_test_pred, y_pred))
print('Acc       : %.4f' % accuracy)
print('Precision: %.4f' % np.average(precision))
print('Recall    : %.4f' % np.average(recall))
print('F1        : %.4f' % np.average(f1))
print('Support  :', np.sum(support))
```

You should see the following output:

```
Final results...
                precision     recall    f1-score     support

           0         0.84       0.77        0.81         204
           1         0.78       0.85        0.81         196

   micro avg         0.81       0.81        0.81         400
   macro avg         0.81       0.81        0.81         400
weighted avg         0.81       0.81        0.81         400

Acc        : 0.8100
Precision: 0.8117
Recall     : 0.8107
F1         : 0.8099
Support    : 400
```

Figure 5.16: Output showing the accuracy of the model

As you can see from the preceding figure, with data augmentation, we achieve an accuracy of **81%**, which is far better.

19. If we want to load the model that we just trained (dogs versus cats), the following code achieves that:

```
from keras.models import load_model
model = load_model('Models/model_dogs-cats.h5')
```

20. Let's try the model with unseen data. The data can be found in the **Dataset/ testing** folder and the code from *Exercise 17, Building a CNN* will be used (but with different names for the samples):

```
images = ['dog1.jpg', 'dog2.jpg', 'cat1.jpg', 'cat2.jpg']

for number in range(len(images)):
    imgLoaded = cv2.imread('testing/%s'%(images[number]))
    img = cv2.resize(imgLoaded, (rows, cols))
    img = (img.astype(np.float32))/255.0
    img = img.reshape(1, rows, cols, 3)
```

In these lines of code, we are loading an image, resizing it to the expected size (128 x 128), normalizing the image – as we did with the training set – and reshaping it to (1, 128, 128, 3) to fit as input in the neural network.

We continue the for loop:

```
    plt.subplot(1,5,number+1),plt.imshow(cv2.cvtColor(imgLoad ed,cv2.COLOR_
BGR2RGB))
        plt.title(np.argmax(model.predict(img)[0]))
        plt.xticks([]),plt.yticks([])
fig = plt.gcf()
plt.show()
```

Dog	Cat
0	1

Figure 5.17: Prediction of the Oxford Pet dataset with unseen data using CNNs and data augmentation

We can see that the model has made all the predictions well. Note that not all the breeds are stored in the dataset, so not all the cats and dogs will be predicted properly. Adding more types of breeds would be necessary in order to achieve that.

Activity 5: Making Use of Data Augmentation to Classify correctly Images of Flowers

In this activity, you are going to put into practice what you have learned. We are going to use a different dataset, where the images are bigger (150x150). There are 5 classes in this dataset: daisy, dandelion, rose, sunflower, and tulip. There are, in total, 4,323 images, which is fewer when compared to the previous exercises we performed. The classes do not have the same number of images either, but do not worry about that. The images are RGB, so there will be three channels. We have stored them in NumPy arrays of each class, so we will provide a way to load them properly.

The following steps will guide you through this:

1. Load the dataset by using this code, as the data is stored in NumPy format:

```
import numpy as np
classes = ['daisy','dandelion','rose','sunflower','tulip']
X = np.load("Dataset/flowers/%s_x.npy"%(classes[0]))
y = np.load("Dataset/flowers/%s_y.npy"%(classes[0]))
print(X.shape)
for flower in classes[1:]:
    X_aux = np.load("Dataset/flowers/%s_x.npy"%(flower))
    y_aux = np.load("Dataset/flowers/%s_y.npy"%(flower))
    print(X_aux.shape)
    X = np.concatenate((X, X_aux), axis=0)
    y = np.concatenate((y, y_aux), axis=0)
print(X.shape)
print(y.shape)
```

2. Show some samples from the dataset by importing **random** and **matplotlib**, using a random index to access the **X** set.

> **Note**
>
> The NumPy arrays were stored in BGR format (OpenCV format), so in order to show the images properly, you will need to use the following code to change the format to RGB (only to show the image): **image=cv2.cvtColor(image,cv2.COLOR_BGR2RGB)**.
>
> You will need to import **cv2**.

3. Normalize the **X** set and set the labels to categorical (the **y** set).

4. Split the sets into a training and testing set.

5. Build a CNN.

> **Note**
>
> As we have bigger images, you should consider adding more layers, thus reducing the image size, and the first layer should contain a bigger kernel (the kernel should be an odd number when it is bigger than 3).

6. Declare ImageDataGenerator from Keras with the changes that you think will suit the variance of the dataset.

7. Train the model. You can either choose an EarlyStopping policy or set a high number of epochs and wait or stop it whenever you want. If you declare the Checkpoint callback, it will always save only the best validation loss model (if that is the metric you are using).

8. Evaluate the model using this code:

```
from sklearn import metrics
y_pred = model.predict(x_test, batch_size=batch_size, verbose=0)
y_pred = np.argmax(y_pred, axis=1)
y_test_aux = y_test.copy()
y_test_pred = list()
for i in y_test_aux:
    y_test_pred.append(np.argmax(i))
accuracy = metrics.accuracy_score(y_test_pred, y_pred)
print(accuracy)
```

> **Note**
>
> This will print the accuracy of the model. Note that batch_size is the batch size you have set for your training sets and for **x_test** and **y_test**, which are your testing sets.
>
> You can use this code in order to evaluate any model, but first you need to load the model. If you want to load the entire model from a **.h5** file, you will have to use this code:
>
> ```
> from keras.models import load_model
> model = load_model('model.h5')
> ```

9. Try the model with unseen data. In the **Dataset/testing/** folder, you will find five images of flowers that you can load to try it out. Remember that the classes are in this order:

classes=['daisy';'dandelion';'rose';'sunflower';'tulip']

So, the result should look like this:

Figure 5.18: Prediction of roses using CNNs

> **Note**
>
> The solution for this activity can be found on page 313.

State-of-the-Art Models - Transfer Learning

Humans do not learn each and every task that they want to achieve from scratch; they usually take previous knowledge as a base in order to learn tasks much faster.

When training neural networks, there are some tasks that are extremely expensive to train for every individual, such as having hundreds of thousands of images for training and having to distinguish between two or more similar objects, ending up having a cost of days to achieve good performance, for example. These neural networks are trained to achieve this expensive task, and because neural networks are capable of saving that knowledge, then other models can take advantage of those weights to retrain specific models for similar tasks.

Transfer learning does just that – it transfers the knowledge of a pretrained model to your model, so you can take advantage of that knowledge.

So, for example, if you want to make a classifier that is capable of identifying five objects but that task seems too expensive to train (it takes knowledge and time), you can take advantage of a pretrained model (usually trained on the famous **ImageNet** dataset) and retrain the model adapted to your problem. The ImageNet dataset is a large visual database designed for use in visual object recognition research and has more than 14 million images with more than 20,000 categories, which is very expensive for an individual to train.

Technically, you load the model with the weights of the dataset where it was trained, and if you want to achieve a different problem, you only have to change the last layer of the model. If the model is trained on ImageNet, it could have, 1000 classes but you only have 5 classes, so you would change the last layer to a dense layer with only 5 neurons. You could add more layers before the last one, though.

The layers of the model that you have imported (the base model) can be frozen so their weights do not reflect on the training time. Depending on this, there are two types of transfer learning:

- **Traditional**: Freeze all the layers of the base model

- **Fine-tuning**: Freeze only a part of the base model, typically the first layers

In Keras, we can import famous pretrained models such as Resnet50 and VGG16. You can import a pretrained model with or without weights (in Keras, there are only weights for ImageNet), which includes the top of the model or not. The input shape can only be only specified if the top is not included and with a minimum size of 32.

With the following lines of code, you would import the Resnet50 model without the top, with the **imagenet** weights and with a shape of 150x150x3:

```
from keras.applications import resnet50

model = resnet50.ResNet50(include_top=False, weights='imagenet', input_
shape=(150,150,3))
```

If you have included the top of the model because you want to use the last dense layers of the model (let's say your problem is similar to ImageNet but with different classes), then you should write this code:

```
from keras.models import Model
from keras.layers import Dense


model.layers.pop()
model.outputs = [model.layers[-1].output]
model.layers[-1].outbound_nodes = []


x=Dense(5, activation='softmax')(model.output)
model=Model(model.input,x)
```

This code gets rid of the classification layer (the last dense layer) and prepares the model so that you can add your own last layer. Of course, you could add more layers at the end before adding your classification layer.

If you have not added the top of the model, then you should add your own top with this code:

```
from keras.models import Model
from keras.layers import Dense, GlobalAveragePooling2D
x=base_model.output
x=GlobalAveragePooling2D()(x)
x=Dense(512,activation='relu')(x) #dense layer 2
x=Dropout(0.3)(x)
x=Dense(512,activation='relu')(x) #dense layer 3
x=Dropout(0.3)(x)
preds=Dense(5,activation='softmax')(x) #final layer with softmax activation
model=Model(inputs=base_model.input,outputs=preds)
```

Here, **GlobalAveragePooling2D** is like a type of max pooling.

With these kinds of models, you should preprocess the data just as you did with the data that trained those models (if you are using the weights). Keras has a **preprocess_input** method that does that for every model. For example, for ResNet50, it would be like this:

```
from keras.applications.resnet50 import preprocess_input
```

You pass your array of images to that function and then you will have your data ready for training.

The **learning rate** in a model is how fast it should convert the model to a local minimum. Usually, you do not have to worry about this but if you are retraining a neural network, this is a parameter that you have to tweak. When you are retraining a neural network, you should decrease the value of this parameter so that the neural network does not unlearn what it has already learned. This parameter is tweaked when declaring the optimizer. You can avoid tweaking this parameter, although the model may end up not ever converging or overfitting.

With this kind of approach, you could train your network with very little data and get good results overall, because you take advantage of the weights of the model.

You can combine transfer learning with data augmentation as well.

Exercise 19: Classifying €5 and €20 Bills Using Transfer Learning with Very Little Data

This problem is about differentiating €5 bills from €20 bills with very little data. We have 30 images for every class, which is much less than we have had in previous exercises. We are going to load the data, declare the pretrained model, then declare the changes on the data with data augmentation and train the model. After that, we will check how well the model performs with unseen data:

1. Open up your Google Colab interface.

    > **Note**
    >
    > You would need to mount the **Dataset** folder on your drive and set the path accordingly.

2. Declare functions to load the data:

    ```
    import re, os, cv2
    import numpy as np

    def list_files(directory, ext=None):
    //{...}
    ##the detailed code can be found on Github##

    def load_images(path,label):
    //{...}
    ##the detailed code can be found on Github##

        for fname in list_files( path, ext='jpg' ):
            img = cv2.imread(fname)
            img = cv2.resize(img, (224, 224))
    //{...}
    ##the detailed code can be found on Github##
    ```

    Note that the data is resized to 224x224.

3. The data is stored in **Dataset/money/**, where you have both classes in subfolders. In order to load the data, you have to write the following code:

```
X, y = load_images('Dataset/money/20',0)
X_aux, y_aux = load_images('Dataset/money/5',1)
X = np.concatenate((X, X_aux), axis=0)
y = np.concatenate((y, y_aux), axis=0)
print(X.shape)
print(y.shape)
```

The label for the €20 bill is 0 and it's 1 for the €5 bill.

4. Let's show the data:

```
import random
random.seed(42)
from matplotlib import pyplot as plt

for idx in range(5):
    rnd_index = random.randint(0, 59)
    plt.subplot(1,5,idx+1),plt.imshow(cv2.cvtColor(X[rnd_index],cv2.COLOR_
BGR2RGB))
    plt.xticks([]),plt.yticks([])
plt.savefig("money_samples.jpg", bbox_inches='tight')
plt.show()
```

Figure 5.19: Samples of bills

5. Now we are going to declare the pretrained model:

```
from keras.applications.mobilenet import MobileNet, preprocess_input
from keras.layers import Input, GlobalAveragePooling2D, Dense, Dropout
from keras.models import Model

input_tensor = Input(shape=(224, 224, 3))

base_model = MobileNet(input_tensor=input_
tensor,weights='imagenet',include_top=False)

x = base_model.output
x = GlobalAveragePooling2D()(x)
x = Dense(512,activation='relu')(x)
x = Dropout(0.5)(x)
x = Dense(2, activation='softmax')(x)

model = Model(base_model.input, x)
```

In this case, we are loading the MobileNet model with the weights of imagenet. We are not including the top so we should build our own top. The input shape is 224x224x3.

We have built the top of the model by taking the output of the last layer of MobileNet (which is not the classification layer) and start building on top of that. We have added **GlobalAveragePooling2D** for image reduction, a dense layer that we can train for our specific problem, a **Dropout** layer to avoid overfitting, and the classifier layer at the end.

The dense layer at the end has two neurons, as we have only two classes, and it has the **Softmax** activation function. For binary classification, the Sigmoid function can also be used, but it changes the entire process as you should not make the labels categorical and the predictions look different.

Afterward, we create the model that we are going to train with the input of MobileNet as input and the classification dense layer as output.

6. We are going to do fine-tuning. In order to do that, we have to freeze some of the input layers and keep the rest of the trainable data, unchanged:

```
for layer in model.layers[:20]:
    layer.trainable=False
for layer in model.layers[20:]:
    layer.trainable=True
```

7. Let's compile the model with the **Adadelta** optimizer:

```
import keras
model.compile(loss='categorical_crossentropy',optimizer=keras.optimizers.
Adadelta(), metrics=['accuracy'])
```

8. Now we will use the **preprocess_input** method that we imported previously to preprocess the **X** set for MobileNet, and then we convert label **y** to one-hot encoding:

```
from keras import utils as np_utils
X = preprocess_input(X)
#X = (X.astype(np.float32))/255.0
y = np_utils.to_categorical(y)
```

9. We use the **train_test_split** method to split the data into a training set and testing set:

```
from sklearn.model_selection import train_test_split
x_train, x_test, y_train, y_test = train_test_split(X, y, test_size=0.2)
print(x_train.shape)
print(y_train.shape)
print(x_test.shape)
print(y_test.shape)
```

10. We are going to apply data augmentation to our dataset:

```
from keras.preprocessing.image import ImageDataGenerator
train_datagen = ImageDataGenerator(
        rotation_range=90,
        width_shift_range = 0.2,
        height_shift_range = 0.2,
        horizontal_flip=True,
        vertical_flip=True,
        zoom_range=0.4)
train_datagen.fit(x_train)
```

As a bill can be at different angles, we choose to make a rotation range of 90°. The other parameters seem reasonable for this task.

11. Let's declare a checkpoint to save the model when the validation loss decreases and train the model:

```
from keras.callbacks import ModelCheckpoint
ckpt = ModelCheckpoint('Models/model_money.h5', save_best_only=True,
monitor='val_loss', mode='min', save_weights_only=False)
model.fit_generator(train_datagen.flow(x_train, y_train,
                                        batch_size=4),
                    epochs=50,
                    validation_data=(x_test, y_test),
                    callbacks=[ckpt],
                    steps_per_epoch=len(x_train) // 4,
                    workers=4)
```

We have set the batch size to 4 because we have only a few samples of data and we do not want to pass all the samples to the neural network at once, but in batches. We are not using the EarlyStopping callback because the loss goes up and down due to the lack of data and the use of Adadelta with a high learning rate.

12. Check the results:

```
Epoch 1/50
12/12 [==============================] - 20s 2s/step - loss: 1.9433 - acc: 0.6250 - val_loss: 0.7410 - val_acc: 0.8333
Epoch 2/50
12/12 [==============================] - 15s 1s/step - loss: 0.7455 - acc: 0.7917 - val_loss: 0.4823 - val_acc: 0.6667
Epoch 3/50
12/12 [==============================] - 16s 1s/step - loss: 0.8849 - acc: 0.8542 - val_loss: 0.0095 - val_acc: 1.0000
Epoch 4/50
12/12 [==============================] - 16s 1s/step - loss: 1.2643 - acc: 0.7708 - val_loss: 0.8220 - val_acc: 0.6667
Epoch 5/50
12/12 [==============================] - 15s 1s/step - loss: 0.5782 - acc: 0.8125 - val_loss: 0.3651 - val_acc: 0.8333
Epoch 6/50
12/12 [==============================] - 16s 1s/step - loss: 0.2236 - acc: 0.8958 - val_loss: 1.0818 - val_acc: 0.7500
Epoch 7/50
12/12 [==============================] - 16s 1s/step - loss: 0.5183 - acc: 0.8333 - val_loss: 2.9355e-06 - val_acc: 1.0000
Epoch 8/50
12/12 [==============================] - 16s 1s/step - loss: 0.4954 - acc: 0.8958 - val_loss: 7.6321e-05 - val_acc: 1.0000
```

Figure 5.20: Showing the desired output

In the preceding figure, we can see that, in the 7th epoch, we already achieve 100% accuracy with low loss. This is due to the lack of data on the validation set, because with only 12 samples you cannot tell whether the model is performing well against unseen data.

13. Let's run the code to calculate the accuracy of this model:

```
y_pred = model.predict(x_test, batch_size=4, verbose=0)
y_pred = np.argmax(y_pred, axis=1)
y_test_aux = y_test.copy()
y_test_pred = list()
for i in y_test_aux:
    y_test_pred.append(np.argmax(i))

accuracy = metrics.accuracy_score(y_test_pred, y_pred)
print('Acc: %.4f' % accuracy)
```

The output is as follows:

```
Making predictions...
[1 0 1 0 0 0 1 0 0 0 1 1]

Final results...
              precision    recall  f1-score   support

           0       1.00      1.00      1.00         7
           1       1.00      1.00      1.00         5

   micro avg       1.00      1.00      1.00        12
   macro avg       1.00      1.00      1.00        12
weighted avg       1.00      1.00      1.00        12

Acc       : 1.0000
Precision: 1.0000
Recall    : 1.0000
F1        : 1.0000
Support   : 12
```

Figure 5.21: Accuracy achieved of 100%

14. Let's try this model with new data. There are test images in the **Dataset/testing** folder. We have added four examples of bills to check whether the model predicts them well:

> **Note**
>
> Remember that we set the label of €20 to 0 and 1 for €5.

```
images = ['20.jpg','20_1.jpg','5.jpg','5_1.jpg']
model.load_weights('Models/model_money.h5')

for number in range(len(images)):
    imgLoaded = cv2.imread('Dataset/testing/%s'%(images[number]))
    img = cv2.resize(imgLoaded, (224, 224))
    #cv2.imwrite('test.jpg',img)
    img = (img.astype(np.float32))/255.0
    img = img.reshape(1, 224, 224, 3)
    plt.subplot(1,5,number+1),plt.imshow(cv2.cvtColor(imgLoaded,cv2.COLOR_
BGR2RGB))
    plt.title('20' if np.argmax(model.predict(img)[0]) == 0 else '5')
    plt.xticks([]),plt.yticks([])
plt.show()
```

In this code, we have loaded the unseen examples as well, and we have clubbed the output image, which looks like this:

Figure 5.22: Prediction of bills

The model has predicted all the images precisely!

Congratulations! Now you are able to train a model with your own dataset when you have little data, thanks to transfer learning.

> **Note**
>
> The complete code for this exercise is uploaded on GitHub: https://github.com/
> PacktPublishing/Artificial-Vision-and-Language-Processing-for-Robotics/blob/
> master/Lesson05/Exercise19/Exercise19.ipynb.

Summary

CNNs have shown much better performance than fully-connected neural networks when dealing with images. In addition, CNNs are also capable of accomplishing good results with text and sound data.

CNNs have been explained in depth, as have how convolutions work and all the parameters that come along with them. Afterward, all this theory was put into practice with an exercise.

Data augmentation is a technique for overcoming a lack of data or a lack of variation in a dataset by applying simple transformations to the original data in order to generate new images. This technique has been explained and also put into practice with an exercise and an activity, where you were able to experiment with the knowledge you acquired.

Transfer learning is a technique used when there is a lack of data or the problem is so complex that it would take too long to train on a normal neural network. Also, this technique does not need much of an understanding of neural networks at all, as the model is already implemented. It can also be used with data augmentation.

Transfer learning was also covered and put into practice with an exercise where the amount of data was very small.

Learning how to build CNNs is very useful for recognizing objects or environments in computer vision. When a robot is using its vision sensors to recognize an environment, normally, CNNs are employed and data augmentation is used to improve the CNNs performance. In *Chapter 8, Object Recognition to Guide the Robot Using CNNs*, the CNN concepts you have learned about will be applied to a real-world application, and you will be able to recognize an environment using deep learning.

Before applying these techniques to recognize the environment, first you need to learn how to manage a robot that will be able to recognize an environment. In *Chapter 6, Robot Operating System (ROS)*, you will learn how to manage a robot using a simulator by taking advantage of software called ROS.

6

Robot Operating System (ROS)

Learning Objectives

By the end of this chapter, you will be able to:

- Explain Robot Operating System (ROS) essentials and basic concepts
- Create Robot Operating System packages and work with them
- Operate a virtual robot with information obtained from sensors
- Develop and implement working programs for robots

This chapter focuses on ROS and the different ways to work with its packages. You'll also learn how to operate a virtual robot based on the information received from its sensors using ROS.

Introduction

Developing software for robots is not as easy as developing any other type of software. To build robots, you need methods and functions that enable you to access sensor information, control robot parts, and connect with the robot. These methods and functions are present in ROS, making it easier to build a virtual robot.

ROS is a framework that is compatible with Ubuntu (Linux) for writing robot software. It is a set of libraries and tools through which it is possible to build and create various robotic behaviors. One of the most interesting features about this framework is that the developed code can be adapted for any other robot. ROS also gives you a chance to work on several machines simultaneously; for instance, if you want to use a robot to collect apples, you can use a computer to obtain the camera information of the apple and process it, another machine to launch the movement that commands the robot, and finally the robot will pick up the apple. By following this workflow, computers won't perform too many computational tasks, and the execution turns out to be more fluid.

ROS is the most widely used tool for robotics, both for researchers and companies. It is becoming a standard for robotics tasks. Furthermore, ROS is constantly evolving to solve new problems and is adapting to different technologies. All these facts make it a good topic for studying and practicing.

ROS Concepts

As mentioned earlier, working with ROS is not easy the first time round. But just like any other software, you need to know how ROS works and how to perform certain tasks using it. In order to do that and before installing or working with the framework, it is important to understand its basic concepts. The key ideas behind ROS' functions that will help you understand its internal processes are mentioned here:

- **Node**: An ROS node is a process in charge of performing tasks and calculations. They can be combined with each other using topics or other more complex tools.

- **Topic**: Topics can be defined as information channels between nodes that work in a unidirectional way. This is considered a unidirectional workflow because nodes can subscribe to topics, but a topic would not know which nodes are subscribed to it.

- **Master**: The ROS master is a service that provides a name and registration to the remaining nodes. Its main function is to enable individual nodes so that they can locate each other and establish peer-to-peer communication.

- **Package**: Packages are the core of ROS organization. Within these packages, you can find nodes, libraries, datasets, or useful components to build a robotics application.

- **Stack**: An ROS stack is a set of nodes that, all together, provide some functionality. It can be useful for dividing tasks between nodes when the functionality to develop is too complex.

Apart from the aforementioned concepts, there are many other concepts that can be useful when using ROS, but understanding these basic ones will let you implement powerful programs for robots. Let's look at a simple example in order to learn how they would be used in a real situation:

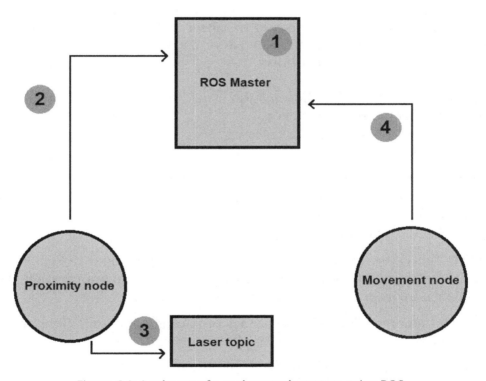

Figure 6.1: A schema of a real example system using ROS

The situation here consists of a robot changing its direction when detecting a close obstacle. This is how it works step by step:

1. The ROS master is enabled. This means the ROS system has been started and can have any node run.

2. The proximity node starts and extracts information from the laser sensor. It advertises the master to publish this obtained information. If there's no problem and the information has the expected type, the master will allow the node to publish through a topic.

3. Once the master allows the node to publish, the information is passed to a topic and published. In this case, the proximity node publishes the information in the laser topic.

4. The movement node asks the master to subscribe to a laser topic. When subscribed, it will obtain the published information and work with it to decide the next action for the robot to perform.

To sum up, both nodes can share information using the master service, which notifies both nodes about each other's existence.

ROS Commands

ROS doesn't have a graphical user interface to work with it; every action must be performed on the command line as it is compatible with Ubuntu. However, before getting your hands on the ROS, you need to learn about its most common commands. Here's a short list of them and their functionality:

- **roscore**: This is the first command to be run when working with ROS. It enables the framework and provides support to any ROS program or operation. It should be launched in order to allow node communication.

- **roscd**: This command switches to a stack or package directory without entering a physical path.

- **rosnode**: These commands manage nodes and obtain information about them. Here, you can see the most used rosnode commands:

- **rosnode list**: This command prints the information of active nodes.

- **rosnode info <node_name>**: This informs the user about the entered node.

- **rosnode kill <node_name>**: The function of this command is to stop a node process.

- **rosrun**: Using this command, you can run any application on your system without switching to its directory.

- **rostopic**: This command allows you to manage and check topic information. There are several other types for this command:

- **rostopic list**: This type prints the information of active topics.

- **rostopic info <topic_name>**: This shows information about a concrete topic.

- **rostopic pub <topic_name> [data...]**: The function of this command is to publish the given data to the entered topic.

- **rqt_graph**: This is a very useful command that can be used to graphically observe active nodes and topics that are being published or subscribed to.

Installation and Configuration

The first thing to consider before installing ROS is the installed Ubuntu version. There are several ROS versions that you will have to choose from depending on your operating system version. In this case, we are explaining the installation of ROS Kinetic Kame, which is compatible with Ubuntu 16.04 LTS (Xenial Xerus).

> ### Note
> If this is not your Ubuntu version, you can head to the ROS website, http://www.ros.org/, and look for the corresponding distribution.

As happens with almost every other tool, it is recommended to always install the latest version, because it may have solved errors or new functionalities; but, as mentioned before, don't worry if you're working with an older version.

> ### Note
> To get detailed steps on how to install ROS, refer to the preface on page vi.

Catkin Workspaces and Packages

This is the last step before coding your first application and program for robots. You have to set up your working environment. To do this, you are going to learn what catkin workspaces and packages are and how to work with them.

A catkin workspace is a ROS directory where catkin packages can be created, compiled, and run. A catkin package is a container for creating ROS nodes and applications. Each of these packages work as a single project that can contain multiple nodes. It is important to know that the ROS code inside catkin packages can only be Python or C++.

Now, let's see how to create the catkin workspace:

> **Note**
>
> Execute these commands in the same terminal window.

1. Create a standard folder containing a subfolder named "**src**." You can choose any location on your system:

   ```
   mkdir -p ~/catkin_ws/src
   cd ~/catkin_ws
   ```

2. Switch to the new **catkin_ws** directory and run the **catkin** compilation command to initialize the new workspace:

   ```
   catkin_make
   ```

   This command must be executed every time you want to compile your workspace when making changes in any package.

By following these simple steps, you will have your catkin workspace ready to work with. But, when working on it, you should always remember to enter this command first:

```
source devel/setup.bash
```

This lets ROS know that there can be ROS executables in the created catkin workspace.

If you have successfully completed the preceding process, you can now create your catkin packages and work on them. Create a package with the steps mentioned here:

1. Go into the "**src**" folder of your catkin workspace:

    ```
    cd ~/catkin_ws/src
    ```

2. Use this command to create a package:

    ```
    catkin_create_pkg <package_name> [dependencies]
    ```

The dependencies are a set of libraries or tools that the package needs to function correctly. For example, in a simple package where you only use Python code, the command will be as follows:

```
catkin_create_pkg my_python_pkg rospy
```

Publishers and Subscribers

When explaining basic ROS concepts, we discussed a few nodes used for publishing data and some others used for subscribing to that data. Knowing this, it is not hard to imagine that nodes can be classified into two groups, depending on the kind of action they perform. They can be **publishers** or **subscribers**. Why do you think it is important to distinguish between these two types of nodes?

As mentioned earlier, publishers are nodes that provide information to other nodes. They usually work with sensors to check the environment status and convert it into valuable outputs for subscribers that can receive this information.

On the other hand, subscribers usually get an understandable input and process it. They then decide which action will be launched depending on the obtained result.

As this is a rarely used type of programming, it will be interesting to follow some examples of how these nodes really work, before starting to use them with robots and simulators. So, let's go through some exercises that will help you understand nodes.

Exercise 20: Publishing and Subscribing

In this example, we will write a simple publisher and subscriber in Python using the following steps:

1. Open a new terminal and enter the **roscore** command to start the ROS service:

    ```
    roscore
    ```

2. Create a new package in your catkin workspace that contains the solution to this exercise. This package will depend on **rospy** and **std_msgs**, so you must create it as follows:

    ```
    catkin_create_pkg exercise20 rospy std_msgs
    ```

    > **Note**
    >
    > **std_msgs** is a package that provides support to ROS primitive data types. You can find more information about it, including the concrete types of managed data, here: http://wiki.ros.org/std_msgs.

3. Switch to the package directory and create a new folder, which will contain publisher and subscriber files, for example:

    ```
    cd ~/catkin_ws/src/exercise20
    mkdir -p scripts
    ```

4. Go into the new folder and create a corresponding Python file for each node:

    ```
    cd scripts
    touch publisher.py
    touch subscriber.py
    ```

5. Provide the executable permission to both files:

    ```
    chmod +x publisher.py
    chmod +x subscriber.py
    ```

6. Begin with the publisher implementation:

    Initialize the Python environment and import the necessary libraries.

    > **Note**
    >
    > This code needs to be added in a **publisher.py** file.

```
#!/usr/bin/env python
import rospy
from std_msgs.msg import String
```

Create a function to publish the message.

```
def publisher():
```

Declare a publisher that publishes a **String** message into a new topic, no matter its name.

```
pub  =rospy.Publisher('publisher_topic', String, queue_size=1)
```

> **Note**
>
> As the ROS publishing process is asynchronous, a queue is created containing published messages. For ROS to register the amount of messages a queue can store, the size value of this queue must be established each time a publisher is created. In this case, we pick a size of 1 because we are going to publish the same message all the time.

Initialize the node with the **init_node** method. It is a good practice to set the anonymous flag to true when initializing a node. This is how naming conflicts can be avoided:

```
rospy.init_node('publisher', anonymous=True)
```

Use the created publisher variable to publish any desired **String**. For instance:

```
pub.publish("Sending message")
```

Finally, detect the program entry and call the created function:

```
if __name__ == '__main__':
    publisher()
```

7. Continue with the subscriber implementation:

Initialize Python and import libraries as you did for your publisher.

> **Note**
>
> This code needs to be added in the **subscriber.py** file.

```
#!/usr/bin/env python
import rospy
from std_msgs.msg import String
```

Create a function to subscribe to the topic:

```
def subscriber():
```

Initialize the node in the same way as you did before:

```
rospy.init_node('subscriber', anonymous=True)
```

Subscribe to **publisher_topic** using this function:

```
rospy.Subscriber('publisher_topic', String, callback)
```

> **Note**
>
> The third parameter of the Subscriber call is a callback function, which means that it is a function not called by the user. The function pointer is passed to other components, the subscriber in this case, which will call the function when it seems appropriate. To sum up, the callback function will be launched every time the subscriber gets a message.

Use the **spin()** function to allow the subscriber to run a **callback** method. This function generates a loop for the program, which does not end the program:

```
rospy.spin()
```

Implement the **callback** function to print a message when it receives any data. For this first exercise, let's kill the subscriber node when receiving the first message from the publisher. This can be done with the **signal_shutdown** method, which is integrated in **rospy** and only needs the shutdown reason as a parameter:

```
def callback(data):
    if(data != None):
        print("Message received")
        rospy.signal_shutdown("Message received")
```

Call the created function from the main execution thread:

```
if __name__ == '__main__':
    subscriber()
```

8. Test the functioning of the created nodes. You can do this as described here:

Open a new terminal and switch to your workspace. Then, run the following command so that ROS checks it for executable files:

```
source devel/setup.bash
```

Run the subscriber node. If the implementation is correct, it should remain under execution until you run your publisher:

```
rosrun exercise20 subscriber.py
```

Open a new terminal and enter the command again.

Run the publisher node:

```
rosrun exercise20 publisher.py
```

If the nodes are well implemented, the subscriber execution ends after executing the publisher node. The output must be the message printed in the callback, in this case: **Message received**.

> **Note**
>
> There is no need to compile the workspace in order to run your package nodes because they are written in Python. If they were coded in C++, you would have to build a package after every change in code.

Exercise 21: Publishers and Subscribers

This exercise is similar to the previous one but is complex. The publisher created before could only send one message per execution. Now, we are going to implement a publisher that won't stop sending data until we terminate it.

The goal of this exercise is to create a number-finding system following these rules:

- The publisher node must publish random numbers into a topic until it is stopped by the user.

- The subscriber node decides a number to look for and searches for it in the received message list. Here, there are two possibilities:

    If the number is found before 1000 tries, a positive message will be printed and the number of tries it took to achieve it too.

If the number is not found in 1000 tries, a negative message will be printed telling the user that it was not possible to find the number.

So, this can be done in the following way:

1. As mentioned earlier, begin by creating the package and files:

    ```
    cd ~/catkin_ws/src
    catkin_create_pkg exercise21 rospy std_msgs
    cd exercise21
    mkdir scripts
    cd scripts
    touch generator.py
    touch finder.py
    chmod +x generator.py finder.py
    ```

2. Begin with the publisher implementation.

    Import the necessary libraries. These libraries are the same as in the preface, but this time, you must change the **String** import for **Int32**, as the node is going to work with numbers. You should also import a random library to generate numbers.

    > **Note**
    >
    > This code needs to be added in the **generator.py** file.

    ```
    #!/usr/bin/env python
    import rospy
    from std_msgs.msg import Int32
    import random
    ```

3. Create the number generator function:

    ```
    def generate():
    ```

4. Declare the publisher and initialize the node as you did in the previous exercise. Note that, this time, the data type is different and the queue size is set to 10, which means that it will be possible to have 10 published numbers. When the eleventh number is published, the first will be dropped from the queue:

    ```
    pub = rospy.Publisher('numbers_topic', Int32, queue_size=10)
    rospy.init_node('generator', anonymous=True)
    ```

5. Configure the rate at which the program loop will iterate. We are setting a rate of 10 (Hz), which is not a very high rate and that will allow us to check the generated numbers:

```
rate = rospy.Rate(10)
```

6. Implement the loop where the numbers will be generated and published. It has to iterate until the user stops it, so you can use the **is_shutdown()** function. Use the sleep function on the declared rate so it can take effect:

```
while not rospy.is_shutdown():
    num = random.randint(1,101)
    pub.publish(num)
    rate.sleep()
```

7. Call the created function from the node entry. Use a try directive so that the user shutdown doesn't produce an error:

```
if __name__ == '__main__':
    try:
        generate()
    except rospy.ROSInterruptException:
        pass
```

8. Continue with the subscriber implementation:

Import the necessary libraries.

> **Note**
>
> This code needs to be added in the **finder.py** file.

```
#!/usr/bin/env python
import rospy
from std_msgs.msg import Int32
```

9. Create a class with two attributes: one for establishing the value of the number to find and the other one for counting the number of tries:

```
class Finder:
    searched_number = 50
    generated_numbers = 0
```

10. Implement the callback function. The logic of the finder has to be coded in this function. There are lots of ways to do this but this is a frequently used one:

```python
def callback(self, data):
    if data.data == self.searched_number:
        print(str(data.data) + ": YES")
        self.generated_numbers += 1
        print("The searched number has been found after " + str(self.
generated_numbers) + " tries")
        rospy.signal_shutdown("Number found")
    elifself.generated_numbers>= 1000:
print("It wasn't possible to find the searched number")
        rospy.signal_shutdown("Number not found")
    else:
        print(str(data.data) + ": NO")
        self.generated_numbers += 1
```

As you can see, it is a simple function that looks for the number and adds one to the counter for each failed try. If the number is found, it prints a positive message. If the counter reaches 1000, the search is aborted and a negative message is shown.

11. Create the function for subscribing. Remember that, this time, the published data type is **Int32**:

```python
def finder(self):
    rospy.init_node('finder', anonymous=True)
    rospy.Subscriber('numbers_topic', Int32, self.callback)
    rospy.spin()
```

12. Finally, from the node entry, create a **Finder** class instance and call the **finder** method:

```python
if __name__ == '__main__':
    find = Finder()
    find.finder()
```

13. Test whether the performed implementation is correct.

   Open a new terminal and run **roscore**.

   Open another terminal and execute the subscriber node:

   ```
   cd ~/catkin_ws
   source devel/setup.bash
   rosrun exercise21 finder.py
   ```

14. In another terminal, run the publisher node so that numbers are generated and the callback function starts working:

   ```
   cd ~/catkin_ws
   source devel/setup.bash
   rosrun exercise21 generator.py
   ```

15. If the searched number, 50 in this case, is found, the output should be similar to this one:

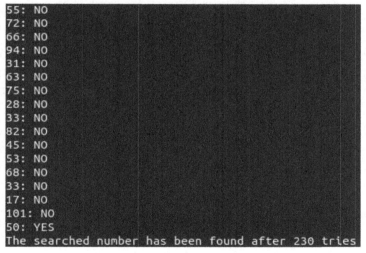

Figure 6.2: Execution example where the number is found

16. Change the searched number to a value higher than 100 when the number is not found. You should obtain an output as follows:

```
58:  NO
43:  NO
41:  NO
32:  NO
85:  NO
101:  NO
95:  NO
86:  NO
48:  NO
38:  NO
35:  NO
1:  NO
5:  NO
62:  NO
99:  NO
24:  NO
It wasn't possible to find the searched number
```

Figure 6.3: Execution example where the number is not found

It will be interesting to use the **rqt_graph** command when both nodes are being executed; this way, you can see the structure you just created graphically. So, open a new terminal and enter the command. The output should be something like this:

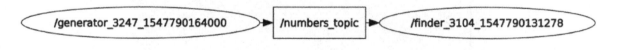

Figure 6.4: Output

Simulators

Simulators are very good tools for developing and testing robotics software. They make robotics affordable for everyone. Imagine that you are working on a robotics project, where you constantly have to test functionality improvements with your robot. It would require connecting the robot for each test, charging it many times, and moving it with you. All of this can be avoided with a simulator, which can be launched in your computer at any time; it can even simulate the nodes and topics generated by the robot. Do you know any simulator for working with robots?

We are going to use Gazebo, a simulator included in the ROS full installation. In fact, if you chose this option while installing it, you can write "**gazebo**" in a terminal and it will launch the simulator. The Gazebo interface is shown in Figure 6.4:

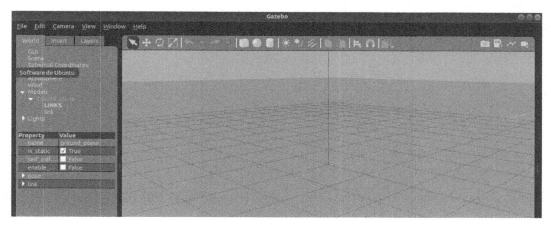

Figure 6.5: The Gazebo start point

The next step is to install and set up the robot that we are going to simulate. In this case, we will use a **Turtlebot**, a wheelie robot that is equipped with sensors such as cameras and lasers. Turtlebot may not be compatible with your ROS distribution (we are using Kinetic Kame); but don't worry, there are lots of robots that you can simulate in Gazebo. You can look up different robots and try to use them with your ROS distribution.

Exercise 22: The Turtlebot configuration

In this exercise, we are going to go through some things you will need to do before using Turtlebot:

1. Install its dependencies:

    ```
    sudo apt-get installros-kinetic-turtlebotros-kinetic-turtlebot-apps
    ros-kinetic-turtlebot-interactions ros-kinetic-turtlebot-simulator
    ros-kinetic-kobuki-ftdiros-kinetic-ar-track-alvar-msgs
    ```

2. Download the **Turtlebot** simulator package in your **catkin** workspace.

> **Note**
>
> If Git is not installed in your local system, use this command to install git: **sudo apt install git**

```
cd ~/catkin_ws/src
git clone https://github.com/PacktPublishing/Artificial-Vision-and-
Language-Processing-for-Robotics/blob/master/Lesson06/turtlebot_simulator.
zip
```

3. After that, you should be able to use Turtlebot with Gazebo.

   Start ROS services:

   ```
   roscore
   ```

   Launch Turtlebot World:

   ```
   cd ~/catkin_ws
   source devel/setup.bash
   roslaunch turtlebot_gazebo turtlebot_world.launch
   ```

4. Now, you should see the same Gazebo world as before, but with a set of objects, including Turtlebot, at the center, as mentioned in figure 6.5:

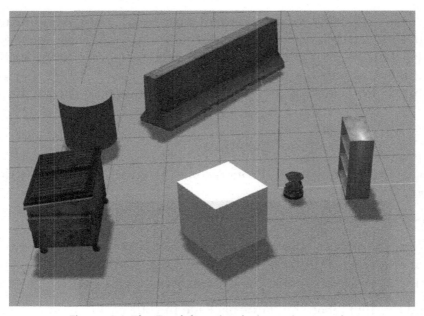

Figure 6.6: The Turtlebot simulation using Gazebo

Once the simulation is correctly running, let's do another exercise for learning how to obtain information from sensors and work with it.

Exercise 23: Simulators and Sensors

In this exercise, we'll create a ROS node that subscribes to the Turtlebot camera to obtain corresponding images. Follow these steps:

1. Create a package with the necessary dependencies and files:

```
cd ~/catkin_ws/src
catkin_create_pkg exercise22 rospy sensor_msgs
cd exercise22
mkdir scripts
cd scripts
touch exercise22.py
chmod +x exercise22.py
```

2. Implement the node.

   Import the necessary libraries. For this exercise, we are going to use **OpenCV** to work with the images obtained from the camera:

```
#!/usr/bin/env python
import rospy
from sensor_msgs.msg import Image
import cv2
from cv_bridge import CvBridge
```

   Create a class and declare an attribute of type **CvBridge**, which will be used later to change the image type to **cv2**:

```
class ObtainImage:
    bridge = CvBridge()
```

   Code the callback function, where you will have to obtain the image and convert it to the cv2 format:

```
def callback(self, data):
    cv_image = self.bridge.imgmsg_to_cv2(data, "bgr8")
    cv2.imshow('Image',cv_image)
    cv2.waitKey(0)
    rospy.signal_shutdown("Finishing")
```

> **Note**
>
> We use the **waitKey()** function so that the image remains on the screen. It will disappear when the user presses any key.

3. Define and implement the subscriber function. Remember that, now, the required data has an Image type:

```
def obtain(self):
        rospy.Subscriber('/camera/rgb/image_raw', Image, self.
callback)
        rospy.init_node('image_obtainer', anonymous=True)
        rospy.spin()
```

> **Note**
>
> If you don't know the name of the topic to which you want to subscribe, you can always enter the **rostopic** list command and check the available nodes. You should see a list like the following:

```
/camera/depth/camera_info
/camera/depth/image_raw
/camera/depth/points
/camera/parameter_descriptions
/camera/parameter_updates
/camera/rgb/camera_info
/camera/rgb/image_raw
/camera/rgb/image_raw/compressed
/camera/rgb/image_raw/compressed/parameter_descriptions
/camera/rgb/image_raw/compressed/parameter_updates
/camera/rgb/image_raw/compressedDepth
/camera/rgb/image_raw/compressedDepth/parameter_descriptions
/camera/rgb/image_raw/compressedDepth/parameter_updates
/camera/rgb/image_raw/theora
/camera/rgb/image_raw/theora/parameter_descriptions
/camera/rgb/image_raw/theora/parameter_updates
```

Figure 6.7: Output of the rostopic list command

4. Call the subscriber function from the program entry:

```
if __name__ == '__main__':
    obt = ObtainImage()
    obt.obtain()
```

5. Check that the node works fine. To do that, you should run **roscore** command, Gazebo with Turtlebot, and created the node in different terminals. Note that you may also run the **source devel/setup.bash** source if you didn't do so earlier:

```
roscore
roslaunch turtlebot_gazebo turtlebot_world.launch
rosrun exercise22 exercise22.py
```

The result should be something like this:

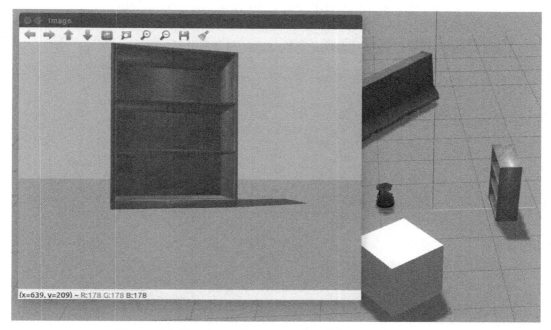

Figure 6.8: The execution example of the exercise node

Activity 6: Simulators and Sensors

Consider the following scenario: you are working for a robotics company that has recently acquired a new client, a security surveillance company. So, you are asked to implement a surveillance system for a robot that guards the store at night. The client wants the robot to stay in the middle of the store and to look around constantly.

You have to simulate the system and you have been asked to use Turtlebot and Gazebo.

1. Implement a node that subscribes to the camera and shows all the images it receives.

2. Implement a node for the robot to turn itself on.

> **Note**
>
> To do that, you will have to publish the /mobile_base/commands/velocity topic, which works with Twist messages. Twist is a type of message included in the **geometry_msgs** library, so you will have to add this as a dependency. To make the robot rotate on itself, create an instance of Twist and modify its **angular.z** value. Then, publish it.

3. Now, run both nodes at the same time.

    At the end of this activity, you will get an output similar to this:

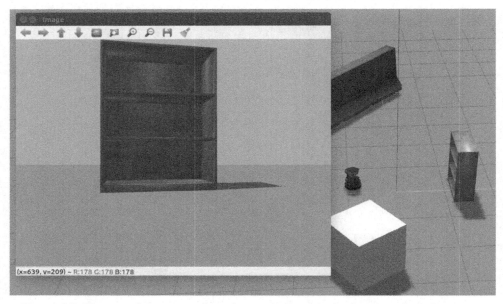

Figure 6.9: The rotating output that shows the images in the virtual environment

> **Note**
>
> The solution for this activity can be found on page 318.

Summary

In this chapter, you learned how to work with ROS, from its installation and configuration to the implementation of nodes. You also worked with simulators and its sensors, obtaining information from them and making the acquired information valuable for solving problems. All the exercises and activities covered in the chapter will be useful for you in the following chapters.

In the next chapter, you will work with natural language processing (NPL) and learn how to build a chatbot. If you build a good one, it could be a very interesting tool to add to a robot. You could even use ROS to develop it.

Build a Text-Based Dialogue System (Chatbot)

Learning Objectives

By the end of this chapter, you will be able to:

- Define the terms GloVe, Word2Vec and Embeddings

- Develop your own Word2Vec

- Select tools to create conversational agents

- Predict the intent of a conversation

- Create a conversational agent

This chapter covers an introduction to terms such as GloVe, Word2Vec, and embeddings and tools that will help you create a conversational agent.

Introduction

One of the latest trends in deep NLP is the creation of conversational agents, also knowns as chatbots. A chatbot is a **text-based dialogue system** that understands human language and can hold a real conversation with people. Many companies use these systems to interact with its customers to obtain information and feedback, for example, opinions on a new product launch.

Chatbots are used as assistants, for example, Siri, Alexa, and Google Home. These can give us real-time information about the weather or traffic.

At this point, the question is how can bots understand us? In the previous chapters, we have reviewed language models and how they work. However, the most important thing in language models (LMs) is the position of a word in a sentence. Each word has a certain probability of appearing in a sentence, depending on the words already in that sentence. But the probability distribution approach is not a good fit for this task. In this case, we need to understand the meaning, not predict the next word, after which, the model will understand the meaning of a word in a given corpus.

A word in itself doesn't make sense unless it is placed within a context or in a corpus. It is important to understand the meaning of a sentence and this dictated by its structure (that is, the position of the words in it). The model will then predict the meaning of words by looking at which words are near to it. But firstly, how is it possible to represent this mathematically?

In *Chapter 4*, *Neural Networks with* NLP, we looked at representing a word using a one-hot encoded vector, which is a vector with 1s and 0s. However, this representation does not provide us with the actual meaning of a word. Let's take a look at an example:

- Dog → [1,0,0,0,0,0]
- Cat → [0,0,0,0,1,0]

A dog and a cat are animals, but their representation in 1s and 0s does not give us any information about the meaning of those words.

But what would happen if these vectors gave us a similarity between two words based on their meaning? Two words with a similar meaning would be placed near to each other in a plane, as opposed to two words without any such relation. For example, the name of a country and its capital are related.

Having this approach, a set of sentences can be related to a conversational intention or a specific topic (also known as intent, this term will be used throughout this chapter). Using this system, we would be able to maintain a sensible conversational dialogue with a human.

The intent of a conversation is the topic of the dialogue. For example, if you were talking about a match between Real Madrid and Barcelona, the intent of the conversation would be football.

Later in this chapter, we will review the fundamental concepts of the representation of a word as a vector, and how to create such vectors and use them to recognize the intent of a conversation.

Word Representation in Vector Space

This section will cover the different architectures for computing a continuous vector representation of words from a corpus. These representations will depend on the similarity of words, in terms of meaning. Also, there will be an introduction to a new Python library (**Gensim**) to do this task.

Word Embeddings

Word embeddings are a collection of techniques and methods to map words and sentences from a corpus and output them as vectors or real numbers. Word embeddings generate a representation of each word in terms of the context in which the word appears. The main task of word embeddings is to perform a dimension reduction from a space with one dimension per word to a continuous vector space.

To better understand what that means, let's have a look at an example. Imagine we have two similar sentences, such as these:

- I am good.

- I am great.

Now, encoding these sentences as one-hot vectors, we have something like this:

- I → [1,0,0,0]

- Am → [0,1,0,0]

- Good → [0,0,1,0]

- Great → [0,0,0,1]

We know the previous two sentences are similar (in terms of their meaning), because "great" and "good" have a similar meaning. But how could we measure the similarity of these two words? We have two vectors representing the words, so let's compute the cosine similarity.

Cosine Similarity

Cosine similarity measures the similarity between two vectors. As the name suggests, this method will state the cosine of the angle between two sentences. Its formula is as follows:

$$\text{similarity} = \cos(\theta) = \frac{\mathbf{A} \cdot \mathbf{B}}{\|\mathbf{A}\|\|\mathbf{B}\|}$$

Figure 7.1: Formula for cosine similarity

Figure 7.1 shows the formula for cosine similarity. A and B are the vectors. Following the previous example, if we compute the similarity between "good" and "great", the result is 0. This is because one-hot encoded vectors are independent and there is no projection along the same dimension (that means there is only a single 1 in a dimension, and the rest are 0s).

Figure 7.2 explains this concept:

Good → [0,0 1,0]
Great → [0,0 0,1]

Figure 7.2: Dimension without projection

Word embeddings solve this problem. There are many techniques to represent word embeddings. But all these techniques are in unsupervised learning algorithms. One of the most famous methods is the Word2Vec model, which is going to be explained next.

Word2Vec

The main goal of Word2Vec is to produce word embeddings. It processes a corpus and then assigns a vector to each unique word in the corpus. This vector, however, does not work like the one-hot vector method. For example, if we have a corpus with 10,000 words, we would have 10,000 dimensions in our one-hot encoded vectors, but Word2Vec can perform dimension reduction, typically of several hundred dimensions.

The core idea of Word2Vec is that a word's meaning is represented by the words that are frequently near to it. When a word appears in a sentence, its context is formed by the set of words it has nearby. This set of words are within a fixed-size window:

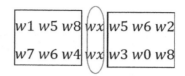

Figure 7.3: Context words of wx

Figure 7.3 shows an example of the context words for wx.

The concept of Word2Vec was created by Tomas Mikolov in 2013. He proposed a framework for learning word vectors. The method works by iterating through a corpus, taking a set of words with a central word (in Figure 7.3, it is wx) and context words (in figure 7.3, the words shown inside the black rectangular box). The vectors of these words keep updating until the corpus ends.

There are two methods for performing Word2Vec:

- **Skip-Gram model**: In this model, the input is the word placed in the center and thereafter it predicts the context of words.

- **CBOW model**: The input of this model are the vectors of the context words, and the output is the central word.

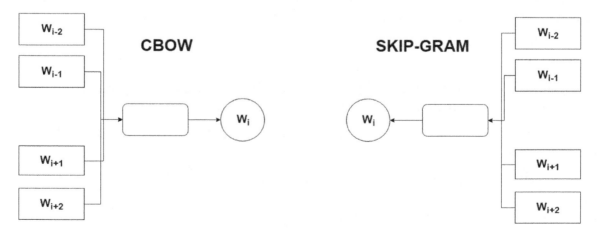

Figure 7.4: CBOW and skip-gram model representation

Both of these models output good results, but the skip-gram model works well with a small amount of data. We will not go into these models in more depth to generate our Word2Vec, but we will be using the Gensim library, which is explained in this chapter.

Problems with Word2Vec

Word2Vec has many advantages for representing words within a vector space. It improves the performance of the task and can capture complex word meanings. But it is not perfect, and does present some problems:

- Inefficiently using statistics: It captures co-occurrences of words one at a time. The problem here is that words that do not occur together within a trained corpus tend to get closer in the plane (this can cause ambiguity) because there's no way to represent their relationships.

- The need to modify the parameters of the model, that is, if the corpus size changes. Doing this, the model will be trained again, and this consumes a lot of time.

Before diving deep in how to solve these problems with Word2Vec, we are going to introduce Gensim, a library for creating Word2Vec models.

Gensim

Gensim is a Python library that provides different NLP methods. It is not like NLTK or spaCy; those libraries are focused on the pre-processing and analysis of data. Gensim provides us with methods to process raw text (which is unstructured).

These are the advantages of Gensim:

- Gensim can be used with a huge corpus. It has memory independence, which means the corpus will not need to be stored in the RAM of your computer. Also, it has memory sharing to store the trained models.

- It can provide efficient vector space algorithms, such as Word2Vec, Doc2Vec, LSI, LSA, and so on.

- Its API is easy to learn.

These are the disadvantages of Gensim:

- It does not provide methods to pre-process text, and it has to be used with NLTK or spaCy to obtain a full NLP pipeline.

Exercise 24: Creation of a Word Embedding

In this exercise, we are going to create our word embedding using a small corpus and use Gensim. Once our model is trained, we will print it on a two-dimensional graph to check the distribution of the words.

Gensim provides the possibility to change some parameters to perform training well on our data. Some useful parameters are as follows:

- **Num_features**: Represents the dimensionality of the vectors (more dimensions equals more accuracy, but is more computationally expensive). In our case, we are going to set this parameter to **2** (vectors of 2 dimensions).

- **Window_size**: Represents the size of the fixed window to contain the context of words. In our case, the corpus is small, so the size here is set to **1**.

- **Min_word_count**: The minimum set word count threshold.

- **Workers**: The threads of your computer running in parallel. In our case, one worker will be good for the size of our corpus.

Let's begin with the exercise:

1. Import the libraries. We are going to use the Gensim model, Word2Vec:

```
import nltk
import gensim.models.word2vec as w2v
import sklearn.manifold
import numpy as np
import matplotlib.pyplot as plt
import pandas as pd
```

2. Define a small random corpus:

```
corpus = ['king is a happy man',
          'queen is a funny woman',
          'queen is an old woman',
          'king is an old man',
          'boy is a young man',
          'girl is a young woman',
          'prince is a young king',
          'princess is a young queen',
          'man is happy,
          'woman is funny,
          'prince is a boy will be king',
          'princess is a girl will be queen']
```

3. Now we will tokenize each sentence with **spaCy**. The concept of **spaCy** was covered in *Chapter 3, Fundamentals of Natural Language Processing*:

```python
import spacy
import en_core_web_sm
nlp = en_core_web_sm.load()
def corpus_tokenizer(corpus):
    sentences = []
    for c in corpus:
        doc = nlp(c)
        tokens = []
        for t in doc:
            if t.is_stop == False:
                tokens.append(t.text)
        sentences.append(tokens)
    return sentences

sentences = corpus_tokenizer(corpus)
sentences
```

4. Now let's define a few variables to create the Word2vec model:

```python
num_features=2
window_size=1
workers=1
min_word_count=1
```

5. Create the model using the Word2Vec method with a seed of 0 (this seed is just a value to initialize the weights of the model; using the same seed to obtain the same results is recommended):

```python
model = w2v.Word2Vec(size=num_features, window=window_
size,workers=workers,min_count=min_word_count,seed=0)
```

6. Now we will build the vocabulary from our corpus. First, we need to have a vocabulary to train our model:

```python
model.build_vocab(sentences)
```

7. Train the model. The parameters here are the sentences of the corpus: total words and epochs. In this case, 1 epoch will be good:

```python
model.train(sentences,total_words=model.corpus_count,epochs=1)
```

8. Now, we can see how the model works when computing the similarity of two words:

```
model.wv['king']
model.wv.similarity('boy', 'prince')
```

0.51534927

Figure 7.5: The computed result stating the similarity of two words

9. Now, to print the model, define a variable with the words of our corpus and an array with the vector of each word:

```
vocab = list(model.wv.vocab)
X = model.wv[vocab]
```

10. Create a **DataFrame** with this data using pandas:

```
df = pd.DataFrame(X, index=vocab, columns=['x', 'y'])
df
```

	x	y
king	0.226001	0.157115
happy	0.077709	-0.038870
man	-0.116079	0.201718
queen	0.191457	-0.091864
funny	-0.055580	-0.144365
woman	0.219265	-0.029579
old	0.093730	-0.247204
boy	-0.012580	-0.033429
young	0.140921	-0.030701
girl	0.221080	-0.238233
prince	0.142078	-0.179534
princess	-0.097676	-0.031869

Figure 7.6: Coordinates of our vectors

11. Create a figure with the location of each word in a plane:

```
fig = plt.figure()
ax = fig.add_subplot(1, 1, 1)

for word, pos in df.iterrows():
    ax.annotate(word, pos)

ax.scatter(df['x'], df['y'])
plt.show()
```

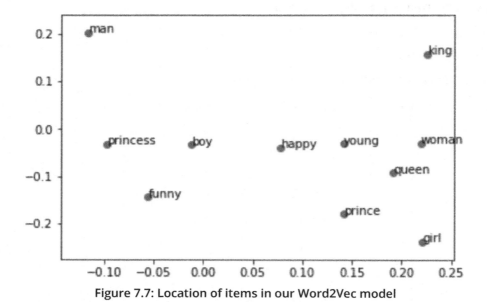

Figure 7.7: Location of items in our Word2Vec model

As you can see in figure 7.7, words can be represented in two dimensions. If you have a smaller corpus, to find out the similarity of two words in terms of meaning, you just need to measure the distances of those two words.

Now you know how to train your own Word2Vec model!

Global Vectors (GloVe)

Global Vectors is a model for word representation. It works just like the Word2Vec model but adds some new features in order to be much more efficient.

Before beginning with this model, it will be beneficial to think of other ways to create a word vector.

The statistics of word occurrences in a corpus is the first source of information we can find to use in unsupervised algorithms, so it is possible to capture the co-occurrence counts directly. To obtain this information, we do not need a processed method; just having the text data will be enough.

Creating a co-occurrence matrix, X, along with a fixed-size window, we can obtain a new representation of words. For example, imagine this corpus:

- I am Charles.
- I am amazing.
- I love apples.

A window-based co-occurrence matrix is as follows:

	I	Am	Charles	amazing	Love	Apples
I	0	2	0	0	1	0
Am	2	0	1	1	0	0
Charles	0	1	0	0	0	0
Amazing	0	1	0	0	0	0
Love	1	0	0	0	0	1
Apples	0	0	0	0	1	0

Figure 7.8: A window-based co-occurrence matrix

The co-occurrence matrix is easy to understand, counting how many times a word appears next to another word in the corpus.

For example, in the first row, with the word "I", the word "am" has the value 2, because there are 2 occurrences of "I am."

This representation improves the one-hot encoding and can capture semantic and syntactic information, but it does have certain problems, such as the size of the model, the sparsity of the vocabulary, and the model is less robust overall.

But in this case, these problems can be solved by reducing the dimension of the matrix using **SVD** (which was explained in *Chapter 3, Fundamentals of Natural Language Processing*) with the following formula:

- A = USVT

The results of doing this are good and the representation of the words do make sense, but this would still be problematic with a large corpus.

The GloVe approach solves the problem of Word2Vec models in the following ways:

- The overall time taken to train the model is reduced if the corpus has a change in it.

- Statistics are used efficiently. It behaves better with words that do not appear many times in the corpus. This was a problem with Word2Vec, that is, unusual words have similar vectors.

GloVe combines the preceding two approaches to achieve fast training. It is scalable to a huge corpus and can achieve better performance with small vectors.

> **Note**
>
> This model was created by Stanford University and is an open source project. You can find more documentation at https://github.com/PacktPublishing/ Artificial-Vision-and-Language-Processing-for-Robotics/tree/master/Lesson07/ Exercise25-26/utils.

In the next exercise, you will learn how to work with GloVe.

Exercise 25: Using a Pretrained GloVe to See the Distribution of Words in a Plane

In this exercise, you will learn how to use GloVe and how to plot a region of a model. We will use the Gensim library once again:

> **Note**
>
> To obtain the model, you will need to download the file from the **utils** folder on GitHub (which is the 50-dimensional model):
>
> https://github.com/TrainingByPackt/Artificial-Vision-and-Language-Processing-for-Robotics/tree/master/Chapter%207/utils

1. Open up your Google Colab interface.

2. Create a folder for the book, download the **utils** folder from GitHub, and upload it to the folder.

3. Import drive and mount it as follows:

```
from google.colab import drive
drive.mount('/content/drive')
```

4. Once you have mounted your drive for the first time, you will have to enter the authorization code by clicking on the URL mentioned by Google and pressing the **Enter** key on your keyboard:

```
[1]  from google.colab import drive
     drive.mount('/content/drive')

     Go to this URL in a browser: https://accounts.google.com/o/oauth2/auth?client_id=947318989803-6bn6qk8qdgf4n4g3pfee6491hc0brc41.apps.googleusercontent.com/

     Enter your authorization code:
     ··········
     Mounted at /content/drive
```

Figure 7.9: Image displaying the Google Colab authorization step

5. Now that you have mounted the drive, you need to set the path of the directory:

```
cd /content/drive/My Drive/C13550/Lesson07/Exercise25/
```

> **Note**
>
> The path mentioned in step 5 may change as per your folder setup on Google Drive. However, the path will always begin with **cd /content/drive/My Drive/**.
>
> The **utils** folder must be present in the path you are setting up.

6. Import the libraries:

```
from gensim.scripts.glove2word2vec import glove2word2vec
from gensim.models import KeyedVectors
import numpy as np
import pandas as pd
```

7. Use the **glove2word2vec** function provided by Gensim to create the **word2vec** model:

```
glove_input_file = 'utils/glove.6B.50d.txt'
word2vec_output_file = 'utils/glove.6B.50d.txt.word2vec'
glove2word2vec(glove_input_file, word2vec_output_file)
```

> **Note**
>
> The **glove.6B.50d.txt** file in this case has been placed within the **utils** folder. If you choose to place it elsewhere, the path will change accordingly.

8. Initialize the model using the file generated by the **glove2word2vec** function:

```
filename = 'utils/glove.6B.50d.txt.word2vec'
model = KeyedVectors.load_word2vec_format(filename, binary=False)
```

9. With GloVe, you can measure the similarity of a pair of words. Check whether the model works by computing the similarity between two words and printing a word vector:

```
model.similarity('woman', 'queen')
```

0.60031056

Figure 7.10: Similarity of woman and queen

10. In *Exercise 24, Creation of a Word Embedding*, we created our own vectors, but here, vectors are already created. To see the representation vector of a word, we just have to do the following:

```
model['woman']
```

```
[-1.8153e-01  6.4827e-01 -5.8210e-01 -4.9451e-01  1.5415e+00  1.3450e+00
 -4.3305e-01  5.8059e-01  3.5556e-01 -2.5184e-01  2.0254e-01 -7.1643e-01
  3.0610e-01  5.6127e-01  8.3928e-01 -3.8085e-01 -9.0875e-01  4.3326e-01
 -1.4436e-02  2.3725e-01 -5.3799e-01  1.7773e+00 -6.6433e-02  6.9795e-01
  6.9291e-01 -2.6739e+00 -7.6805e-01  3.3929e-01  1.9695e-01 -3.5245e-01
  2.2920e+00 -2.7411e-01 -3.0169e-01  8.5286e-04  1.6923e-01  9.1433e-02
 -2.3610e-02  3.6236e-02  3.4488e-01 -8.3947e-01 -2.5174e-01  4.2123e-01
  4.8616e-01  2.2325e-02  5.5760e-01 -8.5223e-01 -2.3073e-01 -1.3138e+00
  4.8764e-01 -1.0467e-01]
```

Figure 7.11: "Woman" vector representation (50 dimensions)

11. We can also see the words most similar to other words. As you can see in steps 4 and 5, GloVe have many functionalities related to word representation:

```
model.similar_by_word(woman)
```

```
[('girl', 0.906528115272522),
 ('man', 0.8860336542129517),
 ('mother', 0.8763704299926758),
 ('her', 0.8613135814666748),
 ('boy', 0.8596119284629822),
 ('she', 0.8430695533752441),
 ('herself', 0.8224567770957947),
 ('child', 0.8108214139938354),
 ('wife', 0.8037394285202026),
 ('old', 0.7982393503189087)]
```

Figure 7.12: Words most similar to woman

12. Now we are going to use Singular Value Decomposition (SVD) to visualize high-dimensional data to plot the words most similar to woman. Import the necessary libraries:

```
from sklearn.decomposition import TruncatedSVD
import pandas as pd
import matplotlib.pyplot as plt
```

13. Initialize an array of 50 dimensions and append the vector of woman. To perform this dimensional reduction, we are going to create a matrix, and its rows will be the vector of each word:

```
close_words=model.similar_by_word('woman')

arr = np.empty((0,50), dtype='f')
labels = ['woman']
#Array with the vectors of the closest words
arr = np.append(arr, np.array([model['woman']]), axis=0)
print("Matrix with the word 'woman':\n", arr)
```

```
Matrix with the word 'woman':
 [[-1.8153e-01  6.4827e-01 -5.8210e-01 -4.9451e-01  1.5415e+00  1.3450e+00
   -4.3305e-01  5.8059e-01  3.5556e-01 -2.5184e-01  2.0254e-01 -7.1643e-01
    3.0610e-01  5.6127e-01  8.3928e-01 -3.8085e-01 -9.0875e-01  4.3326e-01
   -1.4436e-02  2.3725e-01 -5.3799e-01  1.7773e+00 -6.6433e-02  6.9795e-01
    6.9291e-01 -2.6739e+00 -7.6805e-01  3.3929e-01  1.9695e-01 -3.5245e-01
    2.2920e+00 -2.7411e-01 -3.0169e-01  8.5286e-04  1.6923e-01  9.1433e-02
   -2.3610e-02  3.6236e-02  3.4488e-01 -8.3947e-01 -2.5174e-01  4.2123e-01
    4.8616e-01  2.2325e-02  5.5760e-01 -8.5223e-01 -2.3073e-01 -1.3138e+00
    4.8764e-01 -1.0467e-01]]
```

Figure 7.13: Matrix values with the word "woman"

14. Now, we have the word **dog** in the matrix and we need to append every vector of the similar words. Add the rest of the vectors to the matrix:

```
for w in close_words:
    w_vector = model[w[0]]
    labels.append(w[0])
    arr = np.append(arr, np.array([w_vector]), axis=0)
arr
```

This matrix is something like this:

```
Matrix with every word representation:
 [[-0.18153    0.64827   -0.5821    ... -1.3138     0.48764   -0.10467 ]
  [-0.34471    0.69563   -0.78086   ... -1.327      0.37319    0.022389]
  [-0.094386   0.43007   -0.17224   ... -0.97925    0.53135   -0.11725 ]
  ...
  [ 0.30459    0.40631   -0.37512   ... -1.1695     0.33096    0.46469 ]
  [ 0.57651    1.1396    -0.21861   ... -2.0724     0.232      0.37039 ]
  [-0.48533    0.98378   -0.29031   ... -0.95943    0.03837   -0.73304 ]]
```

Figure 7.14: Matrix with the most similar vectors of the "woman" vector

15. Once we have all the vectors in the matrix, let's initialize the TSNE method. It is a function of Sklearn;

```
svd = TruncatedSVD(n_components=2, n_iter=7, random_state=42)
svdvals = svd.fit_transform(arr)
```

16. Transform the matrix into vectors of two dimensions and create a DataFrame with pandas to store them:

```
df = pd.DataFrame(svdvals, index=labels, columns=['x', 'y'])
df
```

	x	y
woman	5.285012	0.626705
girl	5.152245	1.136314
man	4.645061	1.539196
mother	5.343125	-0.823005
her	5.668540	-1.124574
boy	4.728274	1.666479
she	5.222071	-1.117105
herself	4.178489	-1.411256
child	4.677279	-0.202067
wife	4.980629	-1.560086
old	4.398833	1.972819
girl	5.152245	1.136313
man	4.645061	1.539196
mother	5.343125	-0.823005
her	5.668540	-1.124574
boy	4.728274	1.666479
she	5.222071	-1.117105
herself	4.178489	-1.411256
child	4.677280	-0.202067
wife	4.980628	-1.560086
old	4.398833	1.972819

Figure 7.15: Coordinates of our vectors in two dimensions

17. Create a plot to see the words in a plane:

```
fig = plt.figure()
ax = fig.add_subplot(1, 1, 1)

for word, pos in df.iterrows():
    ax.annotate(word, pos)

ax.scatter(df['x'], df['y'])
plt.show()
```

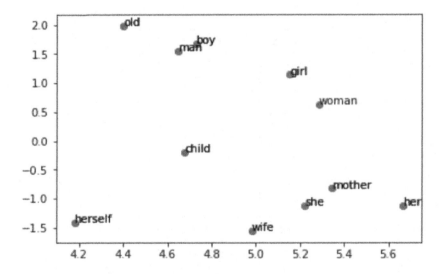

Figure 7.16: Distribution of the words most similar to woman

Here, we reduced the dimensionality of the vectors to get the output in a two-dimensional graph. Here, we can see the similarity relationship between the words.

You have finished exercise 25! You can now choose between using your own word2vec model or a GloVe model.

Dialogue Systems

As we mentioned before, chatbots are becoming more and more popular. They can help humans 24/7, answering questions or just holding a conversation. Dialogue systems can understand topics, give reasonable answers, and detect sentiments in a conversation (such as positive, neutral, or negative sentiment) with a human. The main goal of these systems is to hold a natural dialogue by imitating a human. This capability to behave or think like a human is one of the most important factors in ensuring a good user experience in the conversation. The Loebner Prize is a chatbot contest in which chatbots are tested using many different sentences and questions, and the most human-like system wins. One of the most popular conversational agents is the Mitsuku chatbot (https://www.pandorabots.com/mitsuku/).

Chatbots are commonly used as a text service to give information to users. For example, one of the most popular conversational agents in Spain is Lola, which can give you your zodiac information (https://1millionbot.com/chatbot-lola/). You just need to send a message and wait a few seconds to receive the data. But in 2011, Apple developed Siri, a virtual assistant that understands speech, and now, we have Amazon's Alexa and Google Assistant too. Depending on the input type of a system, they can be classified into two groups: **spoken dialogue systems** and **text-based dialogue systems**, which are explained later in the chapter.

This is not the only way to classify conversational agents. Depending on the type of knowledge they have, they can be divided into goal-oriented and open-domain. We will also review these classifications later in this chapter.

Actually, there are many tools for creating your own chatbot in a few minutes. But in this chapter, you will learn how to create the required system knowledge from scratch.

Tools for Developing Chatbots

Chatbots help a lot of many upcoming companies. But to create a chatbot, do you need to have knowledge of deep NLP? Well, thanks to these tools, a person without any NLP knowledge can create a chatbot in a matter of hours:

- **Dialogflow**: This easily creates a natural-language conversation. Dialogflow is a Google-owned developer that provides voice and conversational interfaces. This system uses Google's machine learning expertise to find the appropriate intents in a dialogue with a user and is deployed on Google Cloud Platform. It supports more than 14 languages and multiple platforms.

- **IBM Watson**: Watson Assistant provides a user-friendly interface to create conversational agents. It works just like Dialogflow but it is deployed on IBM Cloud and it's backed by IBM Watson knowledge. Watson also provides several tools to analyze data generated by conversations.

- **LUIS**: Language Understanding (LUIS) is a Microsoft machine learning-based service for building natural-language apps. This bot framework is hosted on the Azure cloud and uses Microsoft knowledge.

The aforementioned tools are a complex NLP system. In this chapter, we are going to look at a basic method for identifying the intent of a message using a pretrained GloVe. The latest chatbot trends are voice assistants. These tools allow you to implement a chatbot controlled by voice. There are many ways to classify a conversational agent.

Types of Conversational Agents

Conversational agents can be classified into several groups, depending on the type of input-output data and their knowledge limits. When a company orders the creation of a chatbot, the first step is to analyze what its communication channel (text or voice) will be and what the topics of the conversation will be (limited knowledge or without restriction).

Now, we are going to explain many types of groups and the features of each one.

Classification by Input-Output Data Type

A voice-controlled virtual assistant is not like a basic chatbot, which we use text to communicate with. Depending on the input-output type, we can divide them into two groups:

- **Spoken Dialogue System (SDS)**: These models are designed to be voice-controlled, without chat interfaces or keyboards, but with a microphone and speakers. These systems are harder to work with than a normal chatbot because they are composed of different modules:

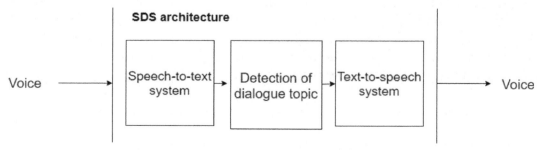

Figure 7.17: Structure of an SDS model

- Figure 7.17 shows the modules of an SDS. An SDS has a higher error probability, because speech-to-text systems need to transform the voice of a human into text, and this can fail. Once speech is converted into text, the conversational agent identifies the intent of the conversation and returns a response. Before the agent returns a response, the answer is converted to voice.

- **Text-Based Dialogue System**: In contrast with an SDS, text-based dialogue systems are based on a chat interface, where the user interacts with the chatbot using a keyboard and a screen. In this chapter, we will be creating a text-based dialogue chatbot.

Classification by System Knowledge

If the chatbot is able to successfully respond to every kind of message using its knowledge or if it is limited to a set of specific questions, these conversational agents can be divided as follows:

- **Closed-Domain or Goal-Oriented (GO)**: The model has been trained to identify a set of intents. The chatbot will only understand sentences related to these topics. If the conversational agent does not identify the intent (intent was explained in the introduction to this chapter), it will return a predefined sentence.

- **Open-Domain**: Not all chatbots have a set of defined intents. If the system can answer every type of sentence using NLG techniques and other data sources, it is classified as an open-domain model. The architecture of these systems is harder to build than a GO model.

- There is a third class of conversational agent, based on its knowledge, that is, the **Hybrid Domain**. It is a combination of the models mentioned previously, therefore, depending on the sentence, the chatbot will have a predefined response (associated intent with many responses) or not.

Creation of a Text-Based Dialogue System

So far, we already know the different classes of a conversational agent and how they can pick or generate a response. There are many other ways to build a conversational agent, and NLP provides many different approaches to achieve this objective. For example, **seq2seq** (sequence-to-sequence) models are able to find an answer when given a question. Also, deep language models can generate responses based on a corpus, that is, if a chatbot has a conversational corpus, it can follow a conversation.

In this chapter, we are going to build a chatbot using Stanford's GloVe. In *Exercise 26, Create Your First Conversational Agent*, you will find a brief introduction to the technique we are going to use, and in the activity, we will create a conversational agent to control a robot.

Scope definition and Intent Creation

Our conversational agent will be a text-based dialogue system and goal-oriented. Therefore, we will interact with our chatbot using the keyboard and it will only understand sentences related to intents created by us.

Before starting with the intent creation, we need to know what the main goal of our chatbot is (maintain a general dialogue, control a device, and obtain information) and what different types of sentences the users may ask.

Once we have analyzed the possible conversations of our chatbot, we can create the intents. Each intent will be a text file with several training sentences. These training sentences are possible interactions of a user with our chatbot. It is really important to define these sentences well because the chatbot could match the wrong intent if there are two similar sentences with different intents.

> **Note**
>
> A good previous analysis of the possible conversations of our chatbot will make intent definition easier. It is obvious the chatbot will not understand all the sentences a user may say, but it must be able to recognize the meaning of sentences related to our intents.

The system will also have a file with the same name as the intent file, but instead of containing the training sentences, it will have responses related to the intent:

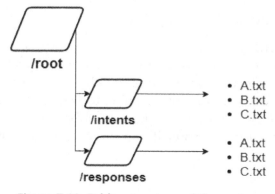

Figure 7.18: Folder structure of the system

In figure 7.18, we can see the structure of our chatbot. The extension of the intents and responses files are `.txt`, but you can also save them as `.json`.

GloVe for Intent Detection

At the beginning of this chapter, the fundamentals of word embeddings, word to vectors, and global vectors were reviewed. GloVe represents each word with a real-valued vector, and these vectors can be used as features in a variety of applications. But for this case – building a conversational agent – we are going to use complete sentences to train our chatbot, not just words.

The chatbot needs to understand that an entire sentence is represented by a set of words as a vector. This representation of a sequence as a vector is called **seq2vec**. Internally, the conversational agent will compare the user's sentence with each intent training phrase to find the most similar meaning.

At this point, there are vectors representing sequences, and these sequences are in a file related to an intent. If the same process mentioned previously is used to join all the sequence vectors into one, we will have a representation of the intent. The main idea is to not just represent a sentence; it is to represent a whole document in a vector, and this is called **Doc2vec**. With this approach, when the user interacts with the chatbot, it will find the intent of that user phrase.

The final structure of our system will look as shown in figure 7.19:

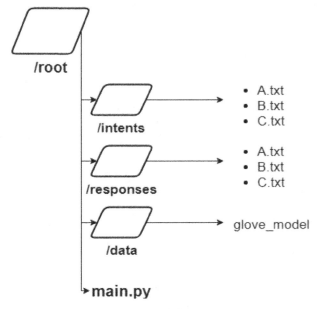

Figure 7.19: Final folder structure

The file named **main.py** will contain the different methods to analyze the input sentence using the GloVe model located in **/data**, creating the document vectors to perform the match between the user's sentence and the intent:

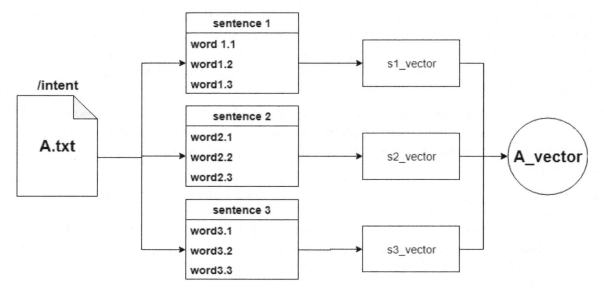

Figure 7.20: Doc2Vec transformation

Figure 7.20 shows the process of transforming a set of sentences in a vector, representing a document. In the example, the **A.txt** file is an intent with three sentences. Each sentence has three words, so each sentence has three vectors. Combining the vectors, we obtain a representation of each set of words, after which, we get the document vector.

The approach of converting sentences into vectors allows a comparison of a sequence of vectors within a document vector without any problem. When the user interacts with the chatbot, the user phrase will be transformed as seq2vec and then it will be compared with each document vector to find the most similar one.

Exercise 26: Create Your First Conversational Agent

> **Note**
>
> Perform exercise 26 in the same folder that you performed exercise 25 in.

In this exercise, you will create a chatbot to understand basic conversation. This exercise will cover the intent and response definition, the transformation of words into a vector, representing a document, and matching the user's sentence with the intent.

Before starting the exercise, please take a look at the folder structure in Google Colab, as shown in figure 7.21:

Figure 7.21: Structure of Exercise 26

The **Exercise26.ipynb** file is the **main.py** file that we came across before, and within the **utils** folder, you will find the folder structure presented as mentioned in the previous exercise:

Figure 7.22: Structure of Exercise 26 (2)

The folder responses have the files with the phrases that the chatbot can output when the user interacts with it. Training is where intents are defined within sentences. To obtain the vectors of each word, we are going to use Stanford's GloVe with five dimensions:

1. First, we need to define the intents and the responses for each intent. This is an introduction exercise, so let's define three intents: welcome, how-are-you, and farewell, and create some related sentences (separated by commas).

   "Welcome" training sentences: Hi friend, Hello, Hi, Welcome.

   "Farewell" training sentences: Bye, Goodbye, See you, Farewell, Have a good day.

   "How are you" training sentences: How are you? What is going on? Are you okay?

2. Once we have the intents created, we will need the responses. Create three files with the same name as the intent files and add responses.

   "Welcome" responses: Hello! Hi.

   "How are you?" responses: I'm good! Very good my friend :)

   "Farewell" responses: See you! Goodbye!

3. Import drive and mount it as follows:

   ```
   from google.colab import drive
   drive.mount('/content/drive')
   ```

4. Once you have mounted your drive for the first time, you will have to enter the authorization code by clicking on the URL mentioned by Google and pressing the **Enter** key on your keyboard:

```
[1]  from google.colab import drive
     drive.mount('/content/drive')

[→  Go to this URL in a browser: https://accounts.google.com/o/oauth2/auth?client_id=947318989803-6bn6qk8qdgf4n4g3pfee6491hc0brc4j.apps.googleusercontent.com

     Enter your authorization code:
     ..........
     Mounted at /content/drive
```

Figure 7.23: The Google Colab authorization step

5. Now that you have mounted the drive, you need to set the path of the directory:

   ```
   /content/drive/My Drive/C13550/Lesson07/Exercise25-26
   ```

6. Import the necessary libraries:

```
from gensim.scripts.glove2word2vec import glove2word2vec
from gensim.models import KeyedVectors
import numpy as np
from os import listdir
```

7. With spaCy, we are going to tokenize the sentences and erase the punctuation marks. Now, create a function that tokenizes every sentence of a document. In this exercise, we will create the Doc2vec from the word vectors by combining all these vectors into one. That is why we are going to tokenize the whole document, returning an array with all the tokens. It is good practice to erase the stopwords too, but in this exercise it is not necessary. The input of this function is an array of sentences:

```
import spacy
import en_core_web_sm
nlp = en_core_web_sm.load()

# return a list of tokens without punctuation marks
def pre_processing(sentences):
    tokens = []
    for s in sentences:
        doc = nlp(s)
        for t in doc:
            if t.is_punct == False:
                tokens.append(t.lower_)
    return tokens
```

8. Load the GloVe model:

```
filename = 'utils/glove.6B.50d.txt.word2vec'
model = KeyedVectors.load_word2vec_format(filename, binary=False)
```

9. Create two lists with the names of the intent files and the response files:

```
intent_route = 'utils/training/'
response_route = 'utils/responses/'

intents = listdir(intent_route)
responses = listdir(response_route)
```

10. Create a function that returns a vector of 100 dimensions representing a document. The input of this function will be a list with the tokens of a document. We need to initialize an empty vector with 100 dimensions. What this function will perform is adding every vector word and then dividing it by the length of the tokenized document:

```
def doc_vector(tokens):
    feature_vec = np.zeros((50,), dtype="float32")
    for t in tokens:
        feature_vec = np.add(feature_vec, model[t])
    return np.array([np.divide(feature_vec,len(tokens))])
```

11. Now, we are ready to read each intent file (located in the training folder), tokenizing them, and creating an array with every document vector:

```
doc_vectors = np.empty((0,50), dtype='f')
for i in intents:
    with open(intent_route + i) as f:
        sentences = f.readlines()
    sentences = [x.strip() for x in sentences]
    sentences = pre_processing(sentences)
    # adding the document vector to the array doc_vectors
    doc_vectors=np.append(doc_vectors,doc_vector(sentences),axis=0)
print("Vector representation of each document:\n",doc_vectors)
```

```
Vector representation of each document:
[[ 0.14770724   0.5464866   -0.16015846 -0.24245347  0.4202002   -0.2871844
  -0.5529633    0.30648416 -0.26304525  0.18462633 -0.37964222  0.19630247
  -0.21136111   0.12203988  0.75448555  0.05365466 -0.05886668 -0.10289577
  -0.3150087   -0.45763    -0.20689546  0.3401133   0.29135     -0.04262844
   0.5196933   -1.4245243  -0.69796884  0.24098887  0.38095883 -0.5922744
   2.7514176    0.62179    -0.4912156   0.33274615 -0.03507556 -0.10477156
   0.31766444   0.00739434  0.03692211 -0.5429275  -0.12317456  0.00449314
  -0.32877222   0.06327023  0.24757276  0.11004833  0.02727033 -0.14340179
  -0.13737655   0.21054223]
 [ 0.4196458    0.0582203   0.070118   -0.19546     0.5108501   -0.11875646
  -0.42002162  -0.13416906 -0.2159363   0.05899461 -0.18535121  0.418683
  -0.3417599    0.0096156   0.76261395  0.588184    0.431321    0.10539579
   0.062165    -0.77512705 -0.25137132  0.27534202  0.58613455  0.3648346
   0.562019    -1.6857541  -0.71831906  0.32524487  0.6571264   -0.8581694
   3.482656     0.483389   -0.32676098 -0.30277604 -0.02907473 -0.1763092
   0.1080915    0.11137016  0.13628599 -0.2416279  -0.29227847  0.0148172
   0.0974369    0.5345739   0.0803531   0.1533238  -0.0486946    0.02074
  -0.0445253    0.45075902]
 [-0.210398     0.681284   -0.0209552   0.21781997 -0.09973179 -0.7236999
  -0.336274    -0.043084   -0.37596998  0.545413    0.09762941  0.38618582
  -0.03290399   0.06879841  0.40217882  0.263802   -0.152566    0.394126
   0.24254799   0.05827668  0.0648665   0.44991398 -0.0497896   0.24755399
   0.54782164  -0.995554   -0.640922    0.04991     0.2009656   -0.79135406
   1.4396639    0.652454   -0.15243599  0.5090066  -0.384622    -0.36758882
   0.07631601  -0.03119398 -0.0378406  -0.44295     0.24170022  -0.019572
   0.11737199  -0.59020996  0.994038   -0.138326   -0.15160021  -0.487186
   0.11172561   0.7248579 ]]
```

Figure 7.24: Documents represented as vectors

12. With a function of **sklearn** called **cosine_similarity**, create a function that finds the most similar intent, comparing a sentence vector with each document vector:

```
from sklearn.metrics.pairwise import cosine_similarity
def select_intent(sent_vector, doc_vector):
    index = -1
    similarity = -1 #cosine_similarity is in the range of -1 to 1
    for idx,v in zip(range(len(doc_vector)),doc_vector):
        v = v.reshape(1,-1)
        sent_vector = sent_vector.reshape(1,-1)
        aux = cosine_similarity(sent_vector, v).reshape(1,)
        if aux[0] > similarity:
            index = idx
            similarity = aux
    return index
```

13. Let's test our chatbot. Tokenize the input of the user and use the last function (**select_intent**) to obtain the related intent:

```
user_sentence = "How are you"

user_sentence = pre_processing([user_sentence])
user_vector = doc_vector(user_sentence).reshape(50,)
intent = intents[select_intent(user_vector, doc_vectors)]
intent
```

```
Intent farewell.txt: 0.8703819513320923
Intent how_are_you.txt: 0.9822492599487305
Intent welcome.txt: 0.5226621031761169

'how_are_you.txt'
```

Figure 7.25: Predicted document intent

14. Create a function that gives a response to the user:

```
def send_response(intent_name):
    with open(response_route + intent_name) as f:
        sentences = f.readlines()
    sentences = [x.strip() for x in sentences]
    return sentences[np.random.randint(low=0, high=len(sentences)-1)]
send_response(intent)
```

15. Check for the output with the test sentence:

```
send_response(intent)
```

The output will look like this:

```
"I'm good!"
```

Figure 7.26: Response of intent how_are_you

16. Check whether the system works with many test sentences.

You have completed exercise 26! You are ready to build a conversational agent to control our virtual robot. As you saw in exercise 26 (step 2), you need a good definition of intents. If you try to add the same sentence in two different intents, the system could fail.

Activity 7: Create a Conversational Agent to Control a Robot

In this activity, we will create a chatbot with many intents. To perform this activity, we will use Stanford's GloVe, as in *Exercise 26, Create Your First Conversational Agent*. We will learn how to create a program that waits for a user sentence, and when the user interacts with the chatbot, it will return a response.

Scenario: You work in a company developing a security system. This security system will be a robot equipped with a camera to see the environment and wheels to move forward or backward. This robot will be controlled via text, so you can type orders and the robot will perform different actions.

1. The robot can perform the following actions:

    Move forward.

    Move backward.

    Rotations:

    45° to the right.

    45° to the left.

2. Identify what the robot can see. This activity is performed in the same way as in *Exercise 26, Create Your First Conversational Agent*. To avoid rewriting code, the **chatbot_intro.py** file has four basic methods:

    Pre_processing: To tokenize sentences

    Doc_vector: To create document vectors

    Select_intent: To find the most similar intent introduced in a sentence

    Send_response: To send a sentence located in the response folder

    Knowing these methods, the core work is done, so the most important thing is the design of the intents.

3. We need to develop four different activities, but the rotation activity has two different types. We are going to define five intents, one per action (two for rotation). You can use these sentences, but you are free to add more training sentences or more actions:

    Backward:

    Move back

    Going backward

    Backward

Go back

Moving backward

Environment:

What can you see?

Environment information

Take a picture

Tell me what you are seeing?

What do you have in front of you?

Forward:

Advance

Move forward

Go to the front

Start moving

Forward

Left:

Turn to the left

Go left

Look to the left

Turn left

Left

Right:

Turn to the right

Go right

Look to the right

Turn right

Right

You can find the files in the activity/training folder:

Figure 7.27: Training sentence files

> **Note**
>
> The solution for this activity is available on page 323.

Summary

Conversational agents, also knowns as chatbots, are text-based dialogue systems that understand human language in order to hold a "real" conversation with people. To achieve a good understanding of what a human is saying, chatbots need to classify dialogue into intents, that is, a set of sentences representing a meaning. Conversational agents can be classified into several groups, depending on the type of input-output data and knowledge limits. This representation of meaning is not easy. To have sound knowledge supporting a chatbot, a huge corpus is needed. Finding the best way to represent a word is a challenge, and one-hot encoding is useless. The main problem with one-hot encoding is the size of the encoded vectors. If we have a corpus of 88,000 words, then the vectors will have a size of 88,000, and without any relationship between the words. This is where the concept of word embeddings enters the picture.

Word embeddings are a collection of techniques and methods to map words and sentences from a corpus into vectors or real numbers. Word embeddings generate a representation of each word in terms of the context in which a word appears. To generate word embeddings, we can use Word2Vec. Word2Vec processes a corpus and assigns a vector to each unique word in the corpus, and it can perform dimension reduction, typically of several hundred dimensions.

The core idea of Word2Vec is that a word's meaning is given by the words that are frequently found near to it. When a word appears in a sentence, its context is formed by the set of words it has nearby. Word2Vec can be implemented using two types of algorithm: skip-gram and CBOW. The idea of Word2Vec is to represent words which is useful, but in terms of efficiency, it has problems. GloVe combines Word2Vec and the statistical information of a corpus. GloVe joins these two approaches to achieve fast training, scalable to huge corpora, and achieve better performance with small vectors. With GloVe, we are capable of giving knowledge to our chatbot, combined with training sentences defining our set of intents.

Chapter 8, Object Recognition to Guide the Robot Using CNNs, will introduce you to object recognition using different pretrained models. Furthermore, it will look at the latest trend in computer vision – the recognition of objects using boxes identifying what is in every part of a picture.

8

Object Recognition to Guide a Robot Using CNNs

Learning Objectives

By the end of this chapter, you will be able to:

- Explain how object recognition works

- Build a network capable of recognizing objects

- Build an object recognition system

This chapter covers how object recognition works by building a network that would be capable of recognizing objects based on a video.

Introduction

Object recognition is an area of computer vision where a robot is capable of detecting objects in an environment using a camera or sensor that is capable of extracting images of the robot's surroundings. From these images, software detects an object within every image and then recognizes the type of object. Machines are capable of recognizing objects from an image or a video captured by the robot's sensors. This allows the robot to be aware of their environment.

If a robot can recognize its environment and obtain this information using object recognition, it will be able to perform more complex tasks, such as grabbing objects or moving around in an environment. In *Chapter 9, Computer Vision for Robotics*, we will look at a robot performing these tasks in a virtual environment.

The task to be performed here is to detect specific objects within an image and recognize those objects. This type of computer vision problem is a bit different from the ones that we have looked at earlier in this book. In order to recognize a specific object, we have seen that labeling those objects and training a convolutional neural network, which was covered in *Chapter 5, Convolutional Neural Networks for Computer Vision*, which would work fine, but what about detecting these objects in the first place?

Previously, we learned that objects we want to recognize have to be labeled with the corresponding class they belong to. Hence, in order to detect those objects within an image, a rectangle-shaped bounding box has to be drawn around them so that their location in the image is properly located. The neural network will then predict the bounding boxes and the label of those objects.

Labeling objects with bounding boxes is a tedious, tough task, so we are not going to show the process for labeling the images in a dataset with bounding boxes, or the process for training a neural network to recognize and detect those objects. Nevertheless, there is a library called **labelImg**, which you can access in this GitHub repository: https://github.com/tzutalin/labelImg. This allows you to create bounding boxes for every object within an image. Once you have the bounding boxes created, which in terms of data are known as coordinates, you can train a neural network to predict the bounding boxes and the corresponding label for every object within an image.

In this chapter, we will be using state-of-the-art methods of the YOLO network, which are ready to use and will save you from having to build your own algorithm.

Multiple Object Recognition and Detection

Multiple object recognition and detection involves detecting and recognizing several objects within an image. This task involves labeling every single object with a bounding box and then recognizing the type of that object.

Because of this, there are many available pre-trained models that detect a lot of objects. The neural network called **YOLO** is one of the best models for this specific task and works in real time. YOLO will be explained in depth in the next chapter for the development of the simulator for the robot.

For this chapter, the YOLO network that we want to use is trained to recognize and detect 80 different classes. These classes are:

person, bicycle, car, motorcycle, airplane, bus, train, truck, boat, traffic light, fire hydrant, stop_sign, parking meter, bench, bird, cat, dog, horse, sheep, cow, elephant, bear, zebra, giraffe, backpack, umbrella, handbag, tie, suitcase, frisbee, skis, snowboard, sports ball, kite, baseball bat, baseball glove, skateboard, surfboard, tennis racket, bottle, wine glass, cup, fork, knife, spoon, bowl, banana, apple, sandwich, orange, broccoli, carrot, hot dog, pizza, donut, cake, chair, couch, potted plant, bed, dining table, toilet, tv, laptop, mouse, remote, keyboard, cell phone, microwave, oven, toaster, sink, refrigerator, book, clock, vase, scissors, teddy bear, hair dryer, toothbrush.

In Figure 8.1, you can see a sample of a street where people, cars, and buses have been detected using YOLO:

Figure 8.1: YOLO detection sample

In this topic, we are going to build a multiple object recognition and detection system for static images.

First, we are going to do so using an OpenCV module called **DNN** (Deep Neural Network), which involves a few lines of code. Later on, we will use a library called **ImageAI**, which does the same but with less than 10 lines of code and will allow you to choose the specific objects you want to detect and recognize.

In order to implement YOLO with OpenCV, you will need to import the image using OpenCV, just like we covered in other chapters of this book.

Exercise 24: Building Your First Multiple Object Detection and Recognition Algorithm

> **Note**
>
> We are going to use a Google Colab notebook as this task does not involve training an algorithm, but rather using one.

In this exercise, we are going to implement a multiple object detection and recognition system using YOLO and OpenCV. We are going to code a detector and a recognizer system that takes an image as input and detects and recognizes objects within that image, then outputs the image with those detections drawn:

1. Open up your Google Colab interface.

2. Import the following libraries:

   ```
   import cv2
   import numpy as np
   import matplotlib.pyplot as plt
   ```

3. To input an image to this network, we need to use the **blobFromImage** method:

> **Note**
>
> This image can be found on GitHub: **Dataset/obj_det/sample.jpg**.
>
> https://github.com/PacktPublishing/Artificial-Vision-and-Language-Processing-for-Robotics/tree/master/Lesson08/Dataset/obj_det

```
image = cv2.imread('Dataset/obj_det/image6.jpg')

Width = image.shape[1]
Height = image.shape[0]
scale = 0.00392
```

We need to load the classes of the dataset, which for YOLO are stored in **Models/yolov3.txt**, which you can find in **Chapter 8/Models** on GitHub. We read the classes like this:

```
# read class names from text file
classes = None
with open("Models/yolov3.txt", 'r') as f:
    classes = [line.strip() for line in f.readlines()]
```

4. Generate different colors for different classes:

```
COLORS = np.random.uniform(0, 255, size=(len(classes), 3))
```

5. Read the pre-trained model and the config file:

```
net = cv2.dnn.readNet('Models/yolov3.weights', 'Models/yolov3.cfg')
```

6. Create an input blob:

```
blob = cv2.dnn.blobFromImage(image.copy(), scale, (416,416), (0,0,0),
True, crop=False)
```

7. Set the input blob for the network:

```
net.setInput(blob)
```

In order to declare the network, we use the **readNet** method from the **DNN** module, and we load **Models/yolov3.weights**, which is the weights of the network, and **Models/yolov3.cfg**, which is the architecture of the model:

Note

The method, class, weight, and architecture files can be found on GitHub in the **Lesson08/Models/** folder.

Now that we have set this up, the only thing that is left in order to recognize and detect all the objects within an image is to run and execute the code, which is explained next.

8. In order to get the output layers of the network, we declare the method mentioned in the following code and then run the interface to obtain the array of output layers, which contains several detections:

```
# function to get the output layer names in the architecture
def get_output_layers(net):

    layer_names = net.getLayerNames()

    output_layers = [layer_names[i[0] - 1] for i in net.
getUnconnectedOutLayers()]

    return output_layers
```

9. Create a function to draw a bounding box around the detected object with the class name:

```
def draw_bounding_box(img, class_id, confidence, x, y, x_plus_w, y_plus_h):

    label = str(classes[class_id])

    color = COLORS[class_id]

    cv2.rectangle(img, (x,y), (x_plus_w,y_plus_h), color, 2)

    cv2.putText(img, label + " " + str(confidence), (x-10,y-10), cv2.FONT_
HERSHEY_SIMPLEX, 0.5, color, 2)
```

10. Execute the code:

```
# run inference through the network
# and gather predictions from output layers
outs = net.forward(get_output_layers(net))
```

> **Note**
>
> 'outs' is an array of predictions. Later on in the exercise, we will see that we have to loop this array in order to get the bounding boxes and the confidences of each detection, along with the type of class.

Object detection algorithms often detect one object several times and that is a problem. This problem can be solved by using **non-max suppression**, which deletes the bounding boxes for every object with less confidence (the probability of the object being in the predicted class), after which the only bounding boxes that will remain are the ones with the highest confidence. After detecting the bounding boxes and the confidences, and declaring the corresponding thresholds, this algorithm can be run as follows:

11. This step is one of the most important ones. Here, we are going to gather the confidence from every detection of every output layer (every object detected), the class ID, and the bounding boxes, but we'll ignore detections with a confidence of less than 50%:

```
# apply non-max suppression
class_ids = []
confidences = []
boxes = []
conf_threshold = 0.5
nms_threshold = 0.4
indexes = cv2.dnn.NMSBoxes(boxes, confidences, conf_threshold, nms_
threshold)
```

12. For each detection from each output layer, get the confidence, the class ID, and bounding box params, and ignore weak detections (confidence < 0.5):

```
for out in outs:
    for detection in out:
        scores = detection[5:]
        class_id = np.argmax(scores)
        confidence = scores[class_id]
        if confidence > 0.5:
            center_x = int(detection[0] * Width)
            center_y = int(detection[1] * Height)
            w = int(detection[2] * Width)
            h = int(detection[3] * Height)
            x = center_x - w / 2
            y = center_y - h / 2
            class_ids.append(class_id)
            confidences.append(float(confidence))
            boxes.append([x, y, w, h])
```

13. We loop over the list of indexes and use the method that we declared for printing to print every bounding box, every label, and every confidence on the input image:

```
for i in indexes:
    i = i[0]
    box = boxes[i]
    x = box[0]
    y = box[1]
    w = box[2]
    h = box[3]

    draw_bounding_box(image, class_ids[i], round(confidences[i],2),
round(x), round(y), round(x+w), round(y+h))
```

14. Finally, we show and save the resulting image. OpenCV has a method for showing it also; there is no need to use Matplotlib:

```
# display output image
plt.axis("off")
plt.imshow(cv2.cvtColor(image, cv2.COLOR_BGR2RGB))

# save output image to disk
cv2.imwrite("object-detection6.jpg", image)
```

The output is as follows:

```
True
```

Figure 8.2: YOLO detection sample

Finally, we have to draw the bounding boxes, its classes, and the confidence.

15. Now let's try some other examples using the steps mentioned previously. You can find the images in the **Dataset/obj-det/** folder. The outputs will be as shown in Figure 8.3:

Figure 8.3: YOLO detection sample

ImageAI

There is another way to achieve this easily. You could use the **ImageAI** library, which is capable of performing object detection and recognition with a few lines of code.

The link to the GitHub repository for this library can be found here:

https://github.com/OlafenwaMoses/ImageAI

In order to install this library, you can do so by using pip with the following command:

```
pip install https://github.com/OlafenwaMoses/ImageAI/releases/download/2.0.2/
imageai-2.0.2-py3-none-any.whl
```

To use this library, we need to import one class:

```
from imageai.Detection import ObjectDetection
```

We import the **ObjectDetection** class, which will work as a neural network.

Afterward, we declare the object of the class that is going to make the predictions:

```
detector = ObjectDetection()
```

The model that we are going to use has to be declared. For this library, we only get to use three models: RetinaNet, YOLOV3, and TinyYOLOV3. YOLOV3 is the same model we used before and has moderate performance and accuracy with a moderate detection time.

As for RetinaNet, it has higher performance and accuracy but a longer detection time.

TinyYOLOV3 is optimized for speed and has moderate performance and accuracy but a much faster detection time. This model will be used in the next topic because of its speed.

You only have to change a couple of lines of code in order to get to work with any of these models. For YOLOV3, these lines are needed:

```
detector.setModelTypeAsYOLOv3()
detector.setModelPath("Models/yolo.h5")
detector.loadModel()
```

The **.h5** file contains the weights and the architecture for the YOLOV3 neural network.

To run the inference and get the corresponding detections, only a line of code is needed:

```
detections = detector.detectObjectsFromImage(input_image="Dataset/obj_det/
sample.jpg", output_image_path="samplenew.jpg")
```

What this line does is take an image as input and detect the bounding boxes of the objects in the image and their classes. It outputs a new image drawn with those detections, as well as a list of the detected objects.

Let's see how it detects the **sample.jpg** image that we used in the last exercise:

Figure 8.4: ImageAI YOLOV3 image detection

ImageAI also allows you to customize which objects you want to recognize. By default, it is also capable of detecting the same classes as YOLO, which is built using OpenCV, that is the 80 classes.

You can customize it to only detect the objects that you want by passing an object as a parameter called **CustomObjects**, where you specify which objects you want the model to detect. Also, the method from the detector for recognizing those objects changes from **detectObjectsFromImage()** to **detectCustomObjectsFromImage()**. It is used like this:

```
custom_objects = detector.CustomObjects(car=True)
```

```
detections = detector.detectCustomObjectsFromImage(custom_objects=custom_
objects, input_image="Dataset/obj_det/sample.jpg", output_image_
path="samplenew.jpg")
```

Figure 8.5: ImageAI YOLOV3 custom image detection

Multiple Object Recognition and Detection in Video

Multiple object recognition and detection in static images sounds amazing, but what about detecting and recognizing objects in a video?

You can download any video from the internet and try to detect and recognize all the objects that show up in the video.

The process to follow would be to get every frame of the video and for every frame, detect the corresponding objects and their labels.

Declare the corresponding libraries first:

```
from imageai.Detection import VideoObjectDetection

from matplotlib import pyplot as plt
```

The **imageai** library contains an object that allows the user to apply object detection and recognition to the video:

```
video_detector = VideoObjectDetection()
```

We need **VideoObjectDetection** so that we can detect objects in video. Moreover, Matplotlib is needed to show the detection process for every frame:

Processing Frame :   6

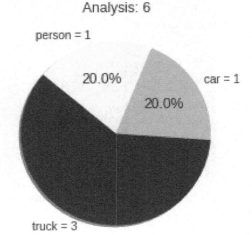

Figure 8.6: ImageAI one-frame object detection process

Now we will first need to load the model. You can decide what model to load, depending on the speed you need the video to be processed at, with the precision required. YOLOV3 is in the middle, between RetinaNet and TinyYOLOV3, RetinaNet being the most precise but the slowest and TinyYOLOV3 the least precise but the fastest. We are going to stick to the YOLOV3 model but feel free to use the other two. The declaration after declaring the video object detection is the same as in the last topic:

```
video_detector.setModelTypeAsYOLOv3()

video_detector.setModelPath("Models/yolo.h5")

video_detector.loadModel()
```

Before running the video detector, we need to declare a function that will be applied to every frame processed. This function does not perform the detection algorithm, but it handles the detection process for every frame. And why do we have to handle the output of every frame after the object detection process? That is because we want to show the detection process frame by frame using Matplotlib..

Before declaring that method, we need to declare the colors that the objects will be printed on:

```
color_index = {'bus': 'red', 'handbag': 'steelblue', 'giraffe': 'orange',
'spoon': 'gray', 'cup': 'yellow', 'chair': 'green', 'elephant': 'pink',
'truck': 'indigo', 'motorcycle': 'azure', 'refrigerator': 'gold', 'keyboard':
'violet', 'cow': 'magenta', 'mouse': 'crimson', 'sports ball': 'raspberry',
'horse': 'maroon', 'cat': 'orchid', 'boat': 'slateblue', 'hot dog': 'navy',
'apple': 'cobalt', 'parking meter': 'aliceblue', 'sandwich': 'skyblue',
'skis': 'deepskyblue', 'microwave': 'peacock', 'knife': 'cadetblue',
'baseball bat': 'cyan', 'oven': 'lightcyan', 'carrot': 'coldgrey',
'scissors': 'seagreen', 'sheep': 'deepgreen', 'toothbrush': 'cobaltgreen',
'fire hydrant': 'limegreen', 'remote': 'forestgreen', 'bicycle': 'olivedrab',
'toilet': 'ivory', 'tv': 'khaki', 'skateboard': 'palegoldenrod', 'train':
'cornsilk', 'zebra': 'wheat', 'tie': 'burlywood', 'orange': 'melon', 'bird':
'bisque', 'dining table': 'chocolate', 'hair drier': 'sandybrown', 'cell
phone': 'sienna', 'sink': 'coral', 'bench': 'salmon', 'bottle': 'brown',
'car': 'silver', 'bowl': 'maroon', 'tennis racket': 'palevilotered',
'airplane': 'lavenderblush', 'pizza': 'hotpink', 'umbrella': 'deeppink',
'bear': 'plum', 'fork': 'purple', 'laptop': 'indigo', 'vase': 'mediumpurple',
'baseball glove': 'slateblue', 'traffic light': 'mediumblue', 'bed': 'navy',
'broccoli': 'royalblue', 'backpack': 'slategray', 'snowboard': 'skyblue',
'kite': 'cadetblue', 'teddy bear': 'peacock', 'clock': 'lightcyan', 'wine
glass': 'teal', 'frisbee': 'aquamarine', 'donut': 'mincream', 'suitcase':
'seagreen', 'dog': 'springgreen', 'banana': 'emeraldgreen', 'person':
'honeydew', 'surfboard': 'palegreen', 'cake': 'sapgreen', 'book':
```

```
'lawngreen', 'potted plant': 'greenyellow', 'toaster': 'ivory', 'stop sign':
'beige', 'couch': 'khaki'}
```

Now we are going to declare the method applied to every frame:

```
def forFrame(frame_number, output_array, output_count, returned_frame):


    plt.clf()


    this_colors = []
    labels = []
    sizes = []


    counter = 0
```

First, as shown, the function is declared and the number of the frame, the array of detections, the number of occurrences of every object detected, and the frame are passed to it. Also, we declare the corresponding variables that we are going to use to print all the detections on every frame:

```
for eachItem in output_count:
    counter += 1
    labels.append(eachItem + " = " + str(output_count[eachItem]))
    sizes.append(output_count[eachItem])
    this_colors.append(color_index[eachItem])
```

In this loop, the objects and their corresponding occurrences are stored. The colors that represent every object are also stored:

```
plt.subplot(1, 2, 1)
plt.title("Frame : " + str(frame_number))
plt.axis("off")
plt.imshow(returned_frame, interpolation="none")
```

```
    plt.subplot(1, 2, 2)

    plt.title("Analysis: " + str(frame_number))

    plt.pie(sizes, labels=labels, colors=this_colors, shadow=True,
startangle=140, autopct="%1.1f%%")


    plt.pause(0.01)
```

In this last piece of code, two plots are printed for every frame: one showing the image with the corresponding detections and the other with a chart containing the number of occurrences of every object detected and its percentage of the total of occurrences.

This output is shown in Figure 8.6.

In the last cell, in order to execute the video detector, we write this couple of lines of code:

```
plt.show()


video_detector.detectObjectsFromVideo(input_file_path="path_to_video.
mp4", output_file_path="output-video" , frames_per_second=20, per_frame_
function=forFrame, minimum_percentage_probability=30, return_detected_
frame=True, log_progress=True)
```

The first line initializes the Matplotlib plot.

The second line starts the video detection. The arguments passed to the function are as follows:

- **input_file_path**: The input video path
- **output_file_path**: The output video path
- **frames_per_second**: Frames per second of the output video
- **per_frame_function**: The callback function after every process of detecting objects within a frame
- **minimum_percentage_probability**: The minimum probability value threshold, where only detections with the highest confidence are considered
- **return_detected_frame**: If set to True, the callback function receives the frame as a parameter
- **log_progress**: If set to True, the process is logged in the console

Activity 8: Multiple Object Detection and Recognition in Video

In this activity, we are going to process a video frame by frame, detecting all possible objects within every frame and saving the output video to disk:

> **Note**
>
> The video we will be using for this activity is uploaded on GitHub, in the **Dataset/ videos/street.mp4** folder:
>
> Url : https://github.com/PacktPublishing/Artificial-Vision-and-Language-Processing-for-Robotics/blob/master/Lesson08/Dataset/videos/street.mp4

1. Open a Google Colab notebook, mount the disk, and navigate to where chapter 8 is located.

2. Install the library in the notebook, as it is not preinstalled, by using this command:

   ```
   !pip3 install https://github.com/OlafenwaMoses/ImageAI/releases/
   download/2.0.2/imageai-2.0.2-py3-none-any.whl
   ```

3. Import the necessary libraries for the development of this activity and set **matplotlib**.

4. Declare the model that you are going to use for detecting and recognizing objects.

> **Note**
>
> You can find that information here:
> https://github.com/OlafenwaMoses/ImageAI/blob/master/imageai/Detection/VIDEO.md
>
> Also note that all models are stored in the **Models** folder.

5. Declare the callback method that is going to be called after every frame is processed.

6. Run Matplotlib and the video detection processes on the **street.mp4** video that is inside the **Dataset/videos/** folder. You can also try out the **park.mp4** video, which is in the same directory.

> **Note**
>
> The solution for this activity is available on page 326.

Summary

Object recognition and detection is capable of identifying several objects within an image, to draw bounding boxes around those objects and predict the types of object they are.

The process of labeling the bounding boxes and their labels has been explained, but not in depth, due to the huge process required. Instead, we used state-of-the-art models to recognize and detect those objects.

YOLOV3 was the main model used in this chapter. OpenCV was used to explain how to run an object detection pipeline using its DNN module. ImageAI, an alternative library for object detection and recognition, has shown its potential for writing an object detection pipeline with a few lines and easy object customization.

Finally, the ImageAI object detection pipeline was put into practice by using a video, where every frame obtained from the video was passed through that pipeline to detect and identify objects from those frames and show them using Matplotlib.

Computer Vision
for Robotics

Learning Objectives

By the end of this chapter, you will be able to:

- Evaluate objects using artificial vision
- Combine external frameworks with ROS
- Use a robot to interact with objects
- Create a robot to understand natural language
- Develop your own end-to-end robotics applications

In this chapter, you'll learn how to work with Darknet and YOLO. You'll also evaluate objects using AI and integrate YOLO and ROS to enable your virtual robot to predict objects in the virtual environment.

Introduction

In previous chapters, you came across many technologies and techniques that may be new to you. You have learned many concepts and techniques that help solve real-world problems. Now, you are going to use all the acquired skills to complete this last chapter and build your own end-to-end robotics application.

In this chapter, you'll use a deep learning framework, Darknet, to build robots that recognize objects in real time. This framework will be integrated with ROS so that the final application can be applied to any robot. Furthermore, it's important to say that object recognition can be used for building different kinds of robotics applications.

The end-to-end applications you are going to build will not only have academic value but will also be useful for real-world problems and live situations. You will even be able to adapt how the application functions depending on circumstances. This will give you a lot of opportunities to solve real-world problems when working with robots.

Darknet

Darknet is an open source neural network framework, which has been written in C and CUDA. It is very fast, as it allows GPU as well as CPU computation. It was developed by Joseph Redmon, a computer scientist focused on artificial vision.

Although we are not going to study all of the functionalities in this chapter, Darknet includes a lot of interesting applications. As we mentioned earlier, we are going to use YOLO, but the following is a list of other Darknet functionalities:

- **ImageNet Classification**: This is an image classifier, which uses known models such as AlexNet, ResNet, and ResNeXt. After classifying some ImageNet images with all these models, a comparison between them is performed. They are based on time, accuracy, weights etc..

- **RNN's**: Recurrent neural networks are used for generating and managing natural language. They use an architecture called a vanilla RNN with three recurrent modules, which achieves good results in tasks such as speech recognition and natural language processing.

- **Tiny Darknet**: Consists of another image classifier, but this time, the generated model is much lighter. This network obtains similar results to Darknet, but the model weight is only 4 MB.

> **Note**
>
> Apart from the preceding, Darknet has some other applications as well. You can get more information about the framework by heading to its website: https://pjreddie.com/darknet/.

Basic Installation of Darknet

The Darknet basic installation won't let you use the entire YOLO power, but it will be enough to check how it works and make your first few object detection predictions. It won't let you use GPU computation to make real-time predictions. For more complex tasks, go to the next section.

> **Note**
>
> For detailed steps regarding the basic and advanced installation of Darknet, refer to the preface, page vii.

YOLO

YOLO is a real-time object detection system based on deep learning and is included in the Darknet framework. Its name comes from the acronym *You Only Look Once*, which references to how fast YOLO can work.

On the website (https://pjreddie.com/darknet/yolo/), the author has added an image where this system is compared to others with the same purpose:

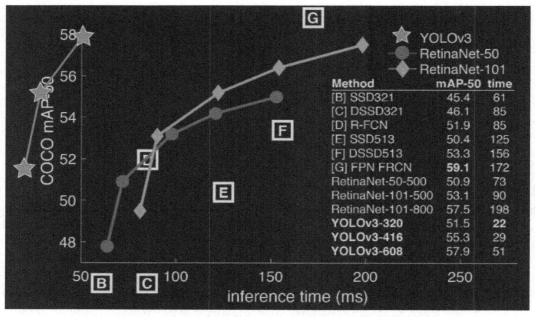

The figure contains the following data table:

Method	mAP-50	time
[B] SSD321	45.4	61
[C] DSSD321	46.1	85
[D] R-FCN	51.9	85
[E] SSD513	50.4	125
[F] DSSD513	53.3	156
[G] FPN FRCN	59.1	172
RetinaNet-50-500	50.9	73
RetinaNet-101-500	53.1	90
RetinaNet-101-800	57.5	198
YOLOv3-320	51.5	22
YOLOv3-416	55.3	29
YOLOv3-608	57.9	51

Figure 9.1: A comparison of object detection systems

In the preceding graphic, the **y** axis represents the **mAP** (mean Average Precision), and the **x** axis represents the time in milliseconds. So, you can see that YOLO achieves a higher mAP in lesser time than the other systems.

It is also important to understand how YOLO works. It uses a neural network, which is applied to the entire image and splits it into different parts, predicting the bounding boxes. These bounding boxes are similar to rectangles marking off certain objects, which will be identified later in the process. YOLO is fast, because it is able to make predictions with only an evaluation of the neural network, while other recognition systems need several evaluations.

The mentioned network has 53 convolutional layers, alternating 3x3 and 1x1 layers. Here's an image of the architecture extracted from a YOLO author's paper (https://pjreddie.com/media/files/papers/YOLOv3.pdf):

	Type	Filters	Size	Output
	Convolutional	32	3 × 3	256 × 256
	Convolutional	64	3 × 3 / 2	128 × 128
	Convolutional	32	1 × 1	
1×	Convolutional	64	3 × 3	
	Residual			128 × 128
	Convolutional	128	3 × 3 / 2	64 × 64
	Convolutional	64	1 × 1	
2×	Convolutional	128	3 × 3	
	Residual			64 × 64
	Convolutional	256	3 × 3 / 2	32 × 32
	Convolutional	128	1 × 1	
8×	Convolutional	256	3 × 3	
	Residual			32 × 32
	Convolutional	512	3 × 3 / 2	16 × 16
	Convolutional	256	1 × 1	
8×	Convolutional	512	3 × 3	
	Residual			16 × 16
	Convolutional	1024	3 × 3 / 2	8 × 8
	Convolutional	512	1 × 1	
4×	Convolutional	1024	3 × 3	
	Residual			8 × 8
	Avgpool		Global	
	Connected		1000	
	Softmax			

Figure 9.2: The YOLO architecture

First Steps in Image Classification with YOLO

In this section, we are going to make our first predictions with YOLO. You are required to complete the basic installation. Let's start recognizing objects in a single image:

1. We are going to use a pretrained model in order to avoid the training process, so the first step is to download the network weights in the Darknet directory:

```
cd <darknet_path>
wget https://pjreddie.com/media/files/yolov3.weights
```

2. After that, we are going to make predictions with YOLO. In this first example, we are trying to recognize a single object, a dog. This is the sample image we are using:

Figure 9.3: Sample image to predict

Save this image as a .jpg file in the Darknet directory and run YOLO on it:

```
./darknet detect cfg/yolov3.cfg yolov3.weights dog.jpg
```

When the execution is finished, you should see an output like the following:

```
Loading weights from yolov3.weights...Done!
dog.jpg: Predicted in 23.796328 seconds.
dog: 100%
```

Figure 9.4: The predicted output

As you can see, YOLO detects that there's a dog in the image with 100% accuracy. It also generates a new file named **predictions.jpg**, where it is possible to see the location of the dog in the image. You can open it from the Darknet directory:

Figure 9.5: Recognized objects in the image

Another possibility when using YOLO is to make predictions for several images with a single execution. To do this, you must enter the same command as before, but this time do not enter the image path:

```
./darknet detect cfg/yolov3.cfg yolov3.weights
```

In this case, you will see the following output:

```
 106 detection
Loading weights from yolov3.weights...Done!
Enter Image Path: █
```

Figure 9.6: The prediction command output

As you can see, it is asking you to enter an image. You could enter, for instance, the same image as before by typing **dog.jpg**. You'll then be asked to enter another image path. This way, you can make predictions for all the images you want. This could be an example:

```
Loading weights from yolov3.weights...Done!
Enter Image Path: data/eagle.jpg
data/eagle.jpg: Predicted in 0.057916 seconds.
bird: 100%
```

Figure 9.7: The output after image prediction

If you do so, you will obtain this image:

Figure 9.8: Image prediction

There's one more interesting command to know when working with YOLO. It can be used to modify the detection threshold.

> **Note**
>
> The detection threshold is an accuracy limit to consider if a prediction is incorrect. For example, if you set your threshold to 0.75, objects detected with a lower accuracy won't be considered as a correct prediction.

By default, YOLO includes an object in its output when it is predicted with an accuracy of 0.25 or higher. You can change the threshold value using the last flag of the following command:

```
./darknet detect cfg/yolov3.cfg yolov3.weights dog2.jpg -thresh 0.5
```

As you may suppose, the preceding command sets the threshold to 0.5. Let's look at a practical example of this. Follow these steps to test the functioning of the threshold modification:

1. Make predictions for images until you find one where an object is predicted with less than 100% accuracy. We are going to use this as an example, where the dog is recognized with 60% accuracy:

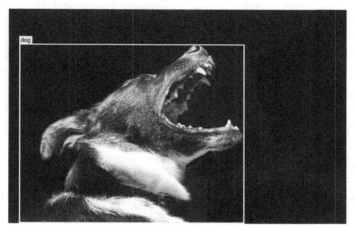

Figure 9.9: Example image with less than 100% accuracy

2. Now, use the **predict** command modifying the detection threshold. As the dog is detected with 60% accuracy, if we change the threshold to 70%, no object should be detected:

```
./darknet detect cfg/yolov3.cfg yolov3.weights dog2.jpg -thresh 0.7
```

3. If we check the **predictions** file, we can confirm that the dog was not detected. Hence, you can see how threshold plays an important role in recognition as well:

Figure 9.10: The final prediction with the modified threshold

YOLO on a Webcam

Once you have made your first predictions with YOLO, it's time to try a more interesting feature of this system. You're going to detect your own real objects by connecting YOLO to your personal webcam. To do this, you must complete the advanced installation because it needs a GPU and OpenCV:

1. Make sure your webcam is connected and can be detected by your system.

2. Enter the following command in the Darknet directory:

```
./darknet detector demo cfg/coco.data cfg/yolov3.cfg yolov3.weights
```

3. Try to recognize an object in your environment; for example, we have detected the books on our shelves:

Figure 9.11: Books recognized using a webcam

Exercise 28: Programming with YOLO

In this exercise, we are going to see how to make predictions with YOLO using Python. We will create a dataset and check how many images containing a certain object are present in the dataset. To build the dataset, check the following images:

Figure 9.12: Images contained in the dataset

As you can see, it is a very simple dataset containing animals and landscape images. The Python program you are going to implement will have to obtain the number of images in which dogs appear.

We will begin by cloning Darknet files from GitHub:

```
git clone https://github.com/pjreddie/darknet
cd darknet
make
```

1. Create a new folder named **dataset** in the Darknet directory.

2. Place these images or others of your choice inside the new folder.

> **Note**
>
> The images can be found in the Chapter 9/exercise28/dataset/ folder on GitHub
>
> URL: https://github.com/PacktPublishing/Artificial-Vision-and-Language-Processing-for-Robotics/tree/master/Lesson09/Exercise28/dataset

3. Create a Python file, **excercise1.py**, and start the implementation.

    Import Python itself and the required libraries:

    ```
    #!usr/bin/env python
    import sys, os
    ```

4. Tell the system where to find the Darknet framework and then import it. If you have created a file inside the Darknet directory, you can do this as follows:

> **Note**
>
> The path set here needs to be the path where you have placed your Darknet directory.

```
sys.path.append(os.path.join(os.getcwd(),'python/'))
import darknet as dn
```

5. Tell Darknet which GPU to use for the program execution:

> **Note**
>
> In Ubuntu, you can obtain an ordered list of your GPUs using the nvidia-smi command. When obtained, check the index of the GPU you want to use and type it into your Python program. If you only have one GPU, you will have to choose the number 0.

```
dn.set_gpu(0)
```

6. Configure the network you are going to use for making your predictions. In this case, we are using the same configuration as before:

```
net = dn.load_net("cfg/yolov3.cfg", "yolov3.weights", 0)
meta = dn.load_meta("cfg/coco.data")
```

> **Note**
>
> Pay attention to the paths entered here; they may change if your Python file is not inside Darknet's folder.

7. Declare the variables to count the total number of images and the number of images containing dogs:

```
dog_images = 0
number_of_images = 0
```

8. Implement a loop for iterating over the files in the dataset:

```
for file in os.listdir("dataset/"):
```

9. Use Darknet's **detect** method to recognize the objects of each image:

```
filename = "dataset/" + file
r = dn.detect(net, meta, filename)
```

10. Iterate over the recognized objects and check whether any of them are dogs. If they are, add one to the dog images counter and stop checking the rest of the objects. Add one to the total counter too:

> **Note**
>
> YOLO returns its predictions as a list of arrays, where each of these arrays represents an object. The data they provide is distributed in the following way:
> - Position 0: Object name
> - Position 1: Accuracy
> - Position 2: Array with the object coordinates in the image

```
for obj in r:
    if obj[0] == "dog":
        dog_images += 1
        break
number_of_images += 1
```

11. Finally, print the obtained results. For example:

```
print("There are " + str(dog_images) + "/" + str(number_of_images) + "
images containing dogs")
```

> **Note**
>
> To execute the code successfully, you need to make changes to the darknet.py file, as follows:
>
> Head to the darknet.py file and modify the line lib = CDLL("<your path>/datrknet/libdarknet.so", RTLD_GLOBAL).

```
cd ..
 wget https://pjreddie.com/media/files/yolov3.weights
python exercise28.py
```

> **Note**
>
> Here the **cd ..** command switches to the directory where your file is located and downloads the weights and run the script.
>
> For example **cd <your_script_location>**

You can test whether it works as expected by running the script. If you used the proposed dataset, the output should be as follows:

```
  106 detection
Loading weights from yolov3.weights...Done!
There are 5/9 images containing dogs
```

Figure 9.13: Exercise 28 final output

ROS Integration

Now, you have already learned how to use YOLO in a common Python program. It's time to see how to integrate it with Robot Operating System (ROS) so that you can use it in real robotics problems. You can combine it with any robot camera to allow the robot to detect and recognize objects, achieving the goal of artificial vision. After the completion of the following exercise, you will be able to do it by yourself.

Exercise 29: ROS and YOLO Integration

This exercise consists of a new ROS node implementation that uses YOLO to recognize objects. We will test it using TurtleBot, the ROS simulator we used in *Chapter 6, Robot Operating System (ROS)*, but it will be easily adaptable for any robot with a camera. These are the steps that must be followed:

1. Create a new package in your catkin workspace to contain the integration node. Do it with this command to include the correct dependencies:

```
cd ~/catkin_ws/
source devel/setup.bash
roscore
cd src
catkin_create_pkg exercise29 rospy cv_bridge geometry_msgs image_transport
sensor_msgs std_msgs
```

2. Switch to the package folder and create a new **scripts** directory. Then, create the Python file and make it executable:

```
cd exercise29
mkdir scripts
cd scripts
touch exercise29.py
chmod +x exercise29.py
```

3. Begin with the implementation.

   Import the libraries you will use for node implementation. You will need **sys** and **os** to import Darknet from its path, **OpenCV** to process images, and **Image** from **sensor_msgs** to publish them:

```
import sys
import os
from cv_bridge import CvBridge, CvBridgeError
from sensor_msgs.msg import Image
```

   Tell the system where to find Darknet:

```
sys.path.append(os.path.join(os.getcwd(), '/home/alvaro/Escritorio/tfg/
darknet/python/'))
```

> **Note**
>
> The above mentioned path may change as per the directories placed in your computer.

Now, import the framework:

```
import darknet as dn
```

Create the class where the node logic will be coded and its constructor:

```
class Exercise29():
    def __init__(self):
```

Code the constructor:

Now, we will initialize the node:

```
rospy.init_node('Exercise29', anonymous=True)
```

Create a bridge object:

```
self.bridge = CvBridge()
```

Subscribe to the camera topic:

```
self.image_sub = rospy.Subscriber("camera/rgb/image_raw", Image,
self.imageCallback)
```

Create the variable to store the obtained images:

```
self.imageToProcess = None
```

Define the corresponding paths for YOLO configuration:

```
cfgPath =  "/home/alvaro/Escritorio/tfg/darknet/cfg/yolov3.cfg"
weightsPath = "/home/alvaro/Escritorio/tfg/darknet/yolov3.weights"
dataPath = "/home/alvaro/Escritorio/tfg/darknet/cfg/coco2.data"
```

> **Note**
>
> The above mentioned path may change as per the directories placed in your computer.

Create YOLO variables for making predictions:

```
self.net = dn.load_net(cfgPath, weightsPath, 0)
self.meta = dn.load_meta(dataPath)
```

Define the name that will be used for storing the images:

```
self.fileName = 'predict.jpg'
```

Implement the callback function to obtain the images with the OpenCV format:

```
def imageCallback(self, data):
    self.imageToProcess = self.bridge.imgmsg_to_cv2(data, "bgr8")
```

Create a function for making predictions over the obtained images. The node must keep making predictions until the user stops the execution. This will be done by storing the image to the disk and making predictions over it using the detection function. Finally, the results will be constantly printed:

```
def run(self):
    while not rospy.core.is_shutdown():
        if(self.imageToProcess is not None):
            cv2.imwrite(self.fileName, self.imageToProcess)
            r = dn.detect(self.net, self.meta, self.fileName)
            print r
```

Implement the main program entry. Here, you will have to initialize Darknet, make an instance of the created class, and call its main method:

```
if __name__ == '__main__':
    dn.set_gpu(0)
    node = Exercise29()
    try:
        node.run()
    except rospy.ROSInterruptException:
        pass
```

4. Test whether the node works as it should.

Open a terminal and start ROS:

```
cd ../../
cd ..
source devel/setup.bash
roscore
```

Open another terminal and run Gazebo with TurtleBot:

```
cd ~/catkin_ws
source devel/setup.bash
roslaunch turtlebot_gazebo turtlebot_world.launch
```

Insert YOLO recognizable objects and make TurtleBot **look at** them. You can insert new objects by clicking on the **insert** button located in the upper-left corner. You could insert, for example, a bowl:

Figure 9.14: Inserted bowl in Gazebo

5. Open a new terminal and run the created node:

```
cd ~/catkin_ws
source devel/setup.bash
rosrun exercise29 exercise29.py
```

If you used a bowl, check that you get an output like the one that follows:

```
[('bowl', 0.7104724049568176, (352.04852294921875, 344.7698669433594
, 76.55792999267578, 31.363014221191406))]
[('bowl', 0.696557879447937, (352.01055908203125, 344.83770751953125
, 76.56439208984375, 31.41343879699707))]
[('bowl', 0.7058066129684448, (351.9707946777344, 344.8869323730469,
 76.7359848022461, 31.645347595214844))]
[('bowl', 0.6935019493103027, (351.9503173828125, 344.8268737792969,
 76.54244995117188, 31.239303588867188))]
[('bowl', 0.6676342487335205, (351.9901123046875, 344.8103942871094,
 76.46720886230469, 31.15680694580078))]
[('bowl', 0.6695064902305603, (351.8796081542969, 344.81585693359375
, 76.3839340209961, 31.182811737060547))]
[('bowl', 0.6725053787231445, (351.87506103515625, 344.8595886230469
, 76.35908508300781, 31.181182861328125))]
[('bowl', 0.6542823314666748, (351.75732421875, 344.78326416015625,
76.5813980102539, 31.1123046875))]
```

Figure 9.15: Object predicted by the node

Activity 9: A Robotic Security Guard

Let's suppose a scenario similar to the one in the *Chapter 6, Activity 6, Simulator and Sensors* activity: You are working for a robotics company that has recently got a new client, a shopping center. The client wants your company to provide some robots for the shopping center at night to avoid robbery. These robots must consider any person a thief and alert the client if they detect one.

Use Gazebo to give the desired functionality to TurtleBot or any other simulator. You should follow these steps:

1. Create a catkin package for storing the required nodes.

2. Now, implement the first node. It should obtain the images from the robot camera and run YOLO on them.

3. Next, it should publish the list of detected objects in string format.

4. Implement the second node. It should subscribe to the topic where the detected objects are being published and obtain them. Finally, it should check whether a person is one of these objects and print an alert message if it is.

5. Run both nodes simultaneously.

> **Note**
>
> Although it's not the main goal of this activity, it would be interesting to combine the execution of these nodes with another one to move the robot (you can use the one implemented in *Chapter 6, Robot Operating System (ROS)*).
>
> The solution of this activity can be found on page 330.

Summary

We have now achieved the objective of this book and built an end-to-end application for a robot. This has only been an example application; however, you could use the techniques that you learned during this book to build other applications for robotics. In this chapter, you also learned how to install and work with Darknet and YOLO. You worked through evaluating objects using AI and integrating YOLO and ROS to enable your virtual robot to predict objects.

You have learned how to control the robot with natural language processing commands, along with studying various models in this book, such as Word2Vec, GloVe embedding techniques, and non-numeric data. After this, you worked with ROS and built a conversational agent to manage your virtual robot. You developed the skills needed to build a functional application that could integrate with ROS to extract useful information about your environment. You worked with tools that are not only useful for robotics; you can use artificial vision and language processing as well.

We end this book by encouraging you to start your own robotics projects and practicing with the technologies you most enjoyed during the book. You can now compare different methods used to work with robots and explore computer vision, algorithms, and limits. Always remember that a robot is a machine that can possess the behavior you want it to.

Appendix

About

This section is included to assist the students to perform the activities in the book.
It includes detailed steps that are to be performed by the students to achieve the objectives of
the activities.

Chapter 1: Fundamentals of Robotics

Activity 1: Robot Positioning Using Odometry with Python

Solution

```python
from math import pi


def wheel_distance(diameter, encoder, encoder_time, wheel, movement_time):
    time = movement_time / encoder_time
    wheel_encoder = wheel * time
    wheel_distance = (wheel_encoder * diameter * pi) / encoder


    return wheel_distance


from math import cos,sin


def final_position(initial_pos,wheel_axis,angle):
    final_x=initial_pos[0]+(wheel_axis*cos(angle))
    final_y=initial_pos[1]+(wheel_axis*sin(angle))
    final_angle=initial_pos[2]+angle


    return(final_x,final_y,final_angle)
def position(diameter,base,encoder,encoder_time,left,right,initial_
pos,movement_time):
#First step: Wheels completed distance
    left_wheel=wheel_distance(diameter,encoder,encoder_time,left,movement_
time)
    right_wheel=wheel_distance(diameter,encoder,encoder_time,right,movement_
time)
#Second step: Wheel's central axis completed distance
```

```
    wheel_axis=(left_wheel+right_wheel)/2
#Third step: Robot's rotation angle
    angle=(right_wheel-left_wheel)/base
#Final step: Final position calculus
    final_pos=final_position(initial_pos,wheel_axis,angle)


    returnfinal_pos
```

```
position(10,80,76,5,600,900,(0,0,0),5)
```

> **Note:**
>
> For further observations, you can change the wheels' diameter to 15 cm and check the difference in the output. Similarly, you can change other input values and check the difference in the output.

Chapter 2: Introduction to Computer Vision

Activity 2: Classify 10 Types of Clothes from the Fashion-MNIST Data

Solution

1. Open up your Google Colab interface.

2. Create a folder for the book, download the **Dataset** folder from GitHub, and upload it into the folder.

3. Import the drive and mount it as follows:

```
from google.colab import drive
drive.mount('/content/drive')
```

Once you have mounted your drive for the first time, you will have to enter the authorization code mentioned by clicking on the URL given by Google and pressing the **Enter** key on your keyboard:

Figure 2.38: Image displaying the Google Colab authorization step

4. Now that you have mounted the drive, you need to set the path of the directory:

```
cd /content/drive/My Drive/C13550/Lesson02/Activity02/
```

5. Load the dataset and show five samples:

```
from keras.datasets import fashion_mnist
(x_train, y_train), (x_test, y_test) = fashion_mnist.load_data()
```

The output is as follows:

```
Using TensorFlow backend.
Downloading data from http://fashion-mnist.s3-website.eu-central-1.amazonaws.com/train-labels-idx1-ubyte.gz
32768/29515 [==============================] - 0s 5us/step
Downloading data from http://fashion-mnist.s3-website.eu-central-1.amazonaws.com/train-images-idx3-ubyte.gz
26427392/26421880 [==============================] - 2s 0us/step
Downloading data from http://fashion-mnist.s3-website.eu-central-1.amazonaws.com/t10k-labels-idx1-ubyte.gz
8192/5148 [==============================] - 0s 0us/step
Downloading data from http://fashion-mnist.s3-website.eu-central-1.amazonaws.com/t10k-images-idx3-ubyte.gz
4423680/4422102 [==============================] - 1s 0us/step
```

Figure 2.39: Loading datasets with five samples

```
import random
from sklearn import metrics
from sklearn.utils import shuffle
random.seed(42)
from matplotlib import pyplot as plt
for idx in range(5):
    rnd_index = random.randint(0, 59999)
    plt.subplot(1,5,idx+1),plt.imshow(x_train[idx],'gray')
    plt.xticks([]),plt.yticks([])
plt.show()
```

Figure 2.40: Samples of images from the Fashion-MNIST dataset

6. Preprocess the data:

```
import numpy as np
from keras import utils as np_utils
x_train = (x_train.astype(np.float32))/255.0
x_test = (x_test.astype(np.float32))/255.0
x_train = x_train.reshape(x_train.shape[0], 28, 28, 1)
x_test = x_test.reshape(x_test.shape[0], 28, 28, 1)
y_train = np_utils.to_categorical(y_train, 10)
y_test = np_utils.to_categorical(y_test, 10)
input_shape = x_train.shape[1:]
```

7. Build the architecture of the neural network using **Dense** layers:

```
from keras.callbacks import EarlyStopping, ModelCheckpoint,
ReduceLROnPlateau
from keras.layers import Input, Dense, Dropout, Flatten
from keras.preprocessing.image import ImageDataGenerator
from keras.layers import Conv2D, MaxPooling2D, Activation,
BatchNormalization
```

```python
from keras.models import Sequential, Model
from keras.optimizers import Adam, Adadelta
def DenseNN(inputh_shape):

    model = Sequential()
    model.add(Dense(128, input_shape=input_shape))
    model.add(BatchNormalization())
    model.add(Activation('relu'))
    model.add(Dropout(0.2))

    model.add(Dense(128))
    model.add(BatchNormalization())
    model.add(Activation('relu'))
    model.add(Dropout(0.2))

    model.add(Dense(64))
    model.add(BatchNormalization())
    model.add(Activation('relu'))
    model.add(Dropout(0.2))

    model.add(Flatten())
    model.add(Dense(64))
    model.add(BatchNormalization())
    model.add(Activation('relu'))
    model.add(Dropout(0.2))

    model.add(Dense(10, activation="softmax"))

    return model
model = DenseNN(input_shape)
```

Note:

The entire code file for this activity can be found on GitHub in the Lesson02 | Activity02 folder.

8. Compile and train the model:

```python
optimizer = Adadelta()
model.compile(loss='categorical_crossentropy', optimizer=optimizer,
metrics=['accuracy'])
ckpt = ModelCheckpoint('model.h5', save_best_only=True,monitor='val_loss',
```

```
mode='min', save_weights_only=False)
model.fit(x_train, y_train, batch_size=128, epochs=20, verbose=1,
validation_data=(x_test, y_test), callbacks=[ckpt])
```

The accuracy obtained is **88.72%**. This problem is harder to solve, so that's why we have achieved less accuracy than in the last exercise.

9. Make the predictions:

```
import cv2
images = ['ankle-boot.jpg', 'bag.jpg', 'trousers.jpg', 't-shirt.jpg']
for number in range(len(images)):
    imgLoaded = cv2.imread('Dataset/testing/%s'%(images[number]),0)
    img = cv2.resize(imgLoaded, (28, 28))
    img = np.invert(img)
cv2.imwrite('test.jpg',img)
    img = (img.astype(np.float32))/255.0
    img = img.reshape(1, 28, 28, 1)
    plt.subplot(1,5,number+1),plt.imshow(imgLoaded,'gray')
    plt.title(np.argmax(model.predict(img)[0]))
    plt.xticks([]),plt.yticks([])
plt.show()
```

Output will look like this:

Figure 2.41: Prediction for clothes using Neural Networks

It has classified the bag and the t-shirt correctly, but it has failed to classify the boots and the trousers. These samples are very different from the ones that it was trained for.

Chapter 3: Fundamentals of Natural Language Processing

Activity 3: Process a Corpus

Solution

1. Import the **sklearn TfidfVectorizer** and **TruncatedSVD** methods:

   ```
   from sklearn.feature_extraction.text import TfidfVectorizer
   from sklearn.decomposition import TruncatedSVD
   ```

2. Load the corpus:

   ```
   docs = []
   ndocs = ["doc1", "doc2", "doc3"]
   for n in ndocs:
       aux = open("dataset/"+ n +".txt", "r", encoding="utf8")
       docs.append(aux.read())
   ```

3. With **spaCy**, let's add some new stop words, tokenize the corpus, and remove the stop words. The new corpus without these words will be stored in a new variable:

   ```
   import spacy
   import en_core_web_sm
   from spacy.lang.en.stop_words import STOP_WORDS
   nlp = en_core_web_sm.load()
   nlp.vocab["\n\n"].is_stop = True
   nlp.vocab["\n"].is_stop = True
   nlp.vocab["the"].is_stop = True
   nlp.vocab["The"].is_stop = True
   newD = []
   for d, i in zip(docs, range(len(docs))):
       doc = nlp(d)
       tokens = [token.text for token in doc if not token.is_stop and not
   token.is_punct]
       newD.append(' '.join(tokens))
   ```

4. Create the TF-IDF matrix. I'm going to add some parameters to improve the results:

   ```
   vectorizer = TfidfVectorizer(use_idf=True,
                                ngram_range=(1,2),
                                smooth_idf=True,
                                max_df=0.5)
   X = vectorizer.fit_transform(newD)
   ```

5. Perform the LSA algorithm:

```
lsa = TruncatedSVD(n_components=100,algorithm='randomized',n_
iter=10,random_state=0)
lsa.fit_transform(X)
```

6. With pandas, we are shown a sorted **DataFrame** with the weights of the terms of each concept and the name of each feature:

```
import pandas as pd
import numpy as np
dic1 = {"Terms": terms, "Components": lsa.components_[0]}
dic2 = {"Terms": terms, "Components": lsa.components_[1]}
dic3 = {"Terms": terms, "Components": lsa.components_[2]}
f1 = pd.DataFrame(dic1)
f2 = pd.DataFrame(dic2)
f3 = pd.DataFrame(dic3)
f1.sort_values(by=['Components'], ascending=False)
f2.sort_values(by=['Components'], ascending=False)
f3.sort_values(by=['Components'], ascending=False)
```

The output is as follows:

	Terms	Components
1845	moon	0.338403
272	apollo	0.315843
958	earth	0.180482
2558	space	0.157921
1879	nasa	0.135361

Figure 3.26: Output example of the most relevant words in a concept (f1)

Note:

Do not worry if the keywords are not the same as yours, if the keywords represent a concept, it is a valid result.

Chapter 4: Neural Networks with NLP

Activity 4: Predict the Next Character in a Sequence

Solution

1. Import the libraries we need to solve the activity:

    ```
    import tensorflow as tf
    from keras.models import Sequential
    from keras.layers import LSTM, Dense, Activation, LeakyReLU
    import numpy as np
    ```

2. Define the sequence of characters and multiply it by 100:

    ```
    char_seq = 'qwertyuiopasdfghjklñzxcvbnm' * 100
    char_seq = list(char_seq)
    ```

3. Create a **char2id** dictionary to relate every character with an integer:

    ```
    char2id = dict([(char, idx) for idx, char in enumerate(set(char_seq))])
    ```

4. Divide the sentence of characters into time series. The maximum length of time series will be five, so we will have vectors of five characters. Also, we are going to create the upcoming vector. The y_labels variable is the size of our vocabulary. We will use this variable later:

    ```
    maxlen = 5
    sequences = []
    next_char = []

    for i in range(0,len(char_seq)-maxlen):
        sequences.append(char_seq[i:i+maxlen])
        next_char.append(char_seq[i+maxlen])

    y_labels = len(char2id)
    print("5 first sequences: {}".format(sequences[:5]))
    print("5 first next characters: {}".format(next_char[:5]))
    print("Total sequences: {}".format(len(sequences)))
    print("Total output labels: {}".format(y_labels))
    ```

5. So far, we have the sequences variable, which is an array of arrays, with the time series of characters. char is an array with the upcoming character. Now, we need to encode these vectors, so let's define a method to encode an array of characters using the information of char2id:

```
def one_hot_encoder(seq, ids):
    encoded_seq = np.zeros([len(seq),len(ids)])
    for i,s in enumerate(seq):
        encoded_seq[i][ids[s]] = 1
    return encoded_seq
```

6. Encode the variables into one-hot vectors. The shape of this is x = (2695,5,27) and y = (2695,27):

```
x = np.array([one_hot_encoder(item, char2id) for item in sequences])
y = np.array(one_hot_encoder(next_char, char2id))
x = x.astype(np.int32)
y = y.astype(np.int32)

print("Shape of x: {}".format(x.shape))
print("Shape of y: {}".format(y.shape))
```

```
Shape of x: (2695, 5, 27)
Shape of y: (2695, 27)
```

Figure 4.35: Variables encoded into OneHotVectors

7. Split the data into train and test sets. To do this, we are going to use the **train_test_split** method of sklearn:

```
from sklearn.model_selection import train_test_split

x_train, x_test, y_train, y_test = train_test_split(x, y, test_size=0.2,
shuffle=False)
print('x_train shape: {}'.format(x_train.shape))
print('y_train shape: {}'.format(y_train.shape))
print('x_test shape: {}'.format(x_test.shape))
print('y_test shape: {}'.format(y_test.shape))
```

```
x_train shape: (2156, 5, 27)
y_train shape: (2156, 27)
x_test shape: (539, 5, 27)
y_test shape: (539, 27)
```

Figure 4.36: Splitting the data into train and test sets

8. With the data ready to be inserted in the neural network, create a Sequential model with two layers:

First layer: LSTM with eight neurons (the activation is tanh). input_shape is the maximum length of the sequences and the size of the vocabulary. So, because of the shape of our data, we do not need to reshape anything.

Second layer: Dense with 27 neurons. This is how we successfully complete the activity. Using a LeakyRelu activation will give you a good score. But why? Our output has many zeroes, so the network could fail and just return a vector of zeroes. Using LeakyRelu prevents this problem:

```
model = Sequential()
model.add(LSTM(8,input_shape=(maxlen,y_labels)))
model.add(Dense(y_labels))
model.add(LeakyReLU(alpha=.01))

model.compile(loss='mse', optimizer='rmsprop')
```

9. Train the model. The batch_size we use is 32, and we have 25 epochs:

```
history = model.fit(x_train, y_train, batch_size=32, epochs=25, verbose=1)
```

```
Epoch 1/25
2156/2156 [==============================] - 1s 451us/step - loss: 0.0349
Epoch 2/25
2156/2156 [==============================] - 0s 175us/step - loss: 0.0327
Epoch 3/25
2156/2156 [==============================] - 0s 172us/step - loss: 0.0304
Epoch 4/25
2156/2156 [==============================] - 0s 133us/step - loss: 0.0282
Epoch 5/25
2156/2156 [==============================] - 0s 140us/step - loss: 0.0261
Epoch 6/25
2156/2156 [==============================] - 0s 138us/step - loss: 0.0236
Epoch 7/25
2156/2156 [==============================] - 0s 135us/step - loss: 0.0215
Epoch 8/25
2156/2156 [==============================] - 0s 144us/step - loss: 0.0195
Epoch 9/25
2156/2156 [==============================] - 0s 133us/step - loss: 0.0173
Epoch 10/25
2156/2156 [==============================] - 0s 137us/step - loss: 0.0153
Epoch 11/25
2156/2156 [==============================] - 0s 135us/step - loss: 0.0135
Epoch 12/25
2156/2156 [==============================] - 0s 134us/step - loss: 0.0119
Epoch 13/25
2156/2156 [==============================] - 0s 156us/step - loss: 0.0106
Epoch 14/25
2156/2156 [==============================] - 0s 154us/step - loss: 0.0092
Epoch 15/25
2156/2156 [==============================] - 0s 143us/step - loss: 0.0077
Epoch 16/25
2156/2156 [==============================] - 0s 141us/step - loss: 0.0067
```

Figure 4.37: Training with a batch_size of 32 and 25 epochs

10. Compute the error of your model.

```
print('MSE: {:.5f}'.format(model.evaluate(x_test, y_test)))
```

```
539/539 [==============================] - 0s 271us/step
MSE: 0.00051
```

Figure 4.38: Error shown in the model

11. Predict the test data and see the average percentage of hits. With this model, you will obtain an average of more than 90%:

```
prediction = model.predict(x_test)

errors = 0
for pr, res in zip(prediction, y_test):
    if not np.array_equal(np.around(pr),res):
        errors+=1

print("Errors: {}".format(errors))
print("Hits: {}".format(len(prediction) - errors))
print("Hit average: {}".format((len(prediction) - errors)/
len(prediction)))
```

```
Errors: 0
Hits: 539
Hit average: 1.0
```

Figure 4.39: Predicting the test data

12. To end this activity, we need to create a function that accepts a sequence of characters and returns the next predicted value. To decode the prediction of the model, we first code a decode method. This method just search in the prediction the higher value and take the key character in the char2id dictionary.

```
def decode(vec):
    val = np.argmax(vec)
    return list(char2id.keys())[list(char2id.values()).index(val)]
```

13. Create a method to predict the next character in a given sentence:

```
def pred_seq(seq):
    seq = list(seq)
    x = one_hot_encoder(seq,char2id)
    x = np.expand_dims(x, axis=0)
    prediction = model.predict(x, verbose=0)
    return decode(list(prediction[0]))
```

14. Finally, introduce the sequence 'tyuio' to predict the upcoming character. It will return 'p':

```
pred_seq('tyuio')
```

'p'

Figure 4.40: Final output with the predicted sequence

Congratulations! You have finished the activity. You can predict a value outputting a temporal sequence. This is also very important in finances, that is, when predicting future prices or stock movements.

You can change the data and predict what you want. If you add a linguistic corpus, you will generate text from your own RNN language model. So, our future conversational agent could generate poems or news text.

Chapter 5: Convolutional Neural Networks for Computer Vision

Activity 5: Making Use of Data Augmentation to Classify correctly Images of Flowers

Solution

1. Open your Google Colab interface.

> **Note:**
>
> You will need to mount your drive using the Dataset folder, and accordingly set the path to continue ahead.

```
import numpyasnp
classes=['daisy','dandelion','rose','sunflower','tulip']
X=np.load("Dataset/flowers/%s_x.npy"%(classes[0]))
y=np.load("Dataset/flowers/%s_y.npy"%(classes[0]))
print(X.shape)
forflowerinclasses[1:]:
    X_aux=np.load("Dataset/flowers/%s_x.npy"%(flower))
    y_aux=np.load("Dataset/flowers/%s_y.npy"%(flower))
    print(X_aux.shape)
    X=np.concatenate((X,X_aux),axis=0)
    y=np.concatenate((y,y_aux),axis=0)

print(X.shape)
print(y.shape)
```

2. To output some samples from the dataset:

```
import random
random.seed(42)
from matplotlib import pyplot as plt
import cv2

for idx in range(5):
    rnd_index = random.randint(0, 4000)
    plt.subplot(1,5,idx+1),plt.imshow(cv2.cvtColor(X[rnd_index],cv2.COLOR_
BGR2RGB))
    plt.xticks([]),plt.yticks([])
    plt.savefig("flowers_samples.jpg", bbox_inches='tight')
plt.show()
```

The output is as follows:

Figure 5.23: Samples from the dataset

3. Now, we will normalize and perform one-hot encoding:

```
from keras import utils as np_utils
X = (X.astype(np.float32))/255.0
y = np_utils.to_categorical(y, len(classes))
print(X.shape)
print(y.shape)
```

4. Splitting the training and testing set:

```
from sklearn.model_selection import train_test_split
x_train, x_test, y_train, y_test = train_test_split(X, y, test_size=0.2)
input_shape = x_train.shape[1:]
print(x_train.shape)
print(y_train.shape)
print(x_test.shape)
print(y_test.shape)
print(input_shape)
```

5. Import libraries and build the CNN:

```
from keras.models import Sequential
from keras.callbacks import ModelCheckpoint
from keras.layers import Input, Dense, Dropout, Flatten
from keras.layers import Conv2D, Activation, BatchNormalization
def CNN(input_shape):
    model = Sequential()

    model.add(Conv2D(32, kernel_size=(5, 5), padding='same',
strides=(2,2), input_shape=input_shape))
    model.add(Activation('relu'))
    model.add(BatchNormalization())
    model.add(Dropout(0.2))
```

```
    model.add(Conv2D(64, kernel_size=(3, 3), padding='same',
strides=(2,2)))
    model.add(Activation('relu'))
    model.add(BatchNormalization())
    model.add(Dropout(0.2))

    model.add(Conv2D(128, kernel_size=(3, 3), padding='same',
strides=(2,2)))
    model.add(Activation('relu'))
    model.add(BatchNormalization())
    model.add(Dropout(0.2))

    model.add(Conv2D(256, kernel_size=(3, 3), padding='same',
strides=(2,2)))
    model.add(Activation('relu'))
    model.add(BatchNormalization())
    model.add(Dropout(0.2))

    model.add(Flatten())
    model.add(Dense(512))
    model.add(Activation('relu'))
    model.add(BatchNormalization())
    model.add(Dropout(0.5))
    model.add(Dense(5, activation = "softmax"))

    return model
```

6. Declare ImageDataGenerator:

```
from keras.preprocessing.image import ImageDataGenerator
datagen = ImageDataGenerator(
        rotation_range=10,
        zoom_range = 0.2,
        width_shift_range=0.2,
        height_shift_range=0.2,
        shear_range=0.1,
        horizontal_flip=True
        )
```

7. We will now train the model:

```
datagen.fit(x_train)

model = CNN(input_shape)

model.compile(loss='categorical_crossentropy', optimizer='Adadelta',
metrics=['accuracy'])

ckpt = ModelCheckpoint('Models/model_flowers.h5', save_best_
only=True,monitor='val_loss', mode='min', save_weights_only=False)

//{…}##the detailed code can be found on Github##

model.fit_generator(datagen.flow(x_train, y_train,
                                 batch_size=32),
                    epochs=200,
                    validation_data=(x_test, y_test),
                    callbacks=[ckpt],
                    steps_per_epoch=len(x_train) // 32,
                    workers=4)
```

8. After which, we will evaluate the model:

```
from sklearn import metrics
model.load_weights('Models/model_flowers.h5')
y_pred = model.predict(x_test, batch_size=32, verbose=0)
y_pred = np.argmax(y_pred, axis=1)
y_test_aux = y_test.copy()
y_test_pred = list()
for i in y_test_aux:
    y_test_pred.append(np.argmax(i))

//{…}
##the detailed code can be found on Github##

print (y_pred)

# Evaluate the prediction
accuracy = metrics.accuracy_score(y_test_pred, y_pred)
print('Acc: %.4f' % accuracy)
```

9. The accuracy achieved is **91.68%**.

10. Try the model with unseen data:

```
classes = ['daisy','dandelion','rose','sunflower','tulip']
images = ['sunflower.jpg','daisy.jpg','rose.jpg','dandelion.jpg','tulip
.jpg']
model.load_weights('Models/model_flowers.h5')

for number in range(len(images)):
    imgLoaded = cv2.imread('Dataset/testing/%s'%(images[number]))
    img = cv2.resize(imgLoaded, (150, 150))
    img = (img.astype(np.float32))/255.0
    img = img.reshape(1, 150, 150, 3)
    plt.subplot(1,5,number+1),plt.imshow(cv2.cvtColor(imgLoaded,cv2.COLOR_
BGR2RGB))
    plt.title(np.argmax(model.predict(img)[0]))
    plt.xticks([]),plt.yticks([])
plt.show()
```

Output will look like this:

Figure 5.24: Prediction of roses result from Activity05

Note:

The detailed code for this activity can be found on GitHub - https://github.com/
PacktPublishing/Artificial-Vision-and-Language-Processing-for-Robotics/blob/mas-
ter/Lesson05/Activity05/Activity05.ipynb

Chapter 6: Robot Operating System (ROS)

Activity 6: Simulators and Sensor

Solution

1. We start by creating the packages and files:

```
cd ~/catkin_ws/src
catkin_create_pkg activity1 rospy sensor_msgs
cd  activity1
mkdir scripts
cd scripts
touch observer.py
touch movement.py
chmod +x observer.py
chmod +x movement.py
```

2. This is the implementation of the image obtainer node:

> **Note:**
>
> Add the aforementioned code to the **observer.py** file.

```python
#!/usr/bin/env python
import rospy
from sensor_msgs.msg import Image
import cv2
from cv_bridge import CvBridge

class Observer:
    bridge = CvBridge()
    counter = 0

    def callback(self, data):
        if self.counter == 20:
            cv_image = self.bridge.imgmsg_to_cv2(data, "bgr8")
            cv2.imshow('Image',cv_image)
            cv2.waitKey(1000)
            cv2.destroyAllWindows()
            self.counter = 0
```

```python
        else:
            self.counter += 1

    def observe(self):
        rospy.Subscriber('/camera/rgb/image_raw', Image, self.callback)
        rospy.init_node('observer', anonymous=True)
        rospy.spin()


if __name__ == '__main__':
    obs = Observer()
    obs.observe()
```

As you can see, this node is very similar to the one in *Exercise 21, Publishers and Subscribers*. The only differences are:

3. A counter is used for showing only one image of twenty received.

We enter **1000 (ms)** as the **Key()** parameter so that each image is shown for a second.

This is the implementation of the movement node:

```python
#!/usr/bin/env python
import rospy
from geometry_msgs.msg import Twist

def move():
    pub = rospy.Publisher('/mobile_base/commands/velocity', Twist, queue_size=1)
    rospy.init_node('movement', anonymous=True)
    move = Twist()
    move.angular.z = 0.5
    rate = rospy.Rate(10)
    while not rospy.is_shutdown():
        pub.publish(move)
        rate.sleep()

if __name__ == '__main__':
    try:
        move()
    except rospy.ROSInterruptException:
        pass
```

4. To execute the file, we will execute the code mentioned here.

> **Note:**
>
> Add this code to observer the **.py** file.

```
cd ~/catkin_ws
source devel/setup.bash
roscore
roslaunch turtlebot_gazebo turtlebot_world.launch
rosrun activity1 observer.py
rosrun activity1 movement.py
```

5. Run both nodes and check the system functioning. You should see the robot turning on itself while images of what it sees are shown. This is a sequence of the execution:

The output will look like this:

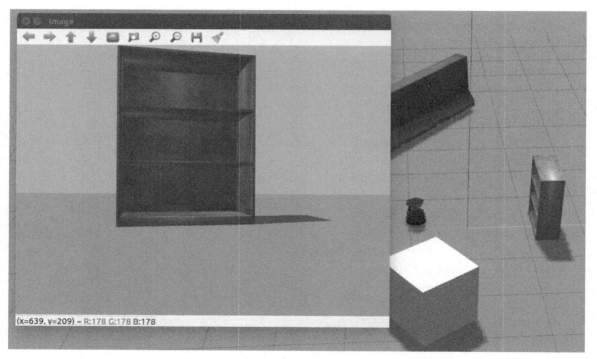

Figure 6.10: The first sequence of the execution of activity nodes

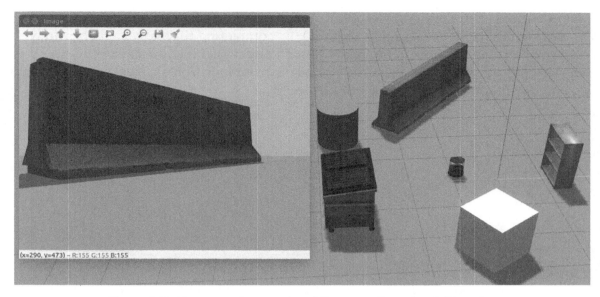

Figure 6.11: The second sequence of the execution of activity nodes

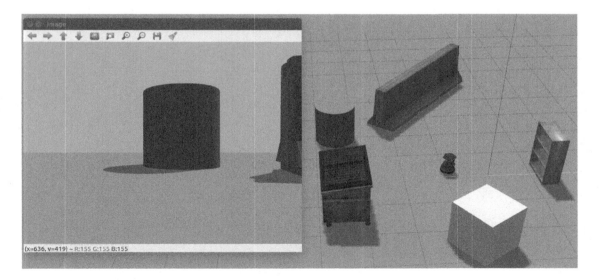

Figure 6.12: The third sequence of the execution of activity nodes

Note:

The output will look similar but not exactly look as the one mentioned in figures 6.10, 6.11, and 6.12.

Congratulations! You have completed the activity and at the end, you will have an output which is like figures 6.8, 6.9, and 6.10. By completing this activity successfully, you have been able to implement and work with nodes that let you subscribe to a camera which will show images in the virtual environment. You also learned to rotate a robot on itself that lets you view these images.

Chapter 7: Build a Text-Based Dialogue System (Chatbot)

Activity 7: Create a Conversational Agent to Control a Robot

Solution

1. Open up your Google Colab interface.

2. Create a folder for the book and download the **utils**, **responses**, and **training** folder from Github and upload it in the folder.

3. Import drive and mount it as follows:

    ```
    from google.colab import drive
    drive.mount('/content/drive')
    ```

    | **Note**
    |
    | Every time you use a new collaborator, mount the drive to the desired folder.

4. Once you have mounted your drive for the first time, you will need to enter the authorization code mentioned by clicking on the URL mentioned by Google and press the Enter key on your keyboard:

Figure 7.28: Image displaying the Google Colab authorization step

5. Now that you have mounted the drive, you need to set the path of the directory.

    ```
    cd /content/drive/My Drive/C13550/Lesson07/Activity01
    ```

    | **Note:**
    |
    | The path mentioned in step 5 may change as per your folder setup on Google
    | Drive. The path will always begin with cd /content/drive/My Drive/

6. Import the chatbot_intro file:

    ```
    from chatbot_intro import *
    ```

7. Define the GloVe model:

```
filename = '../utils/glove.6B.50d.txt.word2vec'
model = KeyedVectors.load_word2vec_format(filename, binary=False)
```

8. List the responses and training sentences files:

```
intent_route = 'training/'
response_route = 'responses/'
intents = listdir(intent_route)
responses = listdir(response_route)

print("Documents: ", intents)
```

```
Documents:  ['backward.txt', 'right.txt', 'environment.txt', 'left.txt', 'forward.txt']
```

Figure 7.29: A list of intent documents

9. Create document vectors:

```
doc_vectors = np.empty((0,50), dtype='f')
for i in intents:
    with open(intent_route + i) as f:
        sentences = f.readlines()
    sentences = [x.strip() for x in sentences]
    sentences = pre_processing(sentences)
doc_vectors= np.append(doc_vectors,doc_vector(sentences,model),axis=0)

print("Shape of doc_vectors:",doc_vectors.shape)
print(" Vector representation of backward.txt:\n",doc_vectors)
```

```
Shape of doc_vectors: (5, 50)
 Vector representation of backward.txt:
 [[-6.07202910e-02 -3.90555531e-01  2.96240002e-01 -5.61776638e-01
    1.42276779e-01 -3.37033987e-01 -6.26757741e-01  9.03290212e-02
   -2.96840459e-01 -1.33693099e-01 -1.55952871e-01  4.51840013e-02
   -8.24113309e-01  1.94479778e-01  2.00248867e-01  4.67142224e-01
    3.89170140e-01 -3.62565696e-01 -2.67985016e-01 -4.58462238e-01
   -1.05254777e-01  2.20742196e-01  8.44515488e-02  1.64389551e-01
    5.83223104e-01 -1.55444455e+00  2.21388876e-01  3.35042506e-01
    6.60393357e-01 -6.60306692e-01  3.16892219e+00  6.72308862e-01
   -1.78230986e-01  1.20764457e-01 -1.16702288e-01 -6.33963272e-02
   -1.68588996e-01  2.74191767e-01  3.96811105e-02 -2.69801974e-01
   -5.43497801e-01  5.43065369e-02  8.82550105e-02  1.54200032e-01
   -3.06477875e-01  4.63499948e-02  5.00185013e-01 -4.89481091e-01
    2.33668815e-02 -2.02015787e-01]
 [ 1.50958434e-01 -1.11912321e-02  6.25830665e-02 -3.13090742e-01
    5.61992288e-01  1.35807067e-01 -4.35773849e-01  1.17024630e-01
   -1.90026194e-01 -1.01508908e-01  3.12561542e-02  1.85585365e-01
```

7.30: Shape of doc_vectors

10. Predict the intent:

```
user_sentence = "Look to the right"

user_sentence = pre_processing([user_sentence])
user_vector = doc_vector(user_sentence,model).reshape(100,)
intent = intents[select_intent(user_vector, doc_vectors)]
intent
```

```
'right.txt'
```

7.31: Predicted intent

Congratulations! You finished the activity. You can add more intents if you want to and train the GloVe model to achieve better results. By creating a function with all the code, you programmed and developing a movement node in ROS, you can order your robot to make movements and turn around.

Chapter 8: Object Recognition to Guide a Robot Using CNNs

Activity 8: Multiple Object Detection and Recognition in Video

Solution

1. Mount the drive:

```
from google.colab import drive
drive.mount('/content/drive')

cd /content/drive/My Drive/C13550/Lesson08/
```

2. Install the libraries:

```
pip3 install https://github.com/OlafenwaMoses/ImageAI/releases/
download/2.0.2/imageai-2.0.2-py3-none-any.whl
```

3. Import the libraries:

```
from imageai.Detection import VideoObjectDetection
from matplotlib import pyplot as plt
```

4. Declare the model:

```
video_detector = VideoObjectDetection()
video_detector.setModelTypeAsYOLOv3()
video_detector.setModelPath("Models/yolo.h5")
video_detector.loadModel()
```

5. Declare the callback method:

```
color_index = {'bus': 'red', 'handbag': 'steelblue', 'giraffe': 'orange',
'spoon': 'gray', 'cup': 'yellow', 'chair': 'green', 'elephant': 'pink',
'truck': 'indigo', 'motorcycle': 'azure', 'refrigerator': 'gold',
'keyboard': 'violet', 'cow': 'magenta', 'mouse': 'crimson', 'sports ball':
'raspberry', 'horse': 'maroon', 'cat': 'orchid', 'boat': 'slateblue',
'hot dog': 'navy', 'apple': 'cobalt', 'parking meter': 'aliceblue',
'sandwich': 'skyblue', 'skis': 'deepskyblue', 'microwave': 'peacock',
'knife': 'cadetblue', 'baseball bat': 'cyan', 'oven': 'lightcyan',
'carrot': 'coldgrey', 'scissors': 'seagreen', 'sheep': 'deepgreen',
'toothbrush': 'cobaltgreen', 'fire hydrant': 'limegreen', 'remote':
'forestgreen', 'bicycle': 'olivedrab', 'toilet': 'ivory', 'tv': 'khaki',
'skateboard': 'palegoldenrod', 'train': 'cornsilk', 'zebra': 'wheat',
'tie': 'burlywood', 'orange': 'melon', 'bird': 'bisque', 'dining table':
'chocolate', 'hair drier': 'sandybrown', 'cell phone': 'sienna', 'sink':
'coral', 'bench': 'salmon', 'bottle': 'brown', 'car': 'silver', 'bowl':
```

```
'maroon', 'tennis racket': 'palevilotered', 'airplane': 'lavenderblush',
'pizza': 'hotpink', 'umbrella': 'deeppink', 'bear': 'plum', 'fork':
'purple', 'laptop': 'indigo', 'vase': 'mediumpurple', 'baseball glove':
'slateblue', 'traffic light': 'mediumblue', 'bed': 'navy', 'broccoli':
'royalblue', 'backpack': 'slategray', 'snowboard': 'skyblue', 'kite':
'cadetblue', 'teddy bear': 'peacock', 'clock': 'lightcyan', 'wine glass':
'teal', 'frisbee': 'aquamarine', 'donut': 'mincream', 'suitcase':
'seagreen', 'dog': 'springgreen', 'banana': 'emeraldgreen', 'person':
'honeydew', 'surfboard': 'palegreen', 'cake': 'sapgreen', 'book':
'lawngreen', 'potted plant': 'greenyellow', 'toaster': 'ivory', 'stop
sign': 'beige', 'couch': 'khaki'}


def forFrame(frame_number, output_array, output_count, returned_frame):

    plt.clf()

    this_colors = []
    labels = []
    sizes = []

    counter = 0

    for eachItem in output_count:
        counter += 1
        labels.append(eachItem + " = " + str(output_count[eachItem]))
        sizes.append(output_count[eachItem])
        this_colors.append(color_index[eachItem])

    plt.subplot(1, 2, 1)
    plt.title("Frame : " + str(frame_number))
    plt.axis("off")
    plt.imshow(returned_frame, interpolation="none")

    plt.subplot(1, 2, 2)
    plt.title("Analysis: " + str(frame_number))
    plt.pie(sizes, labels=labels, colors=this_colors, shadow=True,
startangle=140, autopct="%1.1f%%")

    plt.pause(0.01)
```

6. Run Matplotlib and the video detection process:

```
plt.show()

video_detector.detectObjectsFromVideo(input_file_path="Dataset/videos/
street.mp4", output_file_path="output-video" ,  frames_per_second=20,
per_frame_function=forFrame,  minimum_percentage_probability=30, return_
detected_frame=True, log_progress=True)
```

The output will be as shown in the following frames:

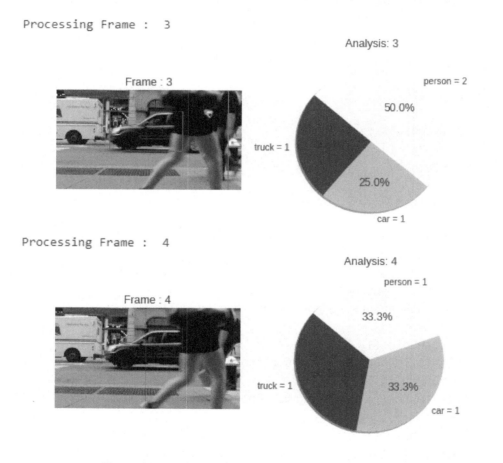

Figure 8.7: ImageAI video object detection output

As you can see, the model detects objects more or less properly. Now you can see the output video in your chapter 8 root directory with all the object detections in it.

> **Note:**
>
> There is an additional video added in the **Dataset/videos** folder – **park.mp4**. You can use the steps just mentioned and recognize objects in this video as well.

Chapter 9: Computer Vision for Robotics

Activity 9: A Robotic Security Guard

Solution

1. Create a new package in your catkin workspace to contain the integration node. Do it with this command to include the correct dependencies:

```
cd ~/catkin_ws/
source devel/setup.bash
roscore
cd src
catkin_create_pkg activity1 rospy cv_bridge geometry_msgs image_transport
sensor_msgs std_msgs
```

2. Switch to the package folder and create a new **scripts** directory. Then, create the Python file and make it executable:

```
cd activity1
mkdir scripts
cd scripts
touch activity.py
touch activity_sub.py
chmod +x activity.py
chmod +x activity_sub.py
```

3. This is the implementation of the first node:

Libraries importation:

```
#!/usr/bin/env python
import rospy
import cv2
import sys
import os
from cv_bridge import CvBridge, CvBridgeError
from sensor_msgs.msg import Image
from std_msgs.msg import String
```

```
sys.path.append(os.path.join(os.getcwd(), '/home/alvaro/Escritorio/tfg/
darknet/python/'))

import darknet as dn
```

> **Note**
>
> The above mentioned path may change as per the directories placed in your computer.

Class definition:

```
class Activity():
    def __init__(self):
```

Node, subscriber, and network initialization:

```
        rospy.init_node('Activity', anonymous=True)
        self.bridge = CvBridge()
        self.image_sub = rospy.Subscriber("camera/rgb/image_raw", Image,
    self.imageCallback)
        self.pub = rospy.Publisher('yolo_topic', String, queue_size=10)
        self.imageToProcess = None
        cfgPath =  "/home/alvaro/Escritorio/tfg/darknet/cfg/yolov3.cfg"
        weightsPath = "/home/alvaro/Escritorio/tfg/darknet/yolov3.weights"
        dataPath = "/home/alvaro/Escritorio/tfg/darknet/cfg/coco2.data"
        self.net = dn.load_net(cfgPath, weightsPath, 0)
        self.meta = dn.load_meta(dataPath)
        self.fileName = 'predict.jpg'
        self.rate = rospy.Rate(10)
```

> **Note**
>
> The above mentioned path may change as per the directories placed in your computer.

Function image callback. It obtains images from the robot camera:

```
def imageCallback(self, data):
    self.imageToProcess = self.bridge.imgmsg_to_cv2(data, "bgr8")
```

Main function of the node:

```
def run(self):
    print("The robot is recognizing objects")

    while not rospy.core.is_shutdown():

        if(self.imageToProcess is not None):
            cv2.imwrite(self.fileName, self.imageToProcess)
```

Method for making predictions on images:

```
r = dn.detect(self.net, self.meta, self.fileName)

objects = ""

for obj in r:
    objects += obj[0] + " "
```

Publish the predictions:

```
self.pub.publish(objects)
self.rate.sleep()
```

Program entry:

```
if __name__ == '__main__':
    dn.set_gpu(0)
    node = Activity()
    try:
        node.run()
    except rospy.ROSInterruptException:
        pass
```

4. This is the implementation of the second node:

Libraries importation:

```python
#!/usr/bin/env python
import rospy
from std_msgs.msg import String
```

Class definition:

```python
class ActivitySub():

    yolo_data = ""

    def __init__(self):
```

Node initialization and subscriber definition:

```python
        rospy.init_node('ThiefDetector', anonymous=True)
        rospy.Subscriber("yolo_topic", String, self.callback)
```

The callback function for obtaining published data:

```python
    def callback(self, data):
        self.yolo_data = data

    def run(self):
        while True:
```

Start the alarm if a person is detected in the data:

```python
            if "person" in str(self.yolo_data):
                print("ALERT: THIEF DETECTED")
                break
```

Program entry:

```python
if __name__ == '__main__':
    node = ActivitySub()
    try:
        node.run()
    except rospy.ROSInterruptException:
        pass
```

5. Now, you need to set the destination to the scripts folder:

```
cd ../../
cd ..
cd src/activity1/scripts/
```

6. Execute the movement.py file:

```
touch movement.py
chmod +x movement.py
cd ~/catkin_ws
source devel/setup.bash
roslaunch turtlebot_gazebo turtlebot_world.launch
```

7. Open a new terminal and execute the command to get the output:

```
cd ~/catkin_ws
source devel/setup.bash
rosrun activity1 activity.py

cd ~/catkin_ws
source devel/setup.bash
rosrun activity1 activity_sub.py

cd ~/catkin_ws
source devel/setup.bash
rosrun activity1 movement.py
```

8. Run both nodes at the same time. This is an execution example:

Gazebo situation:

Figure 9.16: Example situation for the activity

First node output:

The robot is recognizing objects

Figure 9.17: First activity node output

Second node output:

ALERT: THIEF DETECTED

Figure 9.18: Second activity node output

Index

About

All major keywords used in this book are captured alphabetically in this section. Each one is accompanied by the page number of where they appear.

Made in the USA
Columbia, SC
23 February 2020

88314991R00196